Praise for *Welcoming Beginner's Mind*

"As the visual expression of the bodhisattva's journey, the ten ox-herding pictures, which I've loved and studied since my teens, have no equal among the world's artistic and spiritual masterpieces. With Buddhist learning that is insightful and inspiring, experiential and scholarly, Gaylon Ferguson's *Welcoming Beginner's Mind* is an exploration of the oxherding pictures with wise exercises, for which I am deeply grateful."—CHARLES JOHNSON, author of *Oxherding Tale* and *Middle Passage*

"Gaylon Ferguson has harvested a lifetime of deep study, disciplined contemplative practice, and internationally acclaimed teachings to present us with a magnificent tree of Buddhist wisdom. With Chinese Ch'an and Taoism, Japanese Zen, and Tibetan Tantra providing its deep roots and sturdy trunk, this tree also branches out in diverse directions, bearing fragrant blossoms from a rainbow of world cultures and ethnicities. I have been a Buddhist meditator for more than fifty years, and this book has helped me immensely."—DAVID I. ROME, author of *Your Body Knows the Answer* and editor of *Timely Rain: Selected Poetry of Chögyam Trungpa*

"In *Welcoming Beginner's Mind*, Gaylon Ferguson points out that when we resist or shut out parts of our lives, we add to the busyness of them. It works against the practice of non-doing many of us aspire to. Instead, Ferguson suggests a Welcoming Exercise in which life is engaged but not by way of our ideas, goals, and tasks. Using the ancient tale of the oxherding story, he moves us from an intellectual practice to one of discovery. What is it that makes us steer or push the ox? Ultimately this work is a lesson in freedom."—ZENJU EARTHLYN MANUEL, Zen priest and author of *Opening to Darkness*, *Shamanic Bones of Zen*, *Deepest Peace*, and *The Way of Tenderness*

T0038249

"After a long, often painful search, Siddhartha Gautama had a series of insights that came to be called 'enlightenment,' just as he came to be called the Buddha. He taught these insights and demonstrated them in the conduct of his life every day for forty-five years. His students and companions did the same. Because people found this helpful and true, it has continued into the present—having insights and trying to live them—developing through centuries into local, regional, and national styles. So many teachings! So many traditions! Comments upon commentaries. No one navigates this better than Gaylon Ferguson, who pilots readers back to the origin and shows each of us how to get there. Many bows to this skillful teacher!"
—TENSHO DAVID SCHNEIDER, author of Street Zen and Crowded by Beauty and coeditor of Essential Zen

"Gaylon Ferguson's new book is an inviting and rich discussion of the Buddhist path, structured around the traditional series of Zen oxherding pictures. Ferguson distills mindfulness practice to its essence—welcoming and noticing—and by means of simple contemplative exercises gently guides the reader to join him in discovering within the heart the footprints of the Buddha."—JUDITH L. LIEF, editor of The Profound Treasury of the Ocean of Dharma volumes and author of Making Friends with Death

"This insightful and kindhearted book is an important contribution to the development of American Buddhism. Gaylon Ferguson gives much-needed advice for non-doing, non-meditating, and non-becoming. We are invited to see the spiritual journey not as a project of breakthrough and self-improvement but as the manifestation of an ever-deepening process of welcoming immediate, bodyful experience."—ZENKI CHRISTIAN DILLO ROSHI, resident teacher at Boulder Zen Center and author of The Path of Aliveness

WELCOMING BEGINNER'S MIND

Zen and Tibetan Buddhist Wisdom
on Experiencing Our True Nature

GAYLON FERGUSON

FOREWORD BY DAVID CHADWICK

SHAMBHALA

Shambhala Publications, Inc.
2129 13th Street
Boulder, Colorado 80302
www.shambhala.com

Cover art: *When Skies Fall* by Beau Carey
Cover & interior design: Kate E. White

9 8 7 6 5 4 3 2 1

First Edition
Printed in the United States of America

Shambhala Publications makes every effort to print on acid-free, recycled paper.
Shambhala Publications is distributed worldwide by Penguin Random House, Inc.,
and its subsidiaries.

LIBRARY OF CONGRESS CATALOGING-IN-PUBLICATION DATA
Names: Ferguson, Gaylon Jules, author.
Title: Welcoming beginner's mind: Zen and Tibetan Buddhist wisdom on
experiencing our true nature / Gaylon Ferguson.
Description: Boulder: Shambhala Publications, 2024.
Identifiers: LCCN 2023023451 | ISBN 9781645471936 (trade paperback)
Subjects: LCSH: Spiritual life—Zen Buddhism—Introductions. | Meditation—
Buddhism. | Devotional exercises. | Oxen—Religious aspects—Zen Buddhism.
Classification: LCC BQ9268.5 .F47 2024 | DDC 294.3/4432—dc23/eng/20230705
LC record available at https://lccn.loc.gov/2023023451

For Shunryu Suzuki Roshi, great ancestor
—"A solitary rock is majestic."

Contents

Foreword

In the mid-sixties, at the old Sokoji temple on Bush Street in San Francisco, Shunryu Suzuki had concluded his lecture and asked for questions. A woman I didn't recognize raised her hand. She said she was looking for a teacher. She said she had gone to Joshu Sasaki in L.A. and that he had rejected her. She didn't understand why. Suzuki urged her to return to L.A., not to give up on Sasaki so quickly. She burst into tears and sobbed, "Now you reject me!"

"Oh no," said Suzuki, stepping toward her with his arms opening wide, the long sleeves of his robe hanging down like curtains, "I never reject anyone."

In *Welcoming Beginner's Mind*, Gaylon Ferguson explores welcoming as a central Buddhist practice. He does so by taking the reader on an adventure through the famed metaphor of the oxherding pictures, reflecting along the way on the wise words of his teacher, Chögyam Trungpa; on those of Shunryu Suzuki; and on those of other sage ancestors and contemporaries.

Trungpa and Suzuki met at Tassajara Zen Mountain Center in the spring of 1970 when Trungpa visited with Shambhala Publications founders Sam and Hazel Bercholz and a few other students. Trungpa and his party had finished dinner when Suzuki came in to greet them. My mate Dianne and I had served them. I took the plates and serving dishes back to the kitchen. Dianne stayed to make sure all was okay. The room was dark, lit only by some kerosene lamps.

Few words were spoken. As these two teachers sat facing each other, Dianne perceived the room becoming brighter until she could see clearly what had been obscured in darkness.

Suzuki invited Trungpa to give a talk in the meditation hall, which he did, sitting on the edge of the altar with his orthopedic shoes on. Immediately there was a mutual appreciation between Trungpa and Suzuki's students. Later, Trungpa gave talks at the San Francisco Zen Center's City Center. On another occasion, he brought his baby son there to be blessed by Suzuki in the Buddha Hall. The two spoke a few more times, then through letters and visiting students. They talked of founding a Buddhist study center, sharing lecture tapes, and creating a residential program to deal with profoundly troubled students. They spoke of how in America, unlike in their homelands, only the large mountains had names. Suzuki related to no other visiting teacher in this way. Trungpa called Suzuki his American father, and Suzuki said Trungpa was like a son to him.

In October of 1971, Bob Halpern, who had practiced with Suzuki for years, delivered the news to Trungpa that Suzuki had terminal cancer. He said Trungpa cried so hard he burst a blood vessel in an eye. Bob visited Suzuki, bringing word from Trungpa. On Suzuki's bedside table, Bob saw a photo he'd sent of the group's Boulder altar with photos of Trungpa and Suzuki alongside Trungpa's root teacher. Suzuki didn't live long enough to explore with Trungpa their ideas and plans, but their students and teachings spread wide and have continued to intertwine—as in this book, where the two meet again.

Let's look at the title another time: *Welcoming Beginner's Mind*. Suzuki's core teaching of beginner's mind is itself welcoming, and welcoming is beginner's mind, empty and alert, open to whatever comes—not foolishly, but rather like the hunter in stillness, ready to act spontaneously to what comes or doesn't come.

In *Welcoming Beginner's Mind*, Ferguson includes the reader on this path, suggesting various ways to put the book aside and reflect on beginner's mind, on welcoming, on the oxherder, and on the ox. Now let us join them.

—DAVID CHADWICK

Welcoming Beginner's Mind

Introduction
WHY WELCOME?

One day, many years ago, my first Buddhist teacher—a Tibetan master of the art of meditation—looked me over closely and said in a quiet, gentle voice, "You don't have to be embarrassed at who you are." I felt naked—suddenly seen to my core. Silently I wondered to myself, did everyone in Tibet cultivate penetrating X-ray vision?

I had been practicing mindfulness-awareness meditation on a regular basis for two or three years by then. Was it so obvious that this excellent spiritual practice was also another way of avoiding being me? Yes, I was meditating regularly but as a way of avoiding feeling the more uncomfortable aspects of being alive. This is meditation as spiritual bypassing—inwardly moving steadily away from myself under the outer cover story of becoming more intimate with the experience of being human.

This effortful practice of "unwelcoming" myself built and rebuilt an inner wall of self-division. I was diligently doing my daily spiritual work—trying to make sure that all the messy, "bad" parts of myself were efficiently banished to the other side of this partition. In my vision of successfully reaching the fruition of meditation practice, the "good," mindful me would be safely on this side of the wall, while all the distracted, emotionally charged aspects of being human would be held at bay—at least temporarily.

Sound familiar? Many of us practice, in part, because we feel that something in us needs to be fixed, corrected, or improved. Conversely, we may practice because we notice a chronic sense that something outside of us needs to be fixed, corrected, or improved. A friend wrote to me recently that she has never felt much negative self-judgment. Too many contemporary spiritual teachings, she said, seem directed exclusively toward people with low self-esteem, uncertain self-worth, and doubtful feelings of fundamental unworthiness. "I've come to loathe the phrase 'self-loathing,'" she wrote. "What about those of us who suffer from habitual arrogance?"

Ah, yes, a request for equal time: What about those of us too proud to be humble? Still, I wondered, could the self-divided result be the same whether we begin with insecurity or pride, whether I start by feeling one-down or one-up? If I begin practice with the feeling of being at least slightly better than average, then the wishful fantasy of meditative achievement offers the promise of adding yet another spiritual credential to my collection—and perhaps even attaining a position of authority from which I can instruct others. This was once famously called "spiritual materialism." Now I can add spiritual attainment to my life résumé of personal and professional successes.

But let's return our focus to those of us who start from a place of existential embarrassment at feeling one-down—the majority of practitioners, in my experience. All goes swimmingly at first, until inevitably we discover that not all aspects of our inner being are completely on board with this ambitious spiritual project to climb the inner Mount Everest of enlightenment. Even after all these years, there are still so many of these pesky little thoughts and unruly emotions. Some days our otherwise good-enough mind seems to develop a mind of its own, first racing off to this inner movie of resentment (the rerun of an old favorite) and then rushing on to another hopeful dream of falling into the perfect romance. We hope the work we are doing makes a positive difference in the world, and then we fear that it's all too little and too late. Human beings are still killing themselves and each other and destroying other life-forms on the planet at alarming rates. We frown on these erupting emotions and wonder what to do about this stubborn inner enemy—"me."

Whether someone starts from a place of insecurity or of arrogance, we're seeing different starting points leading to the same result: the "good" spiritual me is on one side trying to conquer the "bad" selfish me on the other side. As with many wars, the temptation is to fight harder, to bomb those damn rebels right out of existence. From time to time, there's a still, small voice of sanity inside us whispering, "Good luck with that."

———

Welcoming is our true nature. We human beings enjoy welcoming loved ones into our homes and presence, sharing food and good times together. Many of my favorite childhood memories center on family celebrations of holidays, birthdays, anniversaries. My maternal grandmother—the reigning matriarch of our large family—found great pleasure in welcoming friends and family into our home. "Come in, come in!" she'd call out, warmly greeting them at the door. Isn't something similar found in cultures all over the world?

Welcoming is our true nature. Nowadays a small but growing mountain of neuroscientific research shows that we humans are hardwired for compassion and kindness. Our word kindness descends from the word kin. Evolutionary psychology teaches us that an altruistic instinct for kin selection—based on natural feelings of affection for family—is carried in our genes.

Welcoming is our true nature. We also enjoy welcoming ourselves. Spiritual psychologists call this inwardly friendly embrace "self-acceptance," being kind to oneself. Compassion begins at home. The sitting practice of meditation is, fundamentally, a way of making friends with all our experience. My own experience of the meditative journey is that this simple invitation—to welcome ourselves again and again—turns out to be a lifelong journey. Who knew? Traveling a spiritual path is every bit as complex as we are. Meditation is a wise and gentle life-companion, mirroring and accompanying the daily unfolding of our lives.

That welcoming is our true nature means it isn't the result of years of hard-core spiritual practice (or soft-core persuasion, for that matter). Natural means not manufactured, not produced in a mindfulness factory. Our true nature is like the sky, the ocean, a mountain, the moon, the stars. There is no multinational corporation called Sky, Inc., to send us a bill at the end of the month for how much sky we've enjoyed—not yet, anyway. Nature means, just like the sky above us, not produced by human effort—unconfined and free. Following the awakened ancestors of Buddhist tradition, Zen Buddhist meditation master Shunryu Suzuki called this nature our "original mind."[1] It's what we originally are, our original goodness.

Some years ago, I was part of a large group of concerned citizens gathering to meet the challenge of youth violence in Chicago, contemplating the meaning of what we called "original peace." True nature is what we are from the very beginning, before all thoughts of good and bad, before our fixed concepts of "enemies" to be defeated or "allies" to be welcomed. True nature is the natural truth of being human.

Suzuki Roshi also spoke of this original nature as "beginner's mind." It is here with us at the beginning of any journey, not just in a projected destination of "enlightenment" at which we will finally arrive, somewhere out there at the end of the path. Having in mind a fixed goal to reach narrows the vast field of human potential. As Roshi reminds us, "In the beginner's mind there are many possibilities, in the expert's mind there are few."[2] This is the spacious heart of meditation. Suzuki Roshi called it "the secret of meditation practice."[3] Welcoming is the secret key to meditation. It's an open secret, the secret of basic openness.

WHEN IS BEGINNER'S MIND?

Over fifty years ago, a slender book of Suzuki Roshi's edited talks titled *Zen Mind, Beginner's Mind* was published. The Japanese word *Zen* means "meditation," so one meaning of *Zen* mind is "the mind of meditation." What is that? Is it our state of mind when we are practicing meditation? Maybe that is so sometimes, but as Suzuki Roshi also says, "Not always so." Perhaps *Zen* mind is another name for the nature of our mind, our pristine original mind, the purity of the human mind's true nature. If so, then this is our nature while we are sitting, walking, standing, or lying down. So, yes, this is the mind's true nature while we are meditating but also while we are not meditating. Hearing various traditional teachings about this original mind, we sometimes wonder (as a true beginner might), "What is that?"

Once, in the San Francisco Bay Area, I heard a public talk by a famous meditation teacher who admitted that he waited many years to buy a copy of *Zen Mind, Beginner's Mind* because he did not want to be a beginner. A beginner is someone who admits that they don't know—that they have something to learn. Clearly, there is humility in being willing to be a beginner. Roshi connects this nonconceptual beginner's mind with our capacity to learn: "When we have no thought of achievement, no thought of self, we are true beginners. Then we can really learn something." Yet he also tells us in the book's prologue that the aim, the essential purpose, of meditation practice is to remain with this original not-knowing: "The goal of practice is to always keep our beginner's mind." How is that possible? How is it possible to go on with not-knowing after months, years, or decades of meditation practice and study? Acknowledging the immensity of this challenge, Roshi warns us that "the most difficult thing is always to keep your beginner's mind."

This helpful advice raises more questions than it answers. Why is this the most difficult thing? Some traditions suggest just the opposite: it is also the easiest. "Always to keep"—is this even possible, and if so, how is it possible? If we intentionally hold on to what felt like beginner's mind in yesterday's meditation session, that is the antithesis of being a true beginner. Suddenly we've become experts in beginner's mind. When we feel we already know our original mind, vast openness is fenced in. If we think we know the target and what it is to hit the bull's eye, and we just need to aim carefully to hit it again and again, true learning cannot take place. We never really learn anything new. Stale repetition takes the place of fresh discovery. Keeping our beginner's mind might be more difficult than we initially thought.

Beginner's mind is not the mind we had yesterday or last year or whenever we first began a practice of sitting meditation. As with the poetic phrase, "first thought, best thought," it's not meant literally. Sometimes my first thought is the worst thought—a confused, habitual, reactively selfish thought that just happened to rush to the front of the line.

Timing seems elusive here. Beginner's mind is what is always already here with us. This means that, yes, it was here at the beginning when we began, but it's also here in the middle and will be there at the end. It's basically good at the beginning, good in the middle, good at the end. Calling it "beginner's mind" helpfully reminds us that it's not only found at the end of the road, an attainment at the conclusion of our journey. It's also helpful to remember that beginner's mind is not back there somewhere where we first entered the path. It's present all along—in what we call the past, the present, and the future. As the modern Tibetan Buddhist master Thinley Norbu Rinpoche writes of beginnings, "Whenever we hear from teachers or read in texts that Wisdom Mind is beginningless, we think this means some time before the beginning, far away from this present moment. We must recognize that if from the beginning our Wisdom Mind is beginningless, it has no beginning, no end, and no between, so it is continuous, and always present."[4]

BEGINNER'S MIND, WELCOMING, AND THE OXHERDING IMAGES

My experience is that contemplating the meaning of "beginner's mind" can be frustrating. The more closely I listened into the depths of this apparently simple teaching, the more it began to sound like an impossible conundrum, an unsolvable puzzle, a paradox of contradictions. Zen tradition offers many famous stories of the inscrutable actions of crazy-wise lineage ancestors. Some of these stories have been collected and passed down as koans, case studies for deep contemplation. In some Zen lineages, one sits and sits with a koan to boggle the conceptual mind, to unlock the door that suddenly opens onto a land of freedom, compassion, and flowing spontaneity.

In this book, "beginner's mind" isn't being offered as a koan but as a lead-in to a simple exercise called Welcoming. This Welcoming Exercise—which we'll try for the first time in a moment—will be the experiential thread guiding us throughout this book. This welcoming approach is also a good basis for a developmental journey. Is that surprising? Why shouldn't welcoming include growing and changing or, as some people say, "evolving"? Welcoming is vastness welcoming everything.

This book uses the ancient Zen oxherding images as one example of an unfolding spiritual path. Classical examples of the oxherding images survive in various versions—sometimes there are six, more often ten—but in each case they depict a practitioner in various stages of seeking and relating to an ox. There are early commentaries on the Foundations of Mindfulness Sutra that use similar metaphors: training the mind is like taming an ox. There may also have been earlier Daoist versions. The version of the images that illustrate *Welcoming Beginner's Mind* has been used since the twelfth century as a map of the Buddhist path. In this book, we will explore welcoming in each of the ten stages of awakening represented by the oxherding images.

As you will have noticed, Suzuki Roshi's teachings form an important touchstone for my own comments on welcoming and on the images in this book. I never met Suzuki Roshi, but he was a close friend of my root teacher, the Tibetan meditation master Chögyam Trungpa Rinpoche. In an appreciative essay of loving recollection following Roshi's death in 1971, Rinpoche wrote that meeting Roshi "aroused nostalgia for the past when I was in Tibet working with my teacher. . . . It was amazing that such a compassionate person existed in the midst of so much aggression and passion."[5]

Trungpa Rinpoche was introduced to the Zen oxherding images at the home of his publisher, friend, and student, Samuel Bercholz, in Berkeley in 1971. Inspired by the diverse illuminating sparks between Zen and tantric Buddhist traditions, Rinpoche composed a commentary on these images as stages of the path from awkward beginnings to complete enlightenment. These pithy paragraphs appeared first in a magazine called *Garuda* and then in Rinpoche's early book *Mudra*.[6] That early commentary is the basis for *Welcoming Beginner's Mind*. I offer these gleanings in grateful appreciation of these two vast and profound dharma pioneers.

Without further ado, let's try the Welcoming Exercise.

THE WELCOMING EXERCISE: A BRIEF INTRODUCTION

Now please gently put your book or e-reader aside for a moment, and do the Welcoming Exercise by sitting for three minutes with your eyes open and your hands relaxed in your lap. "Sit for three minutes with your eyes open and your hands relaxed in your lap"—that's it! Just try it and include whatever arises whether you like it or not. There's no target or aim or goal. Remember: this is mainly an experiential journey, so the point is to trust and taste whatever arises—hot, cold, happy, sad, restless, contented—the entire range of feelings, sensations, thoughts, perceptions, and concepts.

WHAT TO DO (AND WHAT NOT TO DO) DURING THE WELCOMING EXERCISE

Welcoming is our true nature. The Welcoming Exercise offers us direct experience of this. It's the immediate application of this gentle approach to our experience. If our natural state is welcoming, we do not require a practice or disciplined training to create or improve this nature, to get to some higher state called "welcoming." This is not an attainment or an achievement. Later, we can, if we like, engage in various trainings to remove the clouds that may temporarily cover our innate brilliance. Note that, even then, we will not be training to manufacture a new, improved sun. This inner sun is always already here. This beginning exercise allows our true nature to express itself directly, just as the radiant light and warmth of the sun outwardly express the inner solar nature. This point is crucial, so let me say it again in a slightly different way: we are not doing the Welcoming Exercise to produce something—a sense of spaciousness, a better mood, or whatever your particular interest may be. We are not welcoming to improve the sky or to get the upgrade of Sky 2.0.

As you may have picked up already, it is much easier to say what we are *not doing* in this exercise than to offer robust descriptions of its content. Clearly, the Welcoming Exercise is not meditation. I often ask groups of experienced meditation practitioners who are engaging in this exercise for the first time to begin by saying to themselves out loud, "Not meditating." Please pause for a moment now and say, "Not meditating." (Thank you.) By saying this, we are reminding ourselves that welcoming is not a meditation technique, another way of training the mind. Training the mind is good and an excellent spiritual discipline. This exercise is slightly upstream from all trainings. There are, of course, many skillful methods of taming and training the mind, but this is not one of them. Instead, we are exploring welcoming itself by allowing it to happen and seeing what happens with this "not-doing." Since we are already familiar with thousands of ways of doing, perhaps it is time for some curiosity about the experience (not the theory or the idea but the felt-sense) of not-doing?

When I say the Welcoming Exercise is not meditation, I mean it. It is not even the same as what is sometimes called open-awareness meditation, in which one does not focus on a single object but allows the attention to move freely from one object to another without distraction. That sounds like a wonderful practice, but, again, welcoming is not cultivating undistracted awareness. If you experience many distracted states, welcome them like a swarm of gnats in the summer. If you experience various nonpeaceful mental states, welcome those as well. This is not a meditation exercise. What is it? The practical answer is, Let's see. This is a suggestion for proceeding by unleashing natural inquisitiveness about all our experiences. What's it like to sit here now . . . and now . . . and now, thinking of past and future and whatever comes up in between?

———————

Essentially, this book is about the experience of welcoming. We will reach no specific goal or higher state by allowing ourselves to sit simply with ourselves for a few moments, exactly as we are, nothing added, nothing taken away. Yet, as we shall see in our exploration of the oxherding images, the Welcoming Exercise is not in any way static or predictable.

One of the benefits of this exercise is that it allows us to sidestep some of the conceptual roadblocks that often pop up when contemplating seemingly paradoxical teachings like beginner's mind. Unlike ordinary highway roadblocks made from concrete and steel, these barriers are constructed from questions about exactly when beginner's mind takes place or what kind of effort is needed to always keep what can never be lost. Bowing respectfully toward these deep questions, we can just do the Welcoming Exercise and, remaining curious throughout, see what our experience is, however it is. What happens when we simply do the exercise? What arises when we do it without expectations or preconceptions of what should happen? We are following the suggestions for doing the exercise, but more importantly, we are being curious—as beginners might—about our experience while doing it. A spiritual expert already knows the point of the Welcoming Exercise before doing it. A beginner's mind has childlike yet sharp inquisitiveness as its leading edge. One teacher called this our "basic innocence."

What can we learn about ourselves through this contemplative journey? This question already suggests a slightly different approach than meditation. Setting aside the idea of hitting the target, achieving the goal, or at least doing the practice "correctly," what is your actual experience from moment to moment? For example, during the various exercises in this book, do you mainly notice sense perceptions (sights and sounds) or thoughts and feelings? Don't start with the assumption that thoughts and feelings are better or worse than sights and sounds. The question guiding your inquiry is not what should you feel or think, hear or see, but what is your experience of yourself sitting simply with minimal effort to change anything that is arising—a thought, a smell, a sound, an emotion? Are you bored, excited, anxious, or sad? Here is an open invitation to do the Welcoming Exercise, realizing that you don't have to solve all the contemplative puzzles or answer all the profound questions beforehand. At least in this instance, you can just do it.

Another benefit of directly engaging in an exercise, of actually doing something, is that it allows us to proceed along this path on the basis of our experience. Perhaps this is another meaning of the old Zen phrase "trust in the heart." Trusting experience, being guided by what we are sensing and feeling, is not the same as having faith in anyone's doctrine or dogma. As with checking on a slowly simmering soup, we can actually taste-test the flavors on our tongue. Not enough salt? Just right? Then we adjust accordingly or leave it alone. We don't have to begin by believing in something called "beginner's mind" or "original nature" or "emptiness" or "awareness." We don't have to have faith that "welcoming is our true nature" or that we even have a true nature. In the spirit of all the great Buddhist practice lineages, we can simply get on with it by finding guidance in our experience, what actually happens, whatever that may be. Our own experience is our guide, our mentor, our counselor and coach. This is not at all the same as being guided by a map or a recipe for what should happen next. We can trust our unfolding experience as an unfailing teacher, a true spiritual friend on our journey.

WELCOMING A SPACIOUS MEADOW

In an early chapter called "Control" in Zen Mind, Beginner's Mind, Suzuki Roshi suggests that we give our sheep or cow a "large, spacious meadow." This spacious meadow is a perfect image for welcoming. Welcoming welcomes—whether our sheep is anxious or angry, tired or well rested, happy or sad. Welcoming welcomes—whether our cow has had a good day and is peaceful and content or is increasingly concerned about the crisis-state of our world. Welcoming welcomes—whether our cow really appreciates the green, spacious meadow today or wishes the other cows were different. Welcoming welcomes—any thoughts, feelings, sensations, or distractions are all welcome.

Many people assume that meditation involves getting rid of thoughts, "emptying the mind." If we aren't able to send thoughts away entirely, then we aim for suppressing or controlling them somehow. Stilling the mind is in fact a good definition of "meditating" in some spiritual traditions. Remember that this Welcoming Exercise is not meditating, so this popular assumption about getting rid of thoughts need not apply here. If you sit for most of the three minutes daydreaming about some pleasurable time from last spring, welcome that. If you remember times of anxiety and grief during the peak of the global pandemic, welcome that. If you are hoping that you'll feel well enough to attend next week's family reunion, welcome that. If you're dreading another tense family gathering and would like to find a way to avoid it, welcome that. Regardless of the techniques you may be familiar with or practice regularly for controlling or disciplining your thoughts in meditation, in the Welcoming Exercise we welcome all thoughts—thoughts of the past, thoughts of the future, thoughts of the present. We are not trying to "be here now." Most definitely not. We are not, for the moment, training the mind to peacefully stay still, to calmly abide. Those are all excellent meditation practices. We are not doing any of that; we are not doing anything. Like a child or a beginner, we are curious and wonder, what's that like? What's our experience of sitting here, feeling, thinking, sensing? What's our experience of being alive as human beings this morning?

In doing this important foundational exercise, there is no expectation that an extraordinary insight into the ultimate nature of reality will arise. (Of course, if it does, welcome that.) There is no promise that you will flash into an altered state of consciousness after two and a half minutes of just welcoming. (If it does, welcome that.) Instead, there is the ongoing welcoming of nothing special. What's that like? How does it feel to lighten up on the compulsive drive toward tasting another special experience, having one more highlight in your day?

QUESTIONS ABOUT THE WELCOMING EXERCISE

Because the Welcoming Exercise is the essential thread we will follow on this entire journey together, it's worth lingering over some of the questions that often arise while engaging in this experiential inquiry. What follows are questions and comments I've heard dozens of times in small and large group retreats held in various contexts—ruggedly spacious contemplative centers way out in the country; in the middle of busy cities like Seattle, Los Angeles, Chicago, and New York; and among those incarcerated for years in federal prisons. These questions raise particular issues, but they also help clarify the overall view of welcoming itself. These questions may help us understand why welcoming is our true nature.

Q1: Even though we agreed (out loud, even) that this is "not meditating," what if I find myself meditating anyway? I know that's the instruction, but the mind is a stubborn animal—it tends to go back again and again to what it's used to doing, what's familiar.

A: Yes. That's a helpful insight: recognizing and acknowledging the power and momentum of our mental habits, even good, healthy habits like meditating. Some Buddhists might say that you're seeing the conditioned effects of many previous causes. If you find yourself, through sheer force of habit, doing what you call "meditating" during this short Welcoming Exercise, first, pause and welcome this familiar old friend ("Ah, here's meditating, back again.") and then drop it, stop doing that activity called "meditating." Stop making a deliberate effort. Stop placing the attention again and again on the body breathing or on whatever other meditative anchor you're used to. Instead, simply return to welcoming as in *not doing anything* and, in particular, not focusing your attention on any specific object like the body or the breath. We're not doing that worthy activity called meditating right now; we can always return to it later, yes? Perhaps our old friend will be delighted to see us again later.

Q2: What if I'm sitting here the entire three minutes making laundry lists of all the things I need to do? I'm a compulsive planner and a very energetic doer. Some people who know me well call me an overachiever. I like to get as many things as possible done in my day so that I can relax later and enjoy the moment. What's wrong with that?

A: To plan ahead, to structure and prioritize one's daily or weekly activities, sounds like a very worthy activity. I'm sure you're a highly productive person, and good for you. Yet the Welcoming Exercise is not really a time to plan the rest of your day or week. Just as planning your retreat in California next summer is not the same as, say, remembering your childhood in day care in Denver, we are giving each activity its due. As it says in an ancient wisdom book, "For everything there is a season." Maybe you remember the old saying "Every dog has its day (and a good dog just might have two days)." Well, let's allow each of these activities—planning, remembering, meditating, and welcoming—its own time. So, if you notice yourself making a mental checklist of things you need to do later, welcome that surely, but then let go of any further deliberate planning activity. When you're planning, then plan deliberately and stick with it. When doing the Welcoming Exercise, don't deliberately do anything.

Q2: Sounds good—at least theoretically—but the proof is in the pudding, right? What if my mind continues to spin out plans for prioritizing and getting things done next week? Like the old-fashioned potter's wheel that keeps spinning even when you're not kicking it to go around again. What then?

A: An excellent analogy. In being true to the spirit of welcoming, first just notice and allow this spinning. Don't try to stop the spinning wheel; that would be doing something, actively trying to put a stop to all this blooming, buzzing mental activity. Here, "not-doing" just means not kicking the wheel to add further speed and momentum to your already spinning discursiveness. If it gradually slows down, welcome that. If it doesn't, if it keeps going with habitual momentum, then welcome that. Beginning to sound familiar? This is what one of my Brazilian friends calls a "one-note samba."

Q2: I'm starting to get lost in the metaphor of the potter's wheel, so could you say it another way?

A: Remember that welcoming is more a matter of not-doing. If we find ourselves habitually or compulsively doing anything, welcome that, of course, but then don't feed it. Contemporary Tibetan Buddhist teacher Yongey Mingyur Rinpoche speaks of "adding wood to the fire." Don't add fuel to that fire the way you would if you were actively engaging in planning your Saturday errands: "After picking up the birthday cake for Bea's party, I have to get some stamps at the post office." Here, "not-doing" means don't do anything deliberately or intentionally. Don't try to stir anything up or make anything go away. Welcoming is a little like going limp, letting up on controlling or directing ourselves this way or that. What does it feel like to not press the accelerator or the brakes just for three minutes? What arises in that fertile space of not-doing? We're often trying to climb another mountain to get to a peak and see the great views we've heard about. Welcoming is curious: what's it like in the valley?

At one point, we tried to teach our family dog to roll over and play dead. Welcoming is a little like pretending to "roll over and play dead" for a few minutes. For three minutes you're not trying, not aiming in any direction. If the mind wanders, let it wander. If the mind sinks, let it sink. If you feel excited that you're about to see your cousin Harvey on that trip to Boston, feel excited. It's as simple as that: a radical simplicity of allowing what is to be as it is.

Q3: What if I simply space out?

A: Good, good. Please say a bit more about what you call "spacing out." Could you describe that?

Q3: I mean what everyone means by "spacing out"—not being present, not being in the present right now and right here, distracted.

A: Right, right. That's what I thought you meant, but could you say a little about what this particular experience of spacing out is like, what it actually feels like rather than what it's like in the negative—"not being present"? Could you describe your experience of spacing out? There must be some positive content to this that you call "spacing out," something you're aware of and truthfully label as "spacing out." What is that? What's that like? For the moment, we're not inquiring into whether it's good or bad, we're just trying to describe the tracking of our moment-to-moment experience in the Welcoming Exercise. As we know, evaluation is not the same as description. What does spacing out feel like? As when we say, this fabric feels smooth or rough, this metal surface feels warm or cold to the touch. For the moment, it's not a matter of whether that fabric is good or better, whether that surface is bad or worse. What is it actually like in your experience?

Q3: Well, my spacing out feels different at different times. Sometimes I feel foggy, sort of like a windshield that's all fogged up. Sometimes I feel slightly sad and not very alert—oops! I'm starting to say again what it's not.

A: Good, it's good that you noticed. Sometimes it's a real challenge to stay with what our experience is rather than prematurely convicting it with a pejorative label of what it's not ("I'm just not alert enough today, dammit!"). This label can then easily slide into further negative comparisons: "I'm not as alert as Carla. I'm not even as alert as I was last year." All of that may be true, and once again, we may wish to practice various trainings for increasing our overall alertness or our kindness, compassion, courage, and so forth. Fine, all fine. The Welcoming Exercise, on the other hand, gives us a rare opportunity to meet ourselves exactly as we are—no additives and no psychological surgeries. We are not removing something called "spacing out" to finally get to the other side of ourselves, the better, healthier side. Welcoming is the ultimate nonviolence, nonaggression toward ourselves. Welcoming welcomes all our experiences as expressions of true nature.

Sometimes I wonder, is deliberately doing nothing challenging or easy? Are there forces shaping our experience of what spiritual teacher Tracee Stanley calls "the toxic culture of grinding it out"?[7] Aside from personal differences, is our moment in collective history

一
尋
牛

1 | SEEKING THE OX

This single person wandering around looking for an ox looks lonely, a bit forlorn. This corresponds to our feelings of frustration while walking the path. We sometimes wonder, when will some tangible achievement finally arrive? As we gaze at this image, the phrase "What's wrong with this picture?" may arise. The feeling-tone is more like "What's missing from this picture?" What are we missing? Everything. We have narrowed our gaze so much that everyone and everything around us seem to fall away as we exhaust ourselves searching for what's painfully absent.

IN MARCH 2005 I was a visiting dharma teacher for a weekend at the San Francisco Zen Center. Suzuki Roshi and his students founded this pioneering Buddhist meditation community in 1962. During the brief period that I practiced with the City Center Zen community, I heard a talk by one of the residents on what is called, in Zen tradition, "the way-seeking mind." This heart-mind is the motive force that moves us on the path, from our first hesitant steps through the challenges of compassionate engagement into the unwavering confidence of complete awakening. In the Indo-Tibetan tradition, this is called the "awakened heart of *bodhichitta*." Roshi also referred to it as "our inmost request."

We are questing, questioning, seeking our own true nature. The teachings of the Buddha suggest that this true nature is the same as the original nature of everything, the basic reality of all that is.

The Welcoming Exercise is offered as an experiential entry, a way station on this winding path of inquiry. What do we find when we welcome? What are we really seeking? Is it experientially true that, as Suzuki Roshi states, "it is wisdom which is seeking wisdom"?[1]

The invitation is to enter further into our experiential inquiry into welcoming. After all, welcoming isn't just a word; it's an experience. Yet what is it really? Is it the same as what Suzuki Roshi, following his teacher and lineage ancestor Dogen, called "beginner's mind"? Is it the same as what some teachers call "mindfulness-awareness" or "panoramic awareness"? Let's find out, not by consulting dharma dictionaries for the real meaning of these terms, but by exploring our own experience as directly as we can. Not only is personally engaging in welcoming a grateful bow toward the experiential essence of all Zen and practice traditions, but we may learn far more from sitting silently with ourselves than from any additional words.

THE WELCOMING EXERCISE

Please pause for two or three minutes now and allow the space of welcoming to unfold. Engage in the Welcoming Exercise by sitting for three minutes with your eyes open and your hands relaxed in your lap.

———————

Doing the Welcoming Exercise allows us to discover many things—as we saw in the questions and comments at the end of the introduction from people who've previously tried this little exercise. We notice, for example, that much of our mental space is often filled with many hopeful and fearful thoughts about what might happen in the future. Remember the saying usually attributed to Mark Twain, "My life has been filled with many terrible things, most of which never even happened." In the open space of welcoming, thousands of thoughts about the past poke their heads up, memories of good times and bad times. One person looked up and smiled after an initial three-minute session of the Welcoming Exercise: "It's crowded in there!" Yes, it often feels jam-packed and busy in our heads. Did someone say, "Bring the noise"?

What else do you notice? What about your body? Sometimes you notice that you're hungry. As you sit welcoming, your stomach growls a few questions: "How long will it be until lunch? How long ago was breakfast?" You might feel an itch and then almost immediately the urge to scratch it. You might want to stretch your arm to relieve some chronic tension. You feel once again the sensations of a sore shoulder or an aching back. You might wish for a cool drink of water or a warm cup of chocolate. You notice sensations in the body—easeful, tense, neutral. You also welcome the feeling that you would like more or less of a particular bodily sensation.

What else? How about other feelings? Even in just three minutes, several emotions may arise, tumbling one after the other, and pass on: "I wish Carmen were here; she's always the life of the party." "I'm not happy that Ed is moving to town, he's so pushy. I don't look forward to seeing him every day."

Welcoming all your mental activity, thoughts, feelings, sense perceptions, and physical sensations is the main point of the Welcoming Exercise. Welcoming all these experiences—just allowing them to arise and to go—is the primary activity, or nonactivity, here. You're being inclusive, allowing whatever momentarily fills the space to arise and whatever leaves the space to leave. If you're doing that, then you've done well (even if you may occasionally wonder, "Done well at what?"). Or you may think, "So what? What's the result of three minutes of doing nothing? What's supposed to come about from this? What's the aim or goal or result?" Notice the ingrained idea, the familiar underlying assumption, that this must be a way to get *to* something else, to change our experience, transforming ourselves from this to that. Why else would anyone do this? Welcoming is an invitation to discover a slightly different motivation. What might that be? Once again, an answer can be found through examining our actual experience. We're not looking for a textbook-correct or an ancient, doctrinal answer. Welcoming is an opportunity to experience a different way of being alive, being human, being with ourselves. Welcoming is a gateless gateway, but if we want to see what's on the other side of that spacious entrance, we have to do it, not just read about it. Experience is essential, the most important ingredient in the soup.

Notice that even in this basic exercise we see clearly our habit of seeking something else again and again. See it? If you don't, taste-test again by sitting still and noticing how long it takes for restless thoughts, discontented feelings, and impulses to arise: "What comes next, and how soon will it get here?" We are almost always searching for our better next-next, and the boringly plain simplicity of the Welcoming Exercise allows us to notice that. It's like a beige canvas background on which the bright and varied colors of our seeking stand out vividly. Often, there's little else to notice. This initial discovery of searching corresponds to the first of the oxherding pictures: someone is looking for a lost ox. In this first image, we only see the searching person gazing here and there. There's no ox in the picture, no footprints or partial glimpses of the ox, nothing. All we see is seeking.

In the spirit of opening again and again to ourselves, please pause a moment now and fully engage in the Welcoming Exercise by sitting for three minutes with your eyes open and your hands relaxed in your lap.

DISCOVERING SEEKING

What we've just seen is one of the first experiential discoveries of the Welcoming Exercise: we are usually not welcoming. We realize this directly for ourselves through our own experience. Instead of welcoming what is arising, we are almost always seeking to get something, to find something *else*. Sometimes our subconscious gossip sounds like this: "Not this same old stuff, surely. When does the really good part kick in? Is this all there is? Really?"

Something arises in our experience—a thought about tomorrow, a feeling about the past, a melancholy memory, a sound. Often, we don't want that bittersweet memory, it's slightly unwelcome, and the telltale sign of our unwelcoming attitude is that we want something else. We would prefer another moment; as it says in a chant from the Buddhist lineages in which I practice, "Always wanting there to be another now." Either we seek a new (mental) place—we're trying to get somewhere else in our practice, or our psychological journey—or we seek to acquire an upgrade, something more valuable and meaningful. To state what is painfully obvious, all our constant seeking is based on a feeling of "lack." This feeling of something missing is also the basis of our spiritual search.

In some commentaries, the ox represents fully awakened mind, our true nature. We search for it because we feel we've lost it. Certainly, we've become cut off from it somehow. The ancient Greek philosopher Heraclitus asserted that we human beings have "lost touch with what is most familiar."[2] Something very close to us, the most intimate aspect of our being, has been misplaced: "Where is it? How can I find it? How can I get it and keep it near me to be happy all the time?"

In some of the old images, the oxherder looks listless, forlorn, and bereft, like a person grieving a loss. Maybe the person has grown tired from so much seeking? In other more modern versions, the searcher looks vigorous, alert, and energized—maybe ready to rush somewhere (where?) to find that ox and post a smiling selfie with it right away. Trungpa Rinpoche's comment on this first image emphasizes the feeling of absence: "The inspiration for this first step . . . is feeling that things are not wholesome, something is lacking."[3] Let's continue our beginning contemplation, then, by exploring that feeling of lack—the basis of our entire meditative journey. This is the necessary first step on the spiritual path of oxherding. Awareness of this feeling of lack—that something vitally important is missing from all our experience—is key to waking up to the noble truth of suffering.

CONTEMPLATING OUR EXPERIENCE OF LACK

One of the best ways to contemplate some of the deeper meanings of "lack" is to examine it from the first-person point of view. For some of us, this is easy. We've grown up with empowering encouragement to "just speak from the heart, be genuine." For others among us who have been trained since childhood not to talk about our feelings in public, this is challenging. It takes quite a bit of courage to feel into our experience and say our truth out loud or even write it down in a journal. Clearly, thinking and speaking from the personal experience and social location of being "me" is not at all the same as speaking objectively from a third-person perspective, as though lack is something that only happens to those over there—to them, to her, to him.

Lack is as close to me as my breathing, as intimate as my own death. Any death can remind us of this primal loss, the looming absence that never leaves us: "When was this inner sense of lack born in me? When did I first come to feel that something is missing?" In my own case, I certainly felt this as an awkward, nerdy Black teenager growing up in racially segregated East Texas. By high school, I remember thinking and feeling, "Something is missing in life, in my life, and maybe something is missing in me." (Scary thought.) Later, in my early twenties, when I heard my first dharma teacher's penetrating comment, "You don't have to be embarrassed about who you are," it felt kind and exposing all at once: when and where had I learned to feel embarrassed about being who I am? You can see that the causes and conditions intertwined here are born from large social systems and collective history, yet they are deeply personal. As it says in the ancient Zen text *Trust in the Heart*, "Not two."

The earliest teachings of the Buddha connect this feeling of lack with the absence of solidity. Something is missing; indeed, we discover that *something is missing in everything*. What's missing is a solid, permanent basis for anything—including a fundamental, unchanging ground or essence to being "me." There is no solid, independent, permanent self. We humans are impermanent, changing beings, arising contingently from our parents and culture, eventually dissolving back into space with the exact time of departure unknown. This pervasive experience of lack is connected with the early Buddhist teachings of "no-self" and—bigger gap here—no solid, enduring ground to any of our experience. People around us change, relationships change, jobs and companies change, laws change, bodies change, minds change, the nature of life on this planet changes faster and faster. Our modern times, in Karl Marx's famous phrase, are when "all that is solid melts into the air."[4] For most of us, all over this planet, life changed abruptly in 2020 with the global COVID-19 pandemic.

Our personal experience shows layer upon layer of absence all the way down to a hollowness at the core of our being. Reality is groundless, and the felt personal sense of this appears as lack, loss, or absence. The Buddhist writer David Loy deftly articulates the link: "This groundlessness usually manifests in our consciousness as a gnawing feeling of lack, the conscious or repressed sense each of us has that 'something is wrong with me.'"[5] This sentence appears in a chapter Loy calls "The Pain of Being Human."

BUDDHA SEEKING

Here, we are close to the ground of the entire Buddhist tradition: Shakyamuni's fearless proclamation of the first noble truth of suffering. The Buddha's awakening and subsequent first teaching were, in some poetic accounts, thundering cosmic events that shook the heavens and the earth. In contemporary terms, enlightenment was a transpersonal moment inaugurating the twenty-five-hundred-year collective spiritual journey of millions. It was also a deeply personal moment—if that word is suitable in this thoroughly egoless context.

As the story goes, the Buddha awakens in a transformative experience under the Bodhi tree and then wanders alone for seven weeks. Eventually, he speaks of his realization to five of his former friends on the spiritual path. These close companions had all abandoned Gautama, the bodhisattva and future buddha, as a lukewarm slacker. They shunned him for his backsliding lack of ascetic rigor and discipline. The Buddha compassionately shares with his old friends the discovery of this brilliant new teaching, the good dharma of awakening. In his first recorded discourse, he tells them that everything, without exception, is suffering. What disappointing news that must have been! One of the friends may have quietly wondered, "Really, Gautama, this is what you've discovered? This is the insight that comes from years of spiritual practice?"

We can imagine ourselves being there for that first discourse. It may have been a warm, slightly sleepy, north Indian afternoon. Suddenly we find ourselves sitting up straight and snapping to alert anticipation, as the Buddha approaches the close circle of spiritual friends. His face radiates peace and compassion. Clearly something deeply transformative has happened to him. What is he going to say? Wait for it. "Suffering. Friends, I have discovered the noble truth of suffering."

What did that mean? It didn't take the Awakened One to tell us that life includes small and large experiences of pain: a splinter in your finger, the sudden death of your mother. The Buddha's proclamation includes what everyone already recognizes as suffering (insert your favorite examples here), but the subtlety and range of his insight include far more than our usual, ordinary experiences of pain; they include the physical, emotional, psychological, social, and political.

Birth is suffering, and death is suffering, of course. Pain is suffering, but pleasure is also suffering (what?). In the midst of experiencing pleasure, we struggle to keep it going, to maintain it as long as possible, as we worry that it won't last. (We're right, it won't.) Getting old and aging in general are suffering. We go through the series of uneasy transitions from child to adolescent to young adult to maturity to middle age to senior; there are no real stops on this one-way express train from birth to death. Death is suffering, but so is being born—being born into new situations, new conditions, new jobs, new relationships, new responsibilities, new configurations of experience. Everything is marked by suffering. It's the universal brand indelibly stamped on all our experiences of life: not solid, impermanent, suffering. Commenting on the first oxherding image, Trungpa Rinpoche says simply, "That feeling of loss produces pain."[6] Yes, that feeling of loss is painful.

Pain is a great motivator. We are moved to action based on the feeling of loss, of lack, of suffering: What is to be done? Surely something must be done, but what? If we contemplate the spiritual journey of the Awakened One, we see that this great sage had already exhausted two popular conventional answers to the great question of life and death, a question we all face. Buddha had already seen that a life dedicated to pleasure—his early life-journey included the loving embrace of family and friends, delicious food and drink, music and dance—is also a life of suffering. A temporarily pleasurable life is not really an answer to the great question of living and dying, not a truly liberating release from the prison of lack. It's just enjoying a more comfortable and entertaining wing of the same prison.

Buddha had also searched for an existential answer to this question through the opposite strategy, following an ascetic path of renouncing food, wealth, and the companionship of friends and family. As a spirit-based alternative to privileged indulgence, the young renunciate energetically embraced the path of yogic hardship, engaging in long fasts and scorching himself in fires. These spiritual experiences were intended to take him completely beyond ordinary pleasure and pain, off the wheel of suffering altogether, all the way to transcendent freedom. In Buddha's experience, all his strenuous ascetic and yogic efforts failed to remove his inner sense of lack. He discovered that this harsh approach to liberation was only digging him deeper into the feeling of basic inadequacy: "What's wrong with me? What's missing here? Why can't I find it?" In Buddha's life, cultivating altered states of consciousness and extreme experiences managed, at best, to hold the inner emptiness at bay temporarily. Eventually, even high spiritual states fall apart—all of them. Neither a life of seeking pleasure nor a life of embracing harsh disciplines leads to true awakening.

In this story, we see the Buddha as the archetypal seeker. He searches and exerts himself wholeheartedly to find the ox of liberation. Finally, he finds himself—alone. Loneliness relaxes into aloneness. Shakyamuni stops desperately searching for a way out of suffering, a way to finally defeat that stubbornly lingering inner sense of emptiness. Instead, he turns toward what he has been fleeing for so long and embraces the reality of pain, the fundamental experience of "something is missing." As we know, this takes tremendous bravery. Talking about it, reading and writing about it, are much easier than actually doing it. Doing it means experiencing for ourselves, again and again, the truth of basic suffering.

One day, in a moment of quiet reflection during a communal festival, Gautama the seeker remembered a childhood experience of natural welcoming when he was neither pushing himself to be better according to the judgments of a relentlessly harsh inner critic, nor indulging every passing whim and chasing after tantalizing objects to gain pleasure. Buddha discovered the innate sanity of a middle way between habitual grasping and rejecting. The rest of the story leads on to what is called "unexcelled, complete, perfect enlightenment."

So, what are we seeing in the Buddha's life story? We see that action motivated by the feeling of inner lack can follow either of two courses. One path leads to behaviors aimed at avoiding this painful feeling of emptiness by acquiring something to fill the gap or renouncing all sense pleasures. The result is increased discontent and, ultimately, more deeply ingrained patterns of suffering. The other path leads to basic well-being by allowing our suffering and joy, pains and pleasures, to arise and to go. In this way, we glimpse an innate awareness that does not come and go. This is a moment of liberation. What are we freed from? We are freed from struggling with our experience. Even a moment of such peace is truly wonderful.

SEEKING: INTERPRETING THE FIRST OXHERDING IMAGE

Trungpa Rinpoche, commenting on this first seeking stage, writes, "You discover that ego's attempt to create an ideal environment is unsatisfactory."[7] This is a vicious circle: loss and lack leading to actions of denial leading to disappointment and even more dissatisfaction than we had at the beginning. Our moment-to-moment investment in avoiding and denying suffering pays big dividends in increased dissatisfaction.

The path of awakening begins with insight into this vicious cycle of avoidance. When we linger with our dissatisfaction, some of our ambitious, neurotic speed to vanquish all discomfort begins to slow down. Welcoming is a space of momentary freedom—allowing our lives to be exactly as bitter and as sweet as they are without manipulation.

By contrast, our frenzied, unsuccessful attempts at complete command and control are part of the materialistic outlook and practice: buying and consuming, getting and spending, 24/7. "The materialistic outlook dominates everywhere," wrote Trungpa Rinpoche in 1968.[8] The essence of the materialistic viewpoint is that we are fundamentally lacking something important. Often, we're not quite sure what that something is, but like the person in this first image seeking the ox, we feel its absence keenly.

Let's linger here a moment to deepen this understanding of the connection between our inner feeling of lack and the outer practice of consumerism. Consuming goods and services is, of course, a major pillar of many contemporary societies. There is also a strong link between consumption and environmental devastation. Dr. Diana Ivanova, research fellow at the University of Leeds' School of Earth and Environment, writes, "We all like to put the blame on someone else, the government, or businesses. . . . But between 60-80 percent of the impacts on the planet come from household consumption. If we change our consumption habits, this would have a drastic effect on our environmental footprint as well."[9] The outlook and daily practice of materialism have devastating consequences.

Buddhist teacher Martine Batchelor notes that the young oxherder is "looking a little lost," "searching for something," and "not even sure what."[10] Perhaps our fundamental uncertainty is connected with the ox's elusiveness. We're not sure. Is there really an ox somewhere, or is life just this way, with every experience marked by basic dissatisfaction? Korean Zen Master Kusan Sunim says of this stage, "However much you try, the way to proceed remains unclear."[11]

This unclear feeling of lack motivates us to search for fulfillment in the outer world: "If something is missing here, maybe if I search hard enough, I can find it over there." First, we search for lasting satisfaction in the physical and emotional realms. We fixate on "food, wealth, companionship, fame, and sensual attachments," according to one Tibetan Buddhist practice text.[12] Batchelor narrates our frustrating search for lasting happiness in changing settings: "We think that if we had enough material things we would be happy. We would like to have a house with a nice garden or enough money to buy whatever takes our fancy. But nothing seems to completely satisfy us. . . . Perhaps we hoped that a good relationship would give us lasting happiness, but it is very hard to find the right person or be the right person, all-loving, all-accepting. Even if we find someone, we discover that one person cannot satisfy all our needs, wishes, and hopes. A worthwhile or highly-paid job might give us security, but again this covers only a certain period of our lives. All these things give us only a fleeting happiness. Something seems to be missing."[13]

Finally, we turn, like Shakyamuni after leaving his family palace, away from seeking outer pleasures toward acquiring more and better inner experiences. We move to spiritual seeking for higher, transcendent states of consciousness, more meditative insights, the blissful streamings of yoga, and more resilience and healing. At first, these seem to be the answer (even if we are not sure what the question is). When spiritual experiences also show their unruly nature, coming and going just like everything else, we spur ourselves on with memories and hope: surely we just need to try a bit harder to find the solution to the problem of life?

Notice that it's our fixation on solidifying various pleasures that eventually leads to frustration. Nothing lasts. There is no permanent happiness to be found in pleasing experiences (or in fending off unpleasant experiences). The problem is not with food or yoga or our companions or spiritual states. The problem that repeatedly gives birth to frustration and disappointment is our futile attempt to build a permanent nest from these transitory materials and experiences. We don't need to renounce the world or our friends and families so much as we need to change our inner attitude. Turns out that, as that wise book title suggests, "Happiness is an inside job."

An old book presciently titled *Cutting Through Spiritual Materialism* states, "There is no need to struggle to be free—absence of struggle is itself freedom."[14] The converse is also true: all our willful struggling, searching, and seeking creates a prison of discontent. Searching is both the way into further experience of the maze of self-frustration and the way into experiencing the spacious meadow that allows life to be lived directly as life.

American Zen teacher Josh Bartok Roshi says of the searching stage pictured in this first image, "This is raising the mind of enlightenment."[15] And as Tibet's great realized poet Milarepa sang, "The Great Awakening of the Bodhi mind can never be achieved by searching and by wanting."[16] If we continue to seek an object—external or internal—to satisfy our inner lack, the path leads to repeated frustration and further seeking. If we turn toward the sense of lack itself, if we search by being willing to linger with the feeling of the impulse to seek, a door to spaciousness opens. Searching is both the confused voice of neurotic entanglement, of chasing our own tails, and the clarion call of basic sanity: "There's no need to seek more over there; look *here*."

COMMENTS ON THE WELCOMING EXERCISE

We are alternating comments on the Zen oxherding pictures with examining our experience doing the Welcoming Exercise. Sometimes this is called contemplating both the dharma of "what has been said or told" and the dharma of "what has been experienced or realized." Contemplating these two aspects can inform and clarify both. For example, it may be clear now—in a way that was not obvious before—that welcoming is not seeking. It's not trying to produce an answer to the great questions of life. It's not trying to understand the mystery of death. It's moving neither toward nor away from our experience. It's not trying to hit the target of a particular peaceful experience of "not suffering," something we glimpsed once in a meditation retreat long ago and have been trying to get back to ever since.

We might even call welcoming a momentary exercise in being. Tsoknyi Rinpoche's suggestion is to "avoid occupying yourself with something all the time. If you are always entertaining yourself, you create the habit of always wanting to do something. You become dependent upon those things you occupy yourself with, and you always need those things around. At some point, it feels impossible to just be."[17] Sound familiar? In the Welcoming Exercise we are becoming intimately familiar both with our restlessness, that feeling of the near impossibility of just being, and with welcoming that restless, searching monkey mind into the space. Surely monkey mind needs loving-kindness and friendliness as well. Let's follow Suzuki Roshi's suggestion and give that monkey mind a spacious meadow to play in.

This learning to be is a developmental process. As Buddhist teacher Charlotte Joko Beck helpfully explained, "Most of us (myself included at times) are like children: we want something or somebody to give us what a small child wants from its parents. We want to be given peace, attention, comfort, understanding. If our life doesn't give us this, we think, 'A few years of Zen practice will do this for me.' No, they won't. That's not what this practice is about. Practice is about opening ourselves so that this little 'I' that wants and wants and wants and wants and wants—that wants the whole world to be its parents, really—grows up."[18] Beautifully said.

Now, it's time once again to stop reading (and writing) and just do it. Please pause a moment and fully engage in the Welcoming Exercise by sitting for three minutes with your eyes open and your hands relaxed in your lap. Remember that this is not meditating (whatever your usual practice of meditation is). Allow space to welcome whatever arises in these next three minutes. Please begin, once again, with beginner's mind.

二
見跡

2 | SEEING THE OX'S FOOTPRINTS

The second oxherding image shows the seeker seeing the footprints of the ox. There's still no ox in the picture, but we're getting closer. We may wonder, getting closer to what? That's the question, isn't it? If we knew with diamond-like clarity and absolute certainty what the ox is (who we are in our essential nature), there would be no need for the spiritual search. Perhaps we're getting closer to understanding the nature of this search. What is all our seeking really about?

LET'S LOOK CLOSELY at this second image of the oxherder discovering footprints. Do you remember times when you felt you were getting closer to experiencing the basic truths of existence? It looks like the oxherder is making big strides, eagerly following those elusive footprints. That feels familiar to me. Renewed exertion on the path is often sparked by glimpses: "Oh, I see! This is what they meant. It's been right here all along. How could I have missed it? It's so obvious." Yet glimpses fade, recede, and disappear into a mist of more questions: "What was it again? What was it I felt I understood during that intensive practice?" We alternate back and forth between seeking and seeing, glimpsing and wondering.

The first two oxherding stages, seeking and seeing, mainly focus on the bad news, the painful truth of searching that leads to constant dissatisfaction. This is the emphasis of what is sometimes called the Buddha's first turning of the wheel of dharma. Yet Trungpa Rinpoche frames this teaching as the inseparability of bad news and good news. Dissatisfaction itself is a sign of a spark of intelligence flashing in the darkness of confusion. Seeing the ox's footprints is an initial sign of this awakened intelligence. Trungpa Rinpoche points a finger at the forceful imprints of the ox. Our dissatisfaction with life is itself a sign of true nature awakening. First, in the early Buddhist teachings and in our own journey, we hear "the bad news: that we are trapped, we are hopeless, we are helpless, and the meaning of life is pain."[1] Then, a little later, we begin to hear "the good news, that even if life is pain and you are trapped in samsaric imprisonment—how do you know that? If you know that, if you have some notion of discovering that, maybe there is something in you that is actually able to see that—which is good news."

With this, we are also getting closer to understanding the truth of suffering and the origin of confused suffering itself. These are the first two of the four noble truths taught by Shakyamuni Buddha in his earliest teaching. They represent an example of the dharma of what has been told or taught, and the corresponding experiential journey is up to us. First, we hear the truth of suffering, and then we make a path of these ancient teachings by closely examining our living experience now. Note that the path of awakening does not arrive ready-made. My first Buddhist teacher repeatedly emphasized to us that we build the road we are walking on.

If we truly hear these teachings, we take them to heart and live them in everyday life. What would be a sign of that embodied understanding? Some days we might notice that we're no longer running away from the painful realities of our lives and the suffering in the lives of those around us. This is softening. As the environmental justice philosopher Dr. Bayo Akomolafe suggests, "The times are urgent. Let us slow down."[2] Neurotic speed tends toward harshness to ourselves and others: "Get outta my way. I've got to get to fully enlightened compassion as quickly as possible—for the benefit of all beings, of course."

In contrast to the subtle (and not so subtle) aggression of seeking to get up and out of here as quickly as possible or rushing to try to see what's ahead, the overall attitude of welcoming allows us to sink slowly into a deeper understanding of what has been called "all-pervasive suffering." This isn't a quick-fix approach, and there are no magic bullets of self-improvement anywhere in sight. (Like many animals, the ox is understandably a bit gun-shy.) This is slow, careful, painstaking work. To the surprise of many, myself included, walking the path turns out to be a hands-on, manual process of feeling into the nitty-gritty details of all our life experience: times of harmony alternating with times of conflict; brief periods marked by few and then many emotionally charged upsets; other times of lots of gray, blah, "meh" moments; and then whole seasons charged with invigorating challenges. The footprints of this ox are everywhere.

As to seeing suffering itself, we begin to notice the struggle to emerge "one-up" from any encounter: who's winning in this conversation, this meeting, this exchange? Whether we are the winners in this game of constant comparing or not, the struggle to always appear "good" or "better" if not "the best" is itself painful compared to the natural ease of not faking it, simply being genuine. We also notice ourselves avoiding any shakiness or uncertainty and making frequent quests for the illusory safety of the familiar and comfortable. Awareness of these tendencies to swerve away is a good beginning. There's no suggestion that we need to be harsh with ourselves by constantly courting discomfort. That was the ascetic alternative the Buddha explored and rejected, finding that it produced no real fruit. It's mindfulness of the subtle suffering of everyday life that's involved here.

The suggestion is that there's an intimate connection between suffering and insight. Novelist Greg Iles was asked in an interview,

"What moves you most in a work of literature?" He responded, "Insight, which as a rule is earned only through suffering. Observation can get you close, but to touch the essence of something, one must see through the eyes of lived experience."[3] It's interesting that Iles uses the word insight to describe the lived experience of suffering. Buddhism writes that equation the same way, encouraging us to see clearly into previously ignored, deeper truths, to feel them directly. This is another facet of the meaning of welcoming. It's not just another contemplative exercise, but an approach, an attitude to be lived out in everyday life.

One ancient Buddhist text compares our increased sensitivity to this underlying suffering to that of a person experiencing a hair on the eyeball. The implied contrast is to the touch of a hair on the hand. The wise feel subtle suffering, the text says, like a stray hair from an eyelash fallen directly on the eye. This sounds like bad news, predicting a painful path to awakening ahead. The good news is that it's the emergence of our basic wakefulness that manifests as this heightened sensing of suffering—a suffering that is present during pleasurable as well as painful times. It's our own innate knowing that notices the constant struggle, the underlying anxiety in everyday life, when we keep asking ourselves, "Am I good? Good enough? Better than yesterday? Better than them? Or (wait for it)— worse?" Awareness notices a watchful inner judge closely monitoring every move we make and harshly criticizing every mistake.

These glimpses of an underlying unease are the footprints of our conflicted ego. We want to win, to be among the best, but not to be perceived as arrogant. We are afraid of losing and being flattened back into that ground-zero lack we were so keenly avoiding, hoping to never feel it again. This ego image–centered approach to living is the opposite of welcoming. We want to engage and feel life fully, yet we either rush to control what is happening ("Let's do this!") or shrink back, waiting to see what will occur ("Let someone else make the first move."). Either approach is fear-based and always slightly out of touch with the real pulse of life, which, like our heartbeat, is never entirely within our control.

Insight into these suffering-causing habits can show up in everyday life—pressing the accelerator too much in an argument or swerving away from acknowledging even the smallest differences with a close friend. The sitting practice of mindfulness meditation can also be an arena where we clearly see these oscillating patterns: first, trying way too hard to stay focused (which agitates the mind further) and then giving up and going back to numbing ourselves through binge-watching internal movies (which also dulls us to the suffering of others). Being brave enough to taste the feeling of lack is a good first step. This is the basic courage of welcoming.

SEEING CONFUSION FEELINGLY

The path of Buddhist meditation engages both our innate mindfulness and awareness.[4] In the first stage, seeking the ox, welcoming allows us a glimpse of the seemingly constant motion of searching. After our short welcoming sessions, the practice in everyday life is to continue that initial glimpse by cultivating mindfulness—in this case, mindfulness of suffering, particularly subtle suffering. This is, in Trungpa Rinpoche's phrase, "understanding suffering as the path."[5]

In everyday life, we also encourage the heart's natural sensitivity. We are not shutting down or tuning out these underground tremors. This is the realm of aroused emotional intelligence—paying close personal attention to feeling states, to the felt-senses of ourselves and others. This is deliberately cultivating our humanity, our human-heartedness. Or as Nobel Prize–winning novelist Toni Morrison writes, "The human project is to remain human."[6]

In the second stage, seeing the ox's footprints, we extend our initial mindfulness of suffering into inquiry: what are the causes of this pervasive suffering? This inquiry is called "insight within," asking where all this seeking is coming from. We are retracing our steps, moving backward from effects to causes, examining the links in the chain of dependent origination. We see clearly that all our seeking comes out of a sense of lack, of loss, of absence. In Shakespeare's play, anguished King Lear says to blind Gloucester, "You see how this world goes." Gloucester replies, "I see it feelingly." In a similar way we clearly feel this insight into lack. Welcoming allows this felt-sense of loss to be here. We're willing to linger with this wounded, broken state, rather than trying to immediately jump over it in search of a fake "wholeness." Our questions and inquisitiveness are aimed at naked, raw experience, feeling more deeply into our dissatisfaction, not bypassing it or covering it over with yet another spiritual concept.

JOINING DIRECT EXPERIENCE WITH UNDERSTANDING THROUGH INFERENCE

Here the path joins immediate experiential contact with valid inferential understanding. If we are holding our hands near an open campfire, that is direct experience of fire. If we see smoke rising above treetops in the distance, we infer the presence of fire somewhere up ahead. The sight of footprints implies that an ox was present. Similarly, we contemplate—in a slow, meditatively thinking inquiry—our experience of suffering and gradually arrive at insight into the lack that motivates it. This insight shows us something about this particular craving and that particular defensiveness as well as the general patterns and origin of samsaric confusion. These are good concepts, based on insight into the cause-and-effect relationships present in our actual experience.

There is sometimes a misunderstanding of the role of valid inference on the Buddhist path. At first, inference sounds merely conceptual and seems beside the main point of awake, mindful presence. In the summer of 2019, a *New York Times* reporter interviewed a Rockland County parent who stated that "Buddhist views prevented her from vaccinating her children unless they became very sick. . . . 'We're taught to live in the present. . . . Right now, my children are healthy.'"[7] Let me respectfully suggest that living in the present can include insight into causes that will have future effects. The earliest teachings of the Buddha emphasize insight into previous causes that produced our current painful realities. The Buddha fully awakened into understanding such causes and conditions on the night of his enlightenment. We do not need to wait until all the horrors of global warming are present before changing our actions. Our personal and collective actions in the present have future consequences for us and our children and our children's children. We understand that some of the effects of climate change are not present, but it would be wise and compassionate to act now.

The larger question here touches on the role of study or contemplation on the path of awakening. Reading and reflecting on the words of the teachings can remind some of us of painful experiences in schools or colleges. Someone may say, "I had a really stressful time in several educational institutions, so I don't want anything more to do with learning concepts. I just want to sit and practice meditation." The other extreme approach shows up in those who regard the Buddha as a kind of superscholar, a supremely erudite person who knew all the eighty-four thousand dharmas. These people may say, "I have no time to meditate. First, I need to finish reading all the Perfection of Wisdom sutras and this great translation of *The Tibetan Book of the Dead*. Did you see that amazing new course on the Six Yogas?"

Both of these extremes are in danger of missing the point. The classic Eightfold Path taught by the Buddha in his first teaching session with friends included ethical conduct (not causing harm and engaging compassionate activity); meditation (right mindfulness and samadhi); and insight (derived in part from studying right view). These are the famous three wheels of training: training in mindful and generous actions, training in sitting practice, and training in contemplative study—a tricycle of fully engaging body, speech, and mind.

Some commentaries stress that seeing the ox's footprints is not the same as seeing the ox itself, and yes, it would be a mistake to take intellectual understanding to be the same as actual awakening. Yet conceptual pointers can be useful guides. We are inspired to continue on the path toward the ox by the many signs and traces left behind, including ancient scriptures, traditional stories, and logical sequences linking states of mind and actions. We understand experientially the connections between craving, grasping, aggression, and suffering.

Commenting on the second oxherding image, Trungpa Rinpoche writes, "You are inspired by unmistakable and logical conclusions rather than blind faith."[8] Blind faith in our ideas of "mindfulness" and "nowness" and "emptiness" may exclude from our awareness a relatively reasonable understanding of causes and effects. Even though death is not yet our direct experience—not something happening right now—we can validly infer that, as with all living beings, we too will die. This is, of course, a classic contemplation in many Buddhist traditions. Our lives are impermanent, and this is a helpful insight on the path to liberation. It reminds us that complacently acting as though we have an infinite life span stretching before us is not realistic. Insight into death and impermanence sparks our motivation and exertion.

Daido Loori Roshi, commenting on this second stage, writes, "You find the traces; . . . you study the subtle signs."[9] The conceptual tracks and traces of the ox lead us into intimate, direct experience. These two—conceptual knowing and nonconceptual, intuitive understanding—are also "not-two." Both can be useful or helpful. The Tibetan Buddhist scholar-yogin Khenpo Tsultrim Rinpoche urges us to rely on the intelligence of listening, reflecting, and meditating as all three can "enhance the other."[10] Hearing the dharma leads to wakeful contemplation of life, and that gives birth to conceptual insight, which dissolves when direct experience arrives. Sometimes this is compared to starting a fire by rubbing two sticks together and then burning the sticks in the fire.

In ancient India, great Buddhist universities like Nalanda and Vikramashila joined contemplative inquiry with experiential insight. Nowadays, students at Naropa University in Colorado, a contemporary educational institution inspired by the shining example of these predecessors, also aspire to join intuition and intellect. Naropa's mission statement articulates this lineage connection and view: "At Nalanda University, Buddhist philosophy and the discipline of meditation provided the environment in which scholars, artists and healers from many Asian countries and religious traditions came to study, debate and learn from one another. Contemporaries knew Nalanda for its joining of intellect and intuition, and for the atmosphere of mutual appreciation and respect among different contemplative traditions."[11]

Studying what has been taught and mixing our contemplation with experience go hand in hand. If we begin by contemplating a traditional topic like death and impermanence, we can eventually let go of the words and feel into the ever-changing river of our lives, in which experiences are arising, being, ceasing, arising, being, and ceasing moment after moment. Dissolving into the flow of experience, we can even let go of the words *arising, being,* and *ceasing.* This is discovering a felt-sense of the stream of change beyond ideas of permanence and impermanence.

At other times, it may be helpful to simply inquire into and directly contemplate our experience itself. What is the current state of this body, mind, and heart? In our own lives, how is the balance of work and family life feeling these days? When we consider the fragility of the natural world, living beings, and ecosystems, many questions arise, leading to action and the question "Personally and collectively, what can be done?"

WHAT IS IT THAT SEES CONFUSION CLEARLY?

Seeing the footprints of the ox suggests that something large first makes its presence known, in part, by its absence. Suzuki Roshi often spoke of all aspects of life as the unfolding of "big mind." As we have seen, welcoming welcomes our small, monkey mind into the circle of kindness. Clearly experiencing small mind reveals a larger, innate spaciousness. It reveals the good news implicit in the bad news.

Let's look closely at the inseparability of confusion and wakefulness, or seeing clearly: that which sees confusion is not itself confused. If it were confused, it would take confusion as enlightenment— a major mistake. Instead, the awareness of suffering as suffering is a necessary step on the liberating path of the Buddha.

Now we need an experiential entry into this same area, so these words do not remain mere words on a screen, or ideas on a page. A contemplative exercise called Natural Noticing explores this inseparability. Here are the instructions, and after engaging in this exercise and answering some questions about it, we will conclude by connecting our experience doing this exercise with the meaning of the second oxherding image.

THE NATURAL NOTICING EXERCISE

The Natural Noticing Exercise is a close relative of the Welcoming Exercise—not exactly a twin, but first cousins at least. In Natural Noticing, as with Welcoming, there is no fixed focus of attention or mindfulness. We are not placing the mind on some activity, like breathing or walking, and returning there again and again, staying as long as we can. That is one form of mindfulness meditation. In this short exercise— unlike most forms of mindfulness practice—we are not cultivating the mind's inherent ability to stay, thereby increasing our mental stability. Instead, in Natural Noticing, we sit, let's say from three to five minutes, and allow ourselves to notice whatever we notice: sights, sounds, smells, the temperature in the room, thoughts in the mind, sensations in the body, feelings in the heart. Again, we are not meditating with a focus. Your attention will probably jump from thing to thing the entire time, and if so, just let it do so and notice that. As you can see, Natural Noticing is quite similar to the Welcoming Exercise, except that in this exercise, there is more emphasis on being curious about what we notice. In Welcoming, as you remember, there is more emphasis on just the act of welcoming.

Please sit for three to five minutes without deliberately doing any formal meditation practice: *don't* meditate. Simply identify what your mind notices as you sit here, or as Beat poet Allen Ginsberg suggested, "Notice what you notice." Again, the guiding question in the Natural Noticing Exercise is "As you sit here, what do you notice?"

QUESTIONS ABOUT THE NATURAL NOTICING EXERCISE

Here are some fairly typical dialogues following experiential sessions of Natural Noticing.

GUIDE: How was that?

PRACTITIONER 1: Fine. It was kind of restful, actually. No big deal, but okay, I guess.

GUIDE: Good. Could you list some of the things you noticed?

PRACTITIONER 1: Well, I noticed the midday sunlight streaming in the windows. I heard a bird singing and wondered what kind of bird—a robin, a finch, an oriole? I remembered being outside in a park once near Bear Mountain and hearing birds like that. Then I noticed the slightly stuffy heat in this room and a feeling of restlessness and wondering, "Has it been three minutes yet?"

GUIDE: Good. What I hear you mentioning is noticing sense perceptions (sights and sounds), thoughts (a memory), and moods that have a feeling-tone (slightly anxious and ready to move on). Does that sound accurate?

PRACTITIONER 1: Yes.

GUIDE: Anything else?

PRACTITIONER 1: Yes, I noticed the sound of cars and trucks going by on the street outside, and I thought I heard laughter in the distance. For some reason, I'm not sure why, at one moment I felt slightly sad. My left foot fell asleep, and I noticed that my body feels a little bit tired—not quite sleepy, but not well rested either.

GUIDE: Very good. Many specific perceptions. If we bundled some of these "noticings" together into a few categories, would it be accurate to say that you mostly noticed sensations in the body, thoughts in the mind, emotions, and sense perceptions?

PRACTITIONER 1: Yes. That covers most of what I noticed, yes.

GUIDE: Anything besides those big four?

PRACTITIONER 1: Well, maybe something like the atmosphere in the room, something like a social field, the feeling of the group energy.

GUIDE: Good.

PRACTITIONER 1: I have one question about this Natural Noticing Exercise. How is this different from what we call "meditating"? It didn't feel that different, you know?

GUIDE: Yes, many people say that. In many forms of meditating, we make an effort to stay with a particular focus (for example, feeling the body breathing or counting breaths). Here the key instruction is not to focus on any particular resting place. Just let the attention run and jump, tumble and turn, leap and fall—wherever it goes is fine. This would not be fine if we were aiming for peaceful stability and focusing on staying with one object. We're not, at least not during this exercise. Later, we could cultivate that steadiness of attention because it's very useful. This is a different exploration. Most forms of meditation involve noticing when the mind has wandered and then returning to either a bodily sensation or a feeling or a mantra. In the Natural Noticing Exercise, we are not returning to anything. There's no target or designated focus. Do you see the difference now?

PRACTITIONER 1: Yes. This is somewhat unusual, elusive. I realize I was following old habits and turning this into a kind of mindfulness meditation practice, forgetting that it's *not meditating*. That's kind of interesting in terms of lack of pliancy, noticing my stuck or rigid habits of mind.

PRACTITIONER 2: I still can't see how this is any different than what's sometimes called "open awareness" or "formless meditation." Isn't this basically the same as *shikantaza* in Zen or *mahamudra* and *dzokchen* in the Tibetan Buddhist traditions?

GUIDE: Well, maybe. Probably it's at least related. I suppose someone would have to practice all those to clarify the similarities and differences in experience—not just in similar sounding words and ideas, right? But in terms of obvious differences, consider this: each of the meditation practices you mentioned lives in a tradition. They are all housed in particular lineages and specific communities of practice. Some of them involve profound transmissions and intensive retreats, dialogues with authorized teachers, and strenuous group practice. Such profundity is like an experience of the bottom of the ocean—deeper than the deepest depths. In comparison, the Welcoming and Natural Noticing exercises are superficial, more like playing at the surface of a bubbling, babbling river. In these brief exercises we are saying to the mind, as Bob Marley sang, "Babble on!"

These exercises don't require any transmissions or esoteric empowerments or meetings of the mind with great teachers in *dokusan* dialogues. We're just exploring the ordinary, conventional, dualistic mind here. We're asking ourselves, "What do I notice when I sit still for a few minutes, making no effort to notice or be aware or mindful or present or any of those excellent practices?"

The most important idea here is naturalness. Meditation techniques all involve training something that is natural, like planting and cultivating a seed. We place pumpkin seeds in the earth, water and weed as needed, and eventually enjoy the delicious fruit. These exercises are all about appreciating the seed itself. They're all-natural, so to speak. This is an appreciative inquiry into natural noticing itself. We are asking ourselves, "What is that raw awareness like before it gets cooked and cultivated by practice?" It's similar to the difference between tasting raw foods and chewing something that's been cooked until it is "well done."

PRACTITIONER 3: So what? I mean what's the point of this stupid exercise really? I feel like I'm just not getting it. I'm not getting anywhere. My experience sitting here doing nothing is boring.

GUIDE: Yes. Boredom is a very important experiential gateway. Some teachers speak of hot and cool boredom in meditation. Notice our old friend seeking from the first oxherding stage in our experience of boredom: "Where's the special experience I've been searching for? When will I get there? Is this all there is?" Remember Tsoknyi Rinpoche's insightful comments about our mental habits of entertaining ourselves, including spiritual entertainment: "If you are always entertaining yourself, you create the habit of always wanting to do something." This "doing something" could include "resting the mind" or "creating space" or "being present"—all fine activities for another time. Right now, we're just noticing the habitual tendency to occupy every moment with doing something.

Do you see that? If not, do the exercise again to the point of feeling boredom, and then look directly into the experience that something (something exciting, dramatic, profoundly meaningful) is missing. Rather than rushing to fill this momentary emptiness, what's it like to linger with the uncomfortable feeling of boredom, lack, or nothing special?

Your question about the point of this exercise is also a good one. All the things we notice during the Natural Noticing Exercise are like footprints. They all point to that which notices. What is it that hears these sounds, notices a memory, drifts along in a fantasy, feels an itch? What is it that notices our experience of irritation or boredom? It is awareness, a natural noticing. This is the same cognitive faculty that senses our suffering. That which sees confusion is not itself confused. Something notices the memory of my grandmother, the yellow of this lily, the sound of robins singing, the rushing river of thoughts. What is that? What is it that notices?

In other words, whatever we perceive, whatever we notice, points back to noticing itself, like fresh footprints on the ground signaling the recent presence of a very large ox. As Suzuki Roshi says of Zen mind, "It is big, big mind. This mind is whatever you see. Your true mind is always with whatever you see. Although you do not know your own mind, it is there—at the very moment you see something, it is there. This is very interesting. Your mind is always with the things you observe."[12] We might extend this to all sense perceptions. At the very moment we hear something, awareness is there. At the very moment we think something, mind is there. Whenever we taste a salty tortilla chip, mind is with that tasting. I agree with Roshi—this dancing duet of mind and its world is very interesting indeed. In chapter 3, we will take the next step in our contemplative journey by inquiring further into the nature of noticing itself.

三　見牛

3 | GLIMPSING THE OX

The third oxherding image shows a person looking at part of an ox. Chinese Buddhist teachers began drawing versions of the oxherding pictures along with writing poetic commentary in the eleventh century during the Sung dynasty. There were different numbers of stages: first four, then six, and then ten. The most popular version that spread in the Japanese Rinzai Zen tradition uses ten images, but even here there are variations in the size and countenance of the ox. In some versions, the ox looms large, and the oxherder is tiny. In the version we are contemplating here, they are of comparable size.

Maybe this variation in the size of the ox corresponds to our own shifting perceptions of enlightened nature. Sometimes true nature seems gigantic, so much larger than our usual preoccupations and a very big mind indeed. At other times it seems that buddha nature is ordinary, really "nothing special" at all, discovered and cultivated in the midst of the ten thousand details of everyday life. Who knows?

FROM SEEKING TO GLIMPSING

After all this searching and seeking and gazing at mere footprints, to glimpse the ox probably brings a feeling of wanting to sing out (with Etta James), "At last!" In some versions of these images, only the ox's rear is visible; we cannot see the head. Daido Roshi commented that the ox "ventures into the thicket and gets stuck. Its head and horns are locked in the twisted strands of the under-growth, and it can't escape. Its rump is sticking out, plainly visible, and we see it. We see the ox. We glimpse our True Self."[1] In other versions, we can only see the head, yet this seems to be no ordinary head. "Look at the size of that thing!" Bartok Roshi wrote. "In our delusion, we think we've seen the whole ox, though all we've seen is the head. But that tiny tail! —what a wonderful thing it is."[2] In the same vein, the ancient Ch'an Buddhist Guo-an's poetic commentary on this third image asks, "What artist can draw that massive head, those majestic horns?"[3]

Whether we're glimpsing a head or a tail, practical emphasis falls on the partial quality of the seeing occurring at this stage. The vastness of the ox renders all our concepts petty. Glimpsing the grandeur of the cosmos, we experience our ideas as puny. We see only parts, not yet the whole. We cannot measure the expanse of the sky by holding up the eye of a needle to count how many across. What's the breadth of this open space? Clearly our true nature is much larger than we thought, perhaps greater than any thinking can comprehend.

Tradition encourages us to celebrate this glimpse ("Finally, yes!") while treading with humility instead of arrogantly assuming there's nothing more to be seen. This is similar to discovering the footprints in the second image—a good sign yet not the same as seeing the ox. In both instances, it would be a big mistake to complacently conclude that "this is all there is." This may be true all along the unfolding of the path, not just here near the beginning, similar to Katherine Hepburn's statement: "The time to make your mind up about someone is . . . never." It's probably premature to presumptively conclude that true nature is this alone and only this. Certainly it is clear awareness, bright sanity, openhearted compassion, and wisdom. Yet, possibly, there is more. Perhaps true nature is endlessly unfolding. This is the attitude of beginner's mind: something new may be freshly emerging in this moment.

Only experts and politicians conclude that they've already seen it all, as in that infamous phrase "If you've seen one redwood tree, you've seen them all."

Calling this stage "glimpses" may sound feeble. So, let's linger a moment to contemplate the importance of experiential glimpses. Perhaps the oxherder, impatient like many of us, wants the whole ox and wants it now. The push-button, instant convenience of our modern culture suggests this possibility. Buddhist teacher Judith Lief notes that the word *glimpses* may seem "to imply that the teachings they contain are superficial or incomplete. But many of our most profound discoveries come about in just this way: as sudden glimpses. In fact, the task of the teacher is to provoke such glimpses."[4] Let us welcome glimpses as well. In terms of our contemplative experience, we're beginning to see clearly into the nature of noticing itself, but thus far we're only seeing part of the ox's complete and perfect nature. Our experience of the ox is partly direct and intimate, but also partly obscured and fragmented. Glimpsing the ox's footprints was more distant, not nearly as vivid as seeing the living, breathing animal itself. Perhaps there is a paradox here: as with a holographic image, seeing part of the ox is seeing the whole. Yet tradition tells us that seeing part of the ox is not nearly as awesome as fully encountering the great beast in totality.

This sequence from seeking the ox to seeing its footprints and now glimpsing it illuminates the step-by-step, gradual unfolding of the spiritual path. In the first stage, we discovered our seemingly constant seeking as revealed by the Welcoming Exercise of doing nothing. Who knew that sitting quietly for a few minutes without a focus could be so illuminating? Doing nothing highlights our seeking, the habitual, compulsiveness of doing something to get somewhere else or gain something. Then we engaged in further contemplative inquiry into this seeking and made an experiential discovery: at the core of all our seeking is a sense of inner emptiness. This leads to mindfulness of this all-pervasive seeking as a subtle form of suffering, a basic anxiety underlying all our experiences of hope as well as fear. The stronger our hope that the "good" moments will last, the greater our fear that they won't.

How does our mindful experience of this subtle but pervasive form of suffering lead us to the third stage? Initially, the sense of something missing is the motivation for our confused attempts to fill the gap with someone or something from outside, the widespread practice of materialism in all its various forms. Over time, however, this same sense of loss—we feel we've somehow lost touch with a basic aspect of being human—also motivates our spiritual search for the ox. All our experiences in everyday life—of pleasure and pain, of sights and sounds—are the footprints of the ox beckoning us to come closer, to come into a more intimate relationship with the ground of our being as it rises before us in the experience of this moment. In this journey, our true nature dawns bit by bit, sometimes by subtle degrees, just as each morning the sun emerges slowly on the horizon. As with the silent transformations of Nature (such as slowly changing seasons), these changes may not be noticeable at first, particularly if we focus exclusively on the high drama of peak experiences.

Sudden approaches to enlightenment are often contrasted with the gentle unfolding of a developmental journey. In the history of Buddhist traditions, there have been many impressive debates about the best path to awakening—gradual or instant. These debates sometimes seem like two children quarreling over the same toy. Sometimes gradual and sudden awakening may go hand in hand, like two children walking together through a playground. This is reflected in what Zentatsu Richard Baker Roshi says of beginner's mind: "It is the kind of mind which can see things as they are, which step by step and in a flash can realize the original nature of everything."[5]

Trungpa Rinpoche comments that we are "startled" at perceiving the ox, and we may even "wonder if it's really there."[6] Is this a sudden glimpse? Of what? He notes the insubstantial quality of the ox, a tantalizing immediacy mixed with stubborn elusiveness. What's that about?

With a glimpse, the ox is in front of us, it's definitely real, and yet we cannot point a finger at it. It's much too big for that. We cannot touch it as we would cradle a red tomato in our hands. It's just not that kind of thing. Perhaps it's not a thing at all? Yet it's not nothing either, most definitely not.

When we see the ox, we see that it's not really out there. It's not an external thing, it's not an object. It feels insubstantial because it's not a substance. We are startled, suddenly freed, because the ox is not at all what we thought it would be: "What is this? Really?" Experience doesn't match our imprisoning concepts and familiar assumptions. The taste of beginner's mind doesn't accord with the expectations and predictions of experts. Here, the oxherder is warmly invited into trusting the unfolding of actual experience rather than relying too literally on any images or maps of what the journey will be like. There is a gentle suggestion that we might only see the ox if we let go of all our existing ideas about what an ox really is, a hint that perhaps the ox has been standing right here in front of us all along. Perhaps the ox is behind us, above and below us, to our left and right sides as well.

Daido Roshi says of the first stage, Searching for the Ox, "With strength depleted, and mind exhausted, you cannot find it."[7] That sounds familiar, an echo of the pervasive frustration and dissatisfaction we first discovered in seeking and explored in the footprints of the second stage. Yet, he continues, "There is only the gentle rustle of maple leaves and the cicadas' evening song." Are these rustling sounds and songs signs of true nature continuously speaking to us? Does what we call "Nature" signal the presence of true nature all around us all the time? Sometimes we cannot see the ox because what we are looking for, desperately seeking with a narrowed gaze, is always already present. According to Suzuki Roshi, "Big mind is something you have, not something to seek for."[8]

Trungpa Rinpoche calls this third stage "perceiving the ox." Direct perception means seeing by relaxing the tight grip of "is" and "is not." We're joining the buddhas, at least momentarily, in seeing beyond the extremes of existence and nonexistence. These solid ideas don't fit the insubstantial, open-sky quality of true nature. The title of Lawrence Weschler's wonderful book about artist Robert Irwin says it well: *Seeing Is Forgetting the Name of What One Sees.*

DRAWING THE TEACHINGS INTO OUR EXPERIENCE

To see the footprints of the ox certainly feels better, more inspiring, than our initial experience of seeking yet seeing nothing. The footprints include the dharma of words, the conceptual teachings handed down to us by our spiritual ancestors. Without the words, we might not know in which direction to search. Is the ox in the East or the West? We contemplate traditional teachings of impermanence and endless change, limitless kindness and compassion.

One challenge is to appreciate what we've heard and read while letting go of these ideas in the face of experience as the dharma leads to glimpses of realization. This marks an important transition from the second stage to the third: glimpsing the ox itself, we shift our focus from the words to the wordless meaning of the words. This juncture contains the first hint that the ox of our true nature is not outside us. *Suffering, patience, awareness*—these words are helpful stepping-stones, but our thirst is to drink something more than the word *water*. When we contemplate the meaning of the words, thinking about the countless ways we experience and avoid impermanence, eventually we glimpse a felt-sense of insight. Impermanence is not out there as a distant event in my future, but the arising and ceasing of each breath I take as I sit here. This is intimate experience of the dharma.

One of the greatest Tibetan Buddhist teachers, Longchenpa, described the practice of contemplating as "drawing the teachings into our experience." This process of slow thinking and rethinking awakens our own insight. We are not relying solely on what was said in the past but are appreciating our daily experience as the path unfolds in new and unexpected ways. Creative discoveries are essential to this journey. Our relationship to the teachings and teachers becomes less "theistic" in the sense of desperately seeking external approval and relying solely on the transcendent authority of others. Slowly yet surely, our inner nature of wakefulness steps forward as teacher and guide. One result is more trust in both the words and our experience, as they are both helpful and necessary. Bartok Roshi comments on this aspect of the third stage, though his comment applies to many stages in this journey: "Here we see for ourselves that the buddhas and ancestors and our own teachers have not been deceiving us."[9] Self-deception fades as genuine experience dawns. Getting closer and then closer, we can almost smell the ox.

Glimpsing the ox may feel as though we are losing ourselves as we find ourselves. Some of our narratives of personal identity may slip and slide a bit as we first encounter the ox in the meadow. Can the elusive ox go hand in hand with our usual stories of who we are and what we are? We all identify with narratives of personal and collective history. Are we both named and nameless? Why not? If, as some say, "awareness has no gender," isn't that another way of saying awareness has and is all genders?

This touches on the inclusive and accommodating aspect of true nature, its warm, welcoming feeling-tone. Our true nature is welcoming. Remember Suzuki Roshi's image of the spacious meadow. It's not merely "empty." Like a fertile valley, it includes and welcomes all. We are invited to settle and take refuge, as Zenju Manuel says, in a "homeless home."[10] Daoist teacher Liu Ming (Charles Belyea) writes of the ground of our being as basically tolerant, fundamentally beyond divisive struggle, and originally peaceful.[11] This spacious aspect of true nature is primordially open yet also friendly, kind, and compassionate—all awakened qualities that are inseparable from truly experiencing emptiness. It's only our idea, our concept of "emptiness" that sounds so cold and unfeeling.

To avoid falling into mere words and sophistry here, let's return to the Natural Noticing Exercise in an upgraded version. These exercises allow us some sight into our own experience—not the map of the traditional sequence outlined here, but glimpses of our living, dynamic journey. These contemplations encourage felt, personal experience. Do the exercise outlined here, and gently feel into the varieties of your experience, like noticing changes in the weather. Rainy and cool, hot and sunny, cloudy, snowy, foggy, hailstorms: all are welcome. Notice the full range of what happens in its highs and lows, shadows and highlights, colors and shapes, smooth or rough textures. Notice the nuances of experience. Our concepts are mostly broad-brushed generalities: "It was a boring day," or "This year was uneventful." Compared to what? Unleash your innate curiosity and enjoy the feast of inquisitiveness. Here our guiding question is "What do we see when we look at awareness itself?" Yes, there is what we are aware of (sights, rustling sounds, busy thoughts), but what is it that is being aware? Let's look and see.

THE NATURAL NOTICING EXERCISE 2

I'll be guiding you toward the exercise by way of an initial dialogue, then we'll try it, return to the dialogue, then do the exercise once more.

Welcoming and Natural Noticing are both more like appreciating a wild meadow than carefully cultivating plants in a greenhouse. One of Tsoknyi Rinpoche's book titles—*Carefree Dignity*—might set the right tone here. Let's inquire into the nature of noticing through a series of questions. Remember, this is an experiential exercise, so the answers to these questions are found in your actual experience, not in a book of meditation teachings or a text on Buddhist psychology. Are you ready?

Practitioner 1: Yes, I'm ready. What comes next?

Guide: Let's first take a gentle on-ramp into the second part of the Natural Noticing Exercise by trying to see if we can determine when this noticing started. When did it begin? After all, from the fact that you awoke, washed and dressed yourself, and got to this point in your day, all of that must have required some innate noticing, right? In other words, it would not be accurate to say that noticing only begins once the Natural Noticing Exercise instructions are given. Not at all. For example, what was the first thing you naturally noticed this morning?

Practitioner 1: Hm, the feel of the cotton bedsheet on my body? The sound of my partner snoring? The morning light streaming into the room? I think I might have remembered . . . I just caught the tail end of a dream about my grandfather, who's been dead many years now.

Guide: Excellent. So, what are we seeing here? We see that noticing is truly natural to us as sentient beings, not something we need to switch on deliberately. Noticing is not an add-on. At the other end of the scale, reach over now and turn your awareness off, like leaving a room and turning the light switch off by the door. Go ahead, please turn your noticing off. *Stop* being aware of anything. Are you doing it? Is it off yet?

Participant 2: Heh, heh. I'm not sure how I would even try to do that, where I would look for the on-off switch. How would I know or notice that I'm not noticing anymore?

Guide: Exactly. Well said. We do not turn awareness on, and we do not know how to turn it off. Where exactly is that switch? If we have a third glass of wine at our cousin's wedding, we don't stop noticing. We notice feeling tipsy, slightly drunk. We notice that suddenly all the wedding guests seem a lot more interesting than they were an hour ago. All over the world, human beings go to sleep and notice something we call "dreaming." *El sueño, le rêve*—there are thousands of words for this basic human experience. It's not only those practicing some form of dream yoga or psychotherapy who notice dreams.

This noticing definitely has a mind of its own. There are many moments when I'm glad it's present, but it also notices the most embarrassing moments of my life. It notices painful memories I'd really rather forget. Noticing is almost always noticing something, whether we're pleased about that noticing or not.

Participant 2: Well, yeah, but it doesn't notice everything, does it?

Guide: No, it doesn't seem to. It seems selective. It's not entirely clear what "noticing everything" would mean.

The main point, as we head deeper into our exercise here, is that this noticing is inherently natural—untamed, uncolonized—in the sense that we neither produce it nor shut it off. This is related to what is sometimes called, in the tradition of Mahayana buddhadharma, the "unborn and unceasing" nature of innate wisdom. The practical importance for our experiential inquiry is that we are, again, not trying to manufacture or produce a particular state of meditation that is calm and mindful, insightful and clear. We are leaving our ordinary dualistic consciousness as it is while looking to see, as clearly as we can, what our noticing itself is like. Can we describe it? How do we articulate its presence in our being, so familiar yet sometimes seemingly elusive?

Now please sit still for three minutes and turn your attention to noticing itself: What is it? Where is it? When does it arise, and where does it go? Proceed to the route.

———

Guide: Please describe your experience of looking into noticing itself.

Participant 3: I found this difficult, surprisingly challenging. It sort of doesn't make any sense—how can awareness notice itself? That would be like the eye seeing itself, which it can't do, at least not without a mirror. So, there was a brief bit of wrestling with that little knot, that entanglement, and then I settled down for a moment and looked. Noticing seems to me to be an awake quality, some kind of alertness.

Guide: Yes, very good. Can you say anything at all about that alertness? What's it like? Is it a bit speedy like after drinking one too many cups of coffee? Is it jangled and jumpy? Can you describe what we call "alertness"?

Participant 3: It didn't seem to have those qualities particularly. It seemed kind of neutral.

Guide: Good. We're just trying to be honest and truthful here. There's no right answer. We're looking and inquiring and then looking again to feel if our descriptions match our experience. We don't want our descriptions to be baggy and huge, like the funny suit David Byrne wears in *Stop Making Sense*. Even though there aren't spiritually correct responses to these questions, there are more or less experiential answers, and that's where we're heading—into the rich, dense thicket of experience. Why? Because that's where the ox lives and thrives. This ox does not live in a book. We're not trying to judge or evaluate this noticing as good or bad, we're just trying to say what it's like. What we're aiming for in our inquiry is more like noticing "That shirt is blue," not whether it's a good shirt or a bad shirt. What is it that notices all colors?

Participant 4: I also found this exercise challenging. What's the difference between Natural Noticing and Natural Noticing 2? I still found myself naturally noticing sounds of birds outside, the temperature of the air in this room, the sound of someone clearing their throat. So, what's the difference?

Guide: That's also a very good question. Here, the metaphor of the mirror of awareness can be helpful. We are not asking, in this second version of the Natural Noticing Exercise, "*What* is reflected in the mirror?" That was the first exercise, in which we noticed sounds and thoughts and colors. If we held up a red rose, it might be clearly reflected in a mirror. This inquiry is not about the rose but about the qualities of the mirror itself. Do you see the difference? If we held up a yellow tulip, it would also be reflected in the mirror. We're not inquiring into yellowness or redness or "flowerness"; we're looking into the mirror itself. What is it? What is it like? What does it feel like?

Participant 5: That's one of its startling qualities right there: it seems willing to reflect a yellow tulip as readily as a red rose. It seems fundamentally unbiased in that way, willing to reflect whatever arises. I have my preferences—to tell you the truth, I don't like roses much; get sick of 'em, particularly around Valentine's Day—but this mirror of awareness seems willing to reflect both the ugly and the beautiful equally.

Guide: Yes, very much so. Again, well said. That seems to be one of the first qualities of this mirror of awareness we might notice: its equanimity, or all-inclusiveness. Our innate awareness has an even quality, a willingness to reflect anything—what we like and what we don't like, all our diverse feelings of attraction and repulsion, that entire spectrum.

———

Now that we've contemplated this metaphor of the mirror, let's do Natural Noticing 2 one more time, looking closely for any other qualities of the mirroring mind. Please sit for three minutes allowing noticing to arise naturally—or to continue arising—and look closely to see the specific characteristics of noticing itself. What do you glimpse of the elusive ox of awareness?

WELCOMING THE OX

I've sometimes wondered if the reason we glimpse only part of the ox at first is its difference from what we're used to perceiving. Unlike most of what we perceive in everyday life, it's not an object like the things our three-year-old granddaughter proudly points out: "That's a banana. That's a car. That's a tree." We are so used to relating to things in our world; everyday life is filled with interactions with things and other living beings. We've practiced becoming familiar with objects throughout our lives. What else is there? Yet the ox of our true nature is not an object, and so it can never be objectified. If we think it's a thing—over there somewhere or deep inside somewhere here—that's our thoroughly trained expert opinion based on years of practice habitually relating with objects. As Suzuki Roshi says of true nature, "The big mind in which you must have confidence is not something which you can experience objectively. It is something which is always with you, always on your side."[12]

We cannot put this ox in a box and keep it for later. It's not out there; it's intimately ours yet it isn't a possession. It cannot be bought or sold. There are many ongoing attempts to commercialize it in the spiritual marketplace, to monetize awareness itself, but whatever is exchanged in the realm of getting and spending cannot be true nature. It can never be a credential: "I have an ox, and you don't." "Her ox is bigger than his." "Their ox is more fully developed." No wonder encountering it is startling. We get stopped in our tracks and wonder, "What is this really?" As a wise bumper sticker reminds us, "The best things in life are not things."

Glimpsing the ox is both humbling and encouraging. Ancestor Guo-an comments that the ox has never been lost, so there is no need to search for it. Some of our ways of seeking raise so much dust that we cannot see the ox standing directly in front of us, or we only glimpse its head or its tail. The good news is that it cannot be lost. The bad news is that, try as we might, we cannot grasp it or hold on to it: "See? I've finally glimpsed the ox. I've found my true nature. Quick, let me take a selfie with it and post it online. I wonder how many likes I'll get by the end of the day?" The other good news is that practice is the direct expression of being human. We are all seasoned practitioners of the ancient art of being human.

The basic attitudes of the Welcoming Exercise and of the two versions of the Natural Noticing Exercise are all the same: allow what is already happening to happen without suppressing or clinging. We are not trying to delete any of our experiences or coax the better ones to stay. This is nonfixation, nonstruggle, practicing with no idea of gain. If we have a vivid glimpse of the ox and a momentary experience of openness or clarity, it's tempting to fixate on making that last. Is there some way to make this experience permanent? What happened, we wonder, to our good experience from yesterday or from last winter's inspiring *sesshin* retreat?

Not fixating is the essence of welcoming. Our spacious meadow allows cows and sheep to arrive, wander freely, chew, ruminate, and take their leave. Taking their time, they proceed in a moment of unconcerned movement. This is "control" in the widest sense. The ox is invited and welcomed as well. Because of this nonfixated welcoming, more of the ox is allowed to appear, and we may begin to suspect that vast spaciousness is one aspect of the ox's true nature. More of the ox shows up. Our usual narrow focus leaves big blind spots of exclusion. We mostly see something dangling like a big carrot ahead of us, forgetting what's behind, above, to the right and left.

Welcoming is a distant cousin of what Trungpa Rinpoche called "panoramic awareness." This is 360-degree expansiveness. Touching awareness in a wide embrace, feeling and tasting it directly, is the next step in our journey.

四

得牛

4 | TOUCHING THE OX

The image for this stage shows the practitioner tethering the ox as closely as possible. This is a somatic, tactile experience. This stage of the spiritual journey demands touching the ox, being more in contact with the whole animal. We've stepped beyond just glimpsing traces here and there: "It was here yesterday, at least I thought I saw it, but where is it now? Where has it gone? I thought I had it, dammit." Now we're not just seeing the tail or the head. In this image, the bodies of ox and oxherder are both fully present.

OUR JOURNEY INTO discovering true nature involves directly contacting both innate compassion and deep insight. These two are inseparably joined, as in the expression "awakened heart." The wisdom of our innate wakefulness has caring as its heart-essence, empathic responsiveness to the suffering all around us. A few years ago, while participating in Mindful Compassion Training at Naropa University, I noticed that empathy for the suffering of others is much more available when I feel an embodied presence. When my experience is dissociated, more like a talking head, I am temporarily numbed and feel less of my own and others' suffering. At this fourth stage of the process, we see that the path of restoring and strengthening our confidence in original nature—both our human nature and the vast nature of Nature—includes directly contacting the body.

Such embodied presence makes for a full-contact journey. We're touching true nature, and the path is touching us. Such an experience can be profoundly enlivening, in part because of its naked intimacy. Many summers ago, I heard an inspiring Zen talk at Naropa University in Colorado. Commenting on Dogen Zenji's profound text *Genjokoan* (*Manifesting Suchness*), Taizan Maezumi Roshi repeated two words again and again and again: "Intimate practice. Intimate practice. Intimate practice."

The experience of intimacy follows naturally from the gradual dissolving of habitual, dualistic barriers separating body and mind, mind and heart, myself and others, self and world. *Intimacy* is an excellent word for the experience of nonduality. Trungpa Rinpoche's commentary suggests that, as the path unfolds, we're less guarded and defensive: "When you begin to accept this perception of nonduality, you relax."[1] We don't have to monitor ourselves so closely, worrying that we'll make a mistake, self-consciously watching and then judging our watcher as well, always asking, "Am I overthinking this or being inconsiderate? Too much? Not enough?" With each steady step into gentleness, we feel less yoked to anxious hypervigilance, more relaxed in the fundamental union of body, mind, and world. This journey is a path of unification.

Trudy Dixon, the editor of the transcribed talks on Zen meditation published as *Zen Mind, Beginner's Mind*, arranged the talks in three main sections for right practice, right attitude, and right understanding. The epigraph for the second part, "Right Attitude," reads, "The point we emphasize is strong confidence in our original nature."[2] Touching the ox is mainly a matter of increased confidence in the continuous presence of original nature. We don't have to anxiously fret and worry that the ox will never show up. It's here.

All along, our primary emphasis has been the naturalness of welcoming and noticing. Awareness is innate, part of our inherent birthright as human beings. Welcoming is our true nature. The Natural Noticing exercises explore this native awareness, which is not an acquisition or an add-on. We discover and develop trust in this powerful and indigenous aspect of being human. The key point, the essence-teaching, is that this wakefulness is who we really are from the very beginning; it is always already present.

Let's pause here to refresh our experience of the Welcoming Exercise. We need to keep alternating tasting our experience with all these words and concepts *about* experience. The words of ancient commentaries can be helpful pointers toward a more intimate relationship with our experience. If, however, we cling to the words for all our nourishment, that would be like subsisting on a steady diet of paper recipes and cardboard menus instead of real food. Here we are joining words and experience, old ideas and fresh intuitions.

REVISITING THE WELCOMING EXERCISE

Please sit for three minutes not doing anything, simply allowing your experience to arise however it arises. Let natural inquisitiveness illuminate the way like the midday summer sun. Allow basic innocence to meet your experience with open-ended curiosity, asking and feeling into this question: What is it like to sit with yourself as you are right now? And now? And now? Be sure not to exclude any moments of memories (dwelling on the past) or prospective thoughts (anticipating the future) that come up. This is not a present-centered mindfulness exercise. This is welcoming yourself as you are and as you are changing, with your mind darting here and there like a bird in flight.

YOU CAN'T TOUCH THE OX WITHOUT YOUR BODY

Since this welcoming spaciousness has been with us from the beginningless beginning, we may wonder how we ever mistakenly thought that we lost it. Why is it necessary to catch it and touch it again and again in order to hold on to it? Conceptually, these may seem like knotty tangles—how can we lose what we actually are? Experientially, however, we feel this loss keenly and daily. Even for someone fairly well established in the fourth stage—someone who has a good hold on the ox—the main discoveries and insights in the first and second stages are not experientially distant. Our constant seeking based on a pervasive feeling of lack remains a primary, foundational insight: our everyday experience is marked by this deep doubt about our original nature. We often feel empty and lost, not full and content. Sometimes we wonder if we are enough and if we will ever be truly worthy human beings. Through all our wandering, we wonder if we will ever fully arrive. Sometimes we suffer the fundamental anxiety of doubting our basic being. Strange as it sounds, we often wonder if this tree has any real roots.

As we have seen, this inner doubt leads directly to searching outside ourselves for someone or something to fill these psychological holes. Doubt leads to jealousy: "She has something I don't have, maybe something I once had but have now lost, I'm not sure. Long story short, I usually feel one-down around her." Doubt and envy can lead to collective aggression: "You and your kind stand in the way of the happiness and well-being of me and my kind. Get back now, or we'll send you back!" Many acts of greed and ruthless destruction arise from this fundamental doubt of basic goodness. David Loy has written insightfully of our collective ego as "wego."[3] Wars have been fought and invasions launched to claim and secure billions in revenue. During the first Iraq war, a cheeky bumper sticker appeared that read, "How did our oil get underneath their sand?"

The earliest teachings of the Buddha attribute all acts of hatred, greed, and delusion to this loss of connection with original nature. In his spiritual journey into deep insight, the Buddha uncovered this deluded sense of disconnection and called it "ignorance" (avidya). Here, "ignoring" means losing touch with our own nature. We do not know ourselves as we truly are. We cannot feel true nature; we've lost contact, so it's as though it's not really here. That's why we think we have to search for it elsewhere, somewhere out there. Having lost touch with what is most familiar, we take our next steps by reinvigorating this natural relationship with our own bodies.

"Body," of course, refers to your personal body, but it also points toward wider arenas of relationship and interdependence. Encouraging us to return to our present felt-experience, Social Presencing Theater cofounder Arawana Hayashi speaks of three bodies: the physical body, a collective social body, and the earth body. Clearly these three are intimately connected.[4] The social visionary Otto Scharmer speaks of three big disconnects in our contemporary global situation: disconnection from ourselves, disconnection from each other, and disconnection from Nature, each of which depends on a fundamental disconnection from our bodies. How else could we be actively leading lives that are destroying life on our planet? The therapist and teacher Resmaa Menakem writes, "The body, not the thinking brain, is where we experience most of our pain, pleasure, and joy.... It is also where we do most of our healing, including our emotional and psychological healing. And it is where we experience resilience and a sense of flow."[5]

The first section of Zen Mind, Beginner's Mind, "Right Practice," concerns the primary importance of posture in the sitting practice of meditation: "To take this posture is itself to have the right state of mind. There is no need to obtain some special state of mind. When you try to attain something, your mind starts to wander about somewhere else."[6] Suzuki Roshi's younger dharma brother Trungpa Rinpoche also emphasized grounding in the body first: "In the practice of meditation, an upright posture is extremely important. Having an upright back is not an artificial posture. It is natural to the human body."[7] Since our bodies are the closest aspect of Nature, our most intimate connection to Nature itself, cultivating the experience of being in the body brings a closer connection with true nature.

When the Buddha awakened on a full moon night sitting under a tree, maras (personifications of the forces of deception) challenged him: "How do we know you are enlightened? Show us your credentials. Which seminars, workshops, and training programs have you completed? Do you have the requisite certificates showing successful completion? If not, who will vouch for you?" According to tradition, the Awakened One calmly touched his hand to the earth, saying, "Earth is my witness." The famous image of Shakyamuni Buddha in "earth-touching mudra" (bhumisparsha) clearly shows us that touching the earth has always been central to this tradition.

Instructions handed down to us from great meditation teachers repeatedly suggest that we touch the ox of original nature by first contacting the body. Of course, we sometimes doubt the body as well. Is it truly trustworthy to be embodied? Given personal and historical trauma, does it feel safe to inhabit this body? These questions can be gateways into embodied experience, an invitation to feel into our actual experience of the body right now, however that feels. If it feels hesitant, reluctant, unsure, then feel that. If it feels like a steady, reliable old friend, feel that. This inclusive approach suggests welcoming our experience of the body as it is, pleasurable or not. This leads to embodied presence. Feeling into the posture of sitting meditation welcomes this most intimate aspect of Nature as the face of our own true nature. In the fourth stage, touching, we apply the welcoming approach to being in the body, with all the varieties of our somatic experience. This stage explores the central insight of Erika Berlant's Sitting: The Physical Art of Meditation: "The practice of meditation is at its core an embodiment practice."[8]

However we begin, however we enter—with rocky challenges or smooth ease or an alternating mix of the two—welcoming our embodied experience leads to a less dualistic experience of our bodies. We are making friends with our bodies—whether that growing relationship feels as awkward as a first date or as comfortable as a seasoned marriage. We have to, as a famous American Buddhist nun teaches, "start where we are." Touching the ox suggests a less dualistic, more intimate, relationship with ourselves, with others, and with Nature.

Whatever happens, ox and oxherder are now journeying together, and this spiritual journey gradually dissolves some of the barriers dividing us. Eventually, a nondualistic question arises: are we catching the ox, or is the ox catching us? Are we reaching out to touch, or is the phenomenal world leaning in, coming close to tickle and touch us? As comedians Abbott and Costello repeatedly asked each other, "Who's on first?" That's always the primary question, isn't it?

AVOIDING TOUCHING OUR TRUE NATURE

Some commentaries on this fourth stage describe it as "catching" rather than "touching" the ox. In these scenarios, the ox is a large, untamed animal, so the oxherder needs to carefully track it through wilderness, catch it, and then bind it tightly with a good, thick rope. (Sometimes these stories sound like outtakes from a "Zen and the Art of the Rodeo" reality TV show.) This big beast is powerful, with a will of its own, and as soon as it sees us, it runs right back to its lair, somewhere out there where the wild things are.

As with the question of who's really in control of this oxherding encounter, we may wonder who is avoiding contact with whom. Is it just that the ox is running away from us? Or is it possible that the oxherder is also secretly avoiding the ox? To take this question seriously requires asking another one: "Why would we avoid coming into intimate connection with our own true nature?" Avoidance often follows directly upon fear. We may fear drawing near our own inner power. There may be aspects of our true nature we are not yet comfortable with. Open spaciousness sounds attractive, but falling in space by definition feels groundless, and groundlessness can make us deeply uncertain and insecure. Likewise, vastness is an appealing idea at first, but moving closer to experiencing it, we may feel small and insignificant, mere grains of sand near an unfathomably deep ocean.

In a similar vein, though having nothing you need to do might sound wonderful, such an experience, perhaps accessed through the Welcoming Exercise, can unleash challenging dimensions of not-doing. If we are not controlling or focusing or directing our experience in any way, then unruly thoughts and emotions may easily arise. If the mind is like an ocean, there may be surly deep-sea creatures that enjoy surfacing from time to time. Welcoming is like an inner releasing—nothing is tethered or confined, repressed or managed. Everything is invited, no RSVP required.

Our true nature includes all the experiential aspects of our being: memories and future fantasies, desires and dramatic rages, moments of quiet peacefulness and long stretches of desertlike boredom. Everything is welcome. Everyone is invited. When we invite our true nature, some uninvited guests may show up as well. These include what psychotherapists call our inner "shadow" material, aspects of our being we have worked hard to repress and ignore. The arrival of more of our true nature signals the lifting of the lid of inner repression.

Here's the kicker: the spiritual activity of searching for the ox, seeking, may be just another way of avoiding direct contact with our basic being in all its complexity. As long as we project a pristine "enlightened nature" that we need to seek out there, we can avoid turning inward to face ourselves as we are right now. This is one description of the widely popular path of spiritual materialism. Our basic humanity is uncertain, constantly changing, sometimes emotional and messy. Often, the tidiness of a neatly arranged meditation hall only highlights, by contrast, the inner currents flowing here and there without apparent order. Spirituality as spiritual bypassing presents a virtuous way of micromanaging our inner lives, particularly in those moments when previously rejected aspects of mind return for a surprise visit: "Hello! We're here now, so get used to us." Then we are all too eager to get back to counting breaths and being dutifully "mindful." This is yet another form of self-deception.

Directly tasting the diverse experiences that arise during the Welcoming Exercise, the Noticing Exercise, or truly open approaches to meditation practice offers us other questions to contemplate: Is the wild ox avoiding us and our confining rope, or are we busily avoiding full contact with the ox? Who's the first one to step into or out of the meadow? Who's on first?

TRUSTING ORIGINAL NATURE

The Welcoming Exercise offers a gentle path into trusting original nature, developing confidence in the basic goodness of all our experience. Welcoming is trusting our experience as it arises, whether it's sour or sweet, salty or spicy. Echoing Psalm 34, Denise Levertov's sensuous poem "O Taste and See" begins, "The world is not with us enough / O taste and see."[9] Welcoming allows direct experience in which we can taste and see for ourselves. We are not proceeding with blind faith in seeking (as in the first stage), nor are we relying entirely on coherent logic and valid inferential understanding (as in the second stage). Now we can say with the certainty of direct experience, "These jalapeño peppers are really hot!"

Efforts to improve or edit our experience, to delete and rewrite our thoughts, feelings, and sensations, are often an expression of anxious doubt: "Is it all right that I feel this way? Is this okay? Right now, in this moment, am I having the right feelings? Are these good meditations? Excellent insights? Is this enough?" Most of these questions are variations on the theme "Is it really okay to be me?"

Some of these questions arise early in life in the heavily gendered context of our society and culture: Is it okay for girls to feel this or want that? Is it all right for boys to cry? Do real men eat quiche? Monica, the lead character in Gina Prince-Bythewood's 2000 film *Love and Basketball*, shocks her childhood friends in the neighborhood by declaring she wants to grow up to be a professional basketball player. Is it all right to want something outside the confines of the current box?

Such questions do not have to be silenced, banished, or pushed to the margins of mind. True doubtlessness includes doubts. Trusting these questions means allowing doubt-filled voices into the mix, not trying to fix them or convince them to be otherwise. Within many American Buddhist communities, cultures form that discourage expressions of difference or doubt. This is also true of all manner of religious, political, and cultural groups where cohesion is overemphasized at the expense of variation. The implicit or explicit messages can be, "Don't ask about that. Such questions are signs of your arrogance and ego. You should be unquestioningly loyal!" Trusting our experience, tasting all the varieties of flavors, expresses strong confidence in the innate basis of being human, our original nature.

Out of a basically good ground, many different thoughts, questions, doubts, feelings, fears, and sensations arise and grow. They all emerge from the same ground. Without exception, these experiences are all the basically good children of a basically good mother. Trungpa Rinpoche often spoke of our "enlightened genes." The word *genes* is related to the word *nature*; both words share a common root. True nature is a name for the basically good ground of life. Even dramatic and turbulent experiences are like massive waves rolling on the surface of a vast and deep ocean. Welcoming, in its radical simplicity, allows us to feel the basic sanity of our experience, the inherent worthiness of being human.

WELCOMING IN THE BEGINNING

To clarify the clear nature of welcoming itself, we might look more closely at welcoming in its beginning, its middle, and its end. In the beginning, welcoming is "unborn." This means it is not produced by any special effort. This is illustrated by the title of the ninth chapter of *Zen Mind, Beginner's Mind*—"Nothing Special." Welcoming is not meditating and not doing. As we have already contemplated, much of our daily doing, our energetic spiritual seeking, arises from an underlying, gnawing, searching discontent. Welcoming is not seeking. Welcoming is quietly content. Welcoming knows that this is enough. Welcoming involves no effort. We are not making something called "welcoming" happen. We don't kick-start the Welcoming Exercise with a little push, a little shove. During the Welcoming Exercise, if you find yourself making some deliberate, intentional, conscious effort to "welcome," just stop. Drop that extra effort. Just forget about it. In some traditions, the sitting practice of meditation is described as "sitting-forgetting," letting go of a remembered goal for meditating. Suzuki Roshi called this "sitting with no gaining idea."[10]

Welcoming is neither an advanced spiritual practice nor a beginner's first meditation project from which we eventually graduate. Welcoming involves no upgrades. Welcoming is not practicing mindfulness. It isn't a practice at all. It sometimes feels more like something that happens to us, less like something we go toward or something we make happen, like a party or a special event. Welcoming is often boring. Trungpa Rinpoche spoke many times of the meditative experience of "cool boredom." Philosophers Martin Heidegger and Giorgio Agamben have both written brilliantly about the experience of what they call "profound boredom."[11] This welcoming is not profound; it's boring and ordinary. Welcoming is not a purposeful journey. It's not going somewhere slowly or quickly. Welcoming is not stepping onto the fast track to complete, perfect enlightenment.

Welcoming is unoriginated, which means it does not have an origin in motivated effort. Motivated effort based in a feeling of lack is the origin of karmic life, leading inevitably to producing more suffering for ourselves and others. Suzuki Roshi's comments on this are pointed and precise, like the hot tip of a burning stick of incense: "If you are trying to attain enlightenment, that is a part of karma, you are creating and being driven by karma, and you are wasting your time on your black cushion."[12] Motivated effort is a necessary link in the chain of dependently arising confusion. Motivated action is what keeps the wheel of samsara spinning. Stepping off this vicious cycle of cause-leading-to-effect-leading-to-another-cause involves boycotting, at least for three minutes, the project of getting more out of or getting away from our experience of our lives. Welcoming is boycotting getting and spending.

WELCOMING IN THE MIDDLE

In the middle, we see that welcoming is not an event. Events are scheduled with a designated starting time and place: "This evening's concert will begin at seven in Berkeley's Greek Theater." "Tonight's Golden State Warriors game starts at five." Welcoming is not like any of those occurrences. In the sense that it's not an event located at a particular place and time, welcoming never "occurs." Concerts, sports events, and theater performances all begin and end. There's no moment when welcoming begins—the beginning of what? Remember, in the Welcoming Exercise we're not doing anything, so how could it have a starting time? Our experience of welcoming is more like tuning in to an unremarkable background sound that was already seamlessly present. Cognitive psychologist Eleanor Rosch once compared it to the continuous drone of the tambura in Indian music.

There's no moment when welcoming ends either. At the end of the Welcoming Exercise, as we rise and move about, some welcoming awareness continues as we reach for the doorknob, turn it to open the door, walk outside, hear the birds and traffic, see the sky. O taste and see.

The question rears its awesome head (with horns) again: are we welcoming the ox, or is the ox welcoming us? Consider that if we are busily doing an activity called "welcoming," that may already be doing too much. As Tibetan Buddhist master Tulku Urgyen would gently ask, "How far do your fingers need to go to touch space?" The fourth stage involves realizing that the effort to touch space with our fingers may rush right past what is already present, the space we ignore in our desperate effort to touch more space. This effort to acquire more "space" may be part of our spiritual materialism, an attempted commodification of what is truly limitless.

If the ox is with us from the very beginning, trying to reach out and touch it may miss what is never lost and never found. Daido Roshi comments on searching for the ox: "[Y]ou cannot find it. There is only the gentle rustle of maple leaves and the cicadas' evening song."[13] Is it possible that the music of these natural sounds is the unnoticed presence of the ox? Could sensing Nature itself be a transmission, our first introduction to true nature?

The question remains: Who is doing this welcoming? If there is a spacious meadow in which our cows and sheep wander freely, who makes this meadow? Has the multinational corporation Sky, Inc. expanded to include a Meadows Division? Sometimes experienced meditators say they need to practice sitting meditation to "create some space," but that effort doesn't seem necessary here. There's quite a bit of space already, exactly as much space as we need for all our experiences to arise. If there weren't enough space for sadness and desire and memories of the past to arise, how could they ever arise? We cannot fit a gigantic ox into a shoebox. There must be space for all our experiences to arise, right? Is there a sense in which space welcomes us? Yes, space welcomes—that's its primary activity, its first gesture.

Welcoming is not caused or produced by any effort. It seems to come along with being alive, without the need for a special upgrade. Welcoming is not the result of any motivated intention. It is an aspect of our basic being, our basic aliveness. Maybe other life-forms also welcome their environment. Who knows?

WELCOMING IN THE END

Finally, welcoming is complete. It includes whatever arises in our experience, rejecting nothing, including everything just as it is.

Welcoming invites and delights in the play of the mind wandering down dusty roads and into muddy swamps.

Welcoming is sustaining. Trying too hard is unsustainable and aggressive, often leading to burnout. This welcoming tames and trains our ox, as though there is a secret affinity between the space of the meadow and the ox's true nature. To our surprise, the ox settles down quietly from time to time—not from force or externally imposed discipline, but from spacious appreciation leading to even more contented spaciousness. Why run over there to the swamps when there is so much room here? Our ox finds contentment in the meadow.

In the end, welcoming keeps faith with the all-inclusive nature of space itself. Welcoming is loyalty to space. This is not the abstract space of physics or outer space. This is a felt-sense of spaciousness, as directly engaged as the taste of pepper on the tongue. We might say, "This is our space," or "We *are* this space accommodating all our life, our ups and downs, ins and outs, births and deaths." It's all-accommodating space. The steady, imperturbable buddha-like composure of an ox arises from this spaciousness. Nothing can threaten space itself, it's both insubstantial and supremely indestructible. Flashing swords may slice through space, but they don't cut it.

Yet our human experience of this inner spaciousness sometimes feels tender and vulnerable. Experiences of ourselves and others touch us, affect us, cheer us up, or pierce us with grief. Uncovering this vast spaciousness underlying everything, the basis of the entire cosmos, is also discovering our inmost request, the awakened heart of compassion, our longing for the liberation of all sentient beings.

As the meditation practice traditions repeatedly warn us, this is not mere philosophy. To test these words, to taste and see for yourself, please pause for a moment and engage in the Welcoming Exercise. Sit with this no-agenda, not-meditating approach to all your experience for three minutes. Give your being in its totality a spacious meadow. Let the spaciousness of welcoming tame the wandering ox of the mind. In *The Opening of the Field*, Robert Duncan's first poem is titled "Often I Am Permitted to Return to a Meadow." He writes of a space "that is a place of first permission."[14] So, go ahead with welcoming now; first permission is granted. Sit for three minutes, hands in your lap, with no focus or aim or direction.

ENTERING THE GREAT WAY OF MAHAYANA

In the *Ten Stages Sutra* (*Dashabhumika Sutra*), the Buddha describes ten stages or spiritual levels we must pass through on the journey to complete awakening or buddhahood. The stages describe the great way of Mahayana buddhadharma, the compassionate path of those "fully dedicated to the awakening of all beings," the brave ones traditionally called bodhisattvas. (*Sattva* means "being," and *bodhi* means "awake.") Each stage, called bhumi in Sanskrit (literally "earth," as in the level of a plateau), involves completely accomplishing one of the ten transcendent acts of a bodhisattva. These begin with generosity (*dana paramita*) at the first stage and progressively move through discipline, patience, and transcendent knowledge up to the perfected wisdom of *jnana paramita* at the tenth stage.

These ten actions are all called "transcendent" (*paramita*) because they pass beyond concepts of an agent, an action, and a recipient of this action. These activities transcend our usual subject-verb-object dualities. For example, a bodhisattva's generosity is free from the fixed concepts of a giver, giving, and a perpetually needy recipient. In this way, compassionate action is less sticky, freed from notions of always being heroic or of others as fundamentally impoverished. Such nonconceptual activity manifests spacious caring in everyday life and allows skillful on-the-spot responsiveness.

What does all this have to do with welcoming and our oxherding journey? A close look at Trungpa Rinpoche's commentary on the oxherding images shows that he interpreted the middle stages through the lens of the bodhisattva path, highlighting the role of welcoming and even mapping some of the oxherding stages to particular bhumis.

Commenting on generosity as the necessary first step on the path of awakened compassion, Trungpa Rinpoche writes, "Welcoming is the first gesture of the bodhisattva."[15] The attitude of welcoming, as we have seen, involves trusting our experience, trusting the phenomenal world's sensuous textures, and trusting the innate goodness of others. Following its injunction, "O taste and see," Psalm 34 goes on to say, "Taste and see and trust in goodness." With welcoming, others and our world feel fundamentally trustworthy. This is an attitude of abundance and richness, the opposite of the mentality of seeking that can never be satisfied. There's an old saying, perhaps from New York's great Yogi Berra: "One can never get enough of what does not satisfy." Welcoming is a gesture of inner freedom and well-being. We feel fundamentally rich enough to open to ourselves and welcome all sentient beings as our guests—just as a bodhisattva would.

Some descriptions of arriving at the first level of this vast openness and abundance suggest an inner spiritual explosion. In the Zen tradition, there are many vivid accounts of sudden breakthroughs into dramatic awakening experiences, often referred to as *kensho* or *satori*. This first spiritual plateau of the Great Way is called "supreme joy" (*pramudita*), the unconditioned joy of true nature. We need not depend on any mental or emotional crutches to stand fully upright. Naturally we celebrate this return to basic healthiness by inviting all beings to dance at the great party. Surprise!

On the other hand, sometimes the experience of emptiness dawns like the sun. It's not a sudden explosion or a big breakthrough. It's an organic process, as natural as a tiny seed sprouting, slowly growing, and eventually flowering as a great expanse. Suzuki Roshi explains it this way: "After you have practiced for a while, you will realize that it is not possible to make rapid, extraordinary progress. Even though you try very hard, the progress you make is always little by little. It is not like going out in a shower in which you know when you get wet. In a fog, you do not know you are getting wet, but as you keep walking you get wet little by little. . . . When you get wet in a fog it is very difficult to dry yourself."[16] This is awakening as nothing special.

Trungpa Rinpoche commented that the third oxherding image corresponds to the first Mahayana Buddhist spiritual level attained by a bodhisattva. This level or bhumi is named "Supreme Joy," and is also described as "arriving on the Path of Seeing." He continues this correlation, connecting the third image with the compassionate acts (paramitas) of generosity and discipline, and then correlating the fourth image with the development of patience and joyful exertion, and finally the fifth image with meditative awareness and transcendent knowledge (prajna).

What are we seeing here? The gradual stages of the Mahayana path begin with partial glimpses of the ox. Glimpsing leads directly to seeing the ox fully and then finally to catching and touching it. We are incrementally moving toward knowing ourselves, knowing our own true nature in a direct and tactile way. If the Greek philosopher Heraclitus was correct in suggesting that we human beings "have lost touch with that with which we are most familiar," now we are fully back in touch. It's like reconnecting with an old friend, warmly shaking their hand, and exclaiming, "Good to see you again! Haven't seen you in a while."

WHOSE OX IS THIS ANYWAY?

Circling and circling, we are contemplating touching the ox as the central theme of this fourth stage. Yes, we finally catch the ox, but we also catch a few questions along the way. Was catching the ox really the result of all our striving? Was finding the ox caused by our desperate seeking, or did searching actually delay finding? How fast and how far did we need to run to get to where we already are? I am reminded of these famous lines from the poem "Little Gidding" by T. S. Eliot: "We shall not cease from exploration / And the end of all our exploring / Will be to arrive where we started / And know the place for the first time."[17]

If the ox catches us just as surely as we catch the ox, one sign of this might be our catching the fever of Mahayana, which turns out to be contagious. What are the signs and symptoms? More than ever, we feel a strong wish, an unshakable resolve, to awaken for the benefit of all beings. Now, with the experience of being near our original nature ("intimate practice"), this desire to liberate beings from suffering feels like the genuine fulfillment of true nature. Suzuki Roshi often spoke of our "inmost desire" to liberate all beings. This is sometimes called the Great Motivation of true nature. From this perspective, earlier projects of self-improvement seem to be determined attempts to fill gaps in our armor of self-esteem—examples of a small or petty motivation.

The ox of true nature cares for all beings. Catching the fever of Mahayana is a sign of the awakening of "a heart as wide as the world," the title of Buddhist teacher Sharon Salzberg's collection of stories about loving-kindness. There is some question about ownership here. True nature is not really mine or yours. True nature is a universal nature, the nature of all beings, the nature of reality, the true nature of Nature. We aspire to welcome and care for all beings with kindness toward them as though they are our kin. We wish and act for the well-being of "all our relations," a phrase used in many Native American prayers. As we move closer to seeing the whole ox clearly, we see that this ox is not just "my ox" or "your ox," rather it belongs to the great family of all sentient beings. Those beings, without exception, all share in the family inheritance of originally awakened nature.

As Boundless Way Zen teacher James Ishmael Ford writes, "This is the universal solvent of the heart. Become as wide as the sky. Let the whole of what is play across the screen of the mind and the heart."[18] Let's focus for a moment on the word play here. Sometimes catching the ox is imagined as a great wrestling match in which we struggle to forcefully subdue a fierce, wild animal. Maybe the journey is like that sometimes, a rough-and-tumble, spiritual rodeo event. There is, however, some possibility that, from the very beginning, the ox just wants to play with us, first in a game of hide-and-seek, then by leaving multiple clues too obvious to miss. If this ox is as large as the whole of existence, it's likely that its footprints are every-where. It's likely you can glimpse it anywhere. And when you finally touch the ox, does it need to be in the manner of beating down a bucking bronco? Or might you succeed as a gentle ox whisperer?

五 牧牛

5 | TAMING THE OX

The fifth oxherding image shows our diligent oxherder leading the ox with a rope. There are no signs of struggle in this picture. These two beings are simply walking along the path together, listening to each other's footsteps. No force is required; gentle persuasion is sufficient. Patience and nonaggressive exertion are essential to the bodhisattva way. Such gentleness is possible because the ox of our true nature is not really a stranger to us. It has been here with us all along this journey of discovery, motivating our search, leaving hints and footprints, popping into and out of our awareness. No wonder the ox sometimes seems like the oxherder's long-lost friend.

THE BASIS OF taming is touching, contact, embodied communication. When ox and oxherder are in such close and sustained contact, their journey resembles two friends making a long cross-continental trip together. A practical question soon arises: how are we going to be together without constantly annoying each other?

Even the closest of friends need regular exchanges to clarify and consolidate their connection. In which direction are we headed? Should we swerve right or left here? Is there enough water for both of us? That seems like a steep ascent up ahead, are you ready? Journeying together is an expression of being in touch with each other. Being in touch with each other leads to a dynamic harmony that includes differences.

IS TAMING CONTROLLING?

Guo-an's ancient verse on the fifth oxherding image explains that "the whip and rope are necessary" because the ox might "stray off down some dusty road."[1] The commentary does not explain why we must not allow straying. Daido Roshi softens this a bit: "The whip and tether cannot be put aside as the ox may wander into mud-filled swamps."[2] This suggests that during later stages of oxherding, we may have no need for the rope or the whip, and we can put both aside. For now though, the main message is the necessity of training and discipline. As with some explanations of strict approaches to good parenting, the justification is that this is for the ox's "own good." Oxen may enjoy rolling around in muddy swamps or aimlessly wandering down dusty roads to nowhere, but we're headed somewhere. We have to keep things on track and under control, or as Trungpa Rinpoche calls it, we need to apply "the sharp whip of transcendental knowledge (*prajna-paramita*)."[3]

In the twenty-first century of our Common Era, I'm wondering what People for the Ethical Treatment of Animals (PETA) might say about all these metaphorical whips and enforced bondage. Even as symbolic images of an inner journey—that is, not as literal objects being used to discipline actual living beings—there's an implicit harshness in this imagery. Perhaps that harshness plays a role in the developmental narrative that's firmly embedded in many depictions of the spiritual path. Or is this a version of the old slogan from gym culture, "No pain, no gain"? Through taming and training, the ox eventually obeys its master. We are promised that then it will follow our way freely. Once the ox is tamed and fully trained, it becomes gentle and can be unfettered. In most commentaries, domination and docile subordination are assumed to be the natural order of things, the only way to true freedom. Is there any other way?

———

As we move beyond occasional glimpses and fleeting touches to on-going direct contact with true nature, taming arises as our next major challenge. Direct experience of ourselves and others reveals more of the whole ox, including a vivid display of unruly desires, jealousies, fears, wounded pride, and lingering shame and guilt. Consistent practice generously invites us to a flavorful feast of unsavory, uncomfortable emotions. Initially, when we hear and contemplate these teachings, welcoming sounds like a plausible method for taming and training ourselves. We think and feel something like, "This welcoming stuff seems to be a sane approach to meditation and inner peace, living a good life of openness and freedom, benefiting others along the way. Yes, I'd like more of that." Soon, however, as we move along the path, other questions arise: "What about all these uninvited guests who show up and linger for weeks, months even, as though hanging around till the next party begins? Is all this inner noise and turbulence also part of the peaceful program?" When diligently sitting day after day, we gradually loosen our tight grip of mental control, slowly lifting the lid of inner repression, what about all the unwelcome thoughts and feelings that bubble to the surface? Grief and sadness for lost loved ones in other places, other times, sincere regrets, old resentments all come back: "Oh, no, not that again. I thought I dealt with that already!"

Our spacious meadow approach to practice and daily life generously invites what was previously unwelcome. These are precisely the rejected aspects of our being that cry out to be included in the warmth of our inner circle. If there have been psychological restrictions—like temporarily crimping the free flow of water in a hose—releasing those limitations (even in the space of a daily twenty-minute sitting) may yield surprising gushes and upsurges.

Contemplating this fifth image, we oxherders may question not the ox but our approach to oxherding. Maybe it is our overly controlling attitude, at least in part, that leads to the ox's unruly wildness. Suddenly, even slightly wild behavior looms large, highlighted by our vigorous efforts to tame. Perhaps some rebellions are the result of repression. Is it possible that one of the elements most in need of taming is our impulse to control and manipulate? "Start where you are" could mean "First things first. Rouse your inner oxherder and then work diligently to domesticate the ox." Yet who's really taming who here? Maybe oxherding is something our teacher and spiritual friend invited us to do so that we might notice and make friends with our own states of mind and heart as we search for and then tend to the ox. Guide: "Could you find and take care of that ox, please?" Practitioner: "Sure, sounds workable. It'll probably take me a few days to completely tame and ride it. I'll see you next week when I've whipped it into good shape."

As we bring more relaxation into our approach to "taming," we may discover more humor in situations that previously seemed stuck or unworkable. Our sense of humor returns, not because things get better, but sometimes because they don't. Oxen are famously stubborn. Space can open around repeated conflicts in a relationship at home or at work, sometimes just because these disagreements suddenly reappear with such familiarly obstinate faces, the unyielding visages of inner mountains of granite. Yes, everything changes—but does it always change at the pace or in the way we'd prefer?

Let's return to Suzuki Roshi's early chapter "Control," since controlling our ox seems to be the main challenge here. Editors placed that chapter in the opening section of Zen Mind, Beginner's Mind, the section on right practice. Roshi talks about the desire to obtain "perfect calmness in your zazen," but first he explores an alternative approach to controlling oneself and others in everyday life: "It is the same with taking care of your everyday life. Even though you try to put people under some control, it is impossible. You cannot do it."[4]

Consider the irony that, as with all the compassionate actions of the bodhisattva path, controlling arises from caring. The great motivation of the Mahayana way of life is taking care of others and ourselves, expanding benevolence from our loved ones to those we do not know and eventually to all the members of the great, extended family of all living beings. Caring is the ground of both unskillful attempts to control and the skillful activity of a bodhisattva.

Even though control may arise from a genuine desire to help, an expansively compassionate motivation that cares for all beings, our efforts—on a meditation cushion and in daily life—may have unintended consequences. Meditation teacher and clinical psychologist Bill Morgan shares results from his research on progress in meditation: "Every subject in my doctoral study reported that the early years of their meditation practice were characterized by striving to control the mind. Each believed that this approach would lead to some life-changing insight; instead, it led to struggle and frustration with meditation."[5] Despite good intentions on all sides, ox and oxherder frequently find themselves swimming in frustration. As Xenophon, a student of Socrates, wrote in his treatise *On Horsemanship*, "What a horse does under compulsion he does blindly, and his performance is no more beautiful than would be that of a ballet-dancer taught by whip and goad."[6]

Suzuki Roshi outlines different approaches to controlling. To ignore people is the worst policy. The second worst is trying to control them. The approach of taking whips to animals may backfire. Perhaps the force of the ox's unruliness is directly linked to our harshness. As with obstacles in meditation practice, some of our mental turbulence may be the result of holding the mind too tightly. Possibly, the ox wants to run off down the road or back into the muddy swamps because the oxherder's tether feels too tight, too restrictive, too limiting. "Don't fence me in!" it thinks. Applying too much pressure in an effort to control our minds and hearts may lead, ironically, to increased agitation, not, as we hope, to the alleviation of stress and greater peace. Framing our ox as "wild" and "animalistic," inclined to stupidly wander off without our tight rope of strict discipline, may be less effective than gently communicating with the ox's own instinctual (that is, innate and natural) intelligence. Like most of us, the ox needs encouragement. Once, at a Zen retreat, a meditator asked Soen Roshi what to do when one feels discouraged. Roshi said, "Encourage others." In the warm, moist atmosphere of gentle encouragement, many flowers bloom that would wilt quickly in a hot, dry desert.

Finally, Suzuki Roshi suggests another possibility: allowing the emergence of a paradoxical, wider sense of control. "The best way to control people is to encourage them to be mischievous. Then they will be in control in its wider sense."[7] This is a different approach altogether than our default perspective of command and control.

In command-and-control approaches to leadership and training, the leader (way up there, somewhere near the top) has a virtual monopoly on insight and intelligence. As with the ox, the rest of the team (over here, a bit lower, the subordinates) will eventually become gentle and see that the designated leader's method is the best way to proceed to move them all in the right direction for accomplishing their mission. The command-and-control approach fits many military situations. In this narrow vision, there is little, if any, appreciation of the innate potential in team members or the overall situation of the group. Wisdom and compassion are not seen to be evenly dispersed throughout the family or team, the community or organization. In this centralized notion of power, voices from the margins hardly matter at all. Taking time to listen to diverse voices— where's the efficiency in that? Why waste time listening when real experts have already decided the best course of action? The absence of deeper listening leads to authoritarian blind spots.

Along with many other organizational development researchers, University of Houston professor Brené Brown has articulated an alternative paradigm of leadership. Asked in an interview to define leadership, she replied, "A leader is anyone who holds her or himself accountable for finding the potential in people and processes. Leadership has nothing to do with position, salary, direct reports, or status anymore. There are leaders at every level of organizations, schools, and communities who, every day, are defining strategy and shaping culture. There are leaders and team members, but it's not the same as the old leader-follower paradigm because everyone on the team can act like a leader by being engaged and showing up with their ideas, even if it means finding the courage to say, 'I think we're headed in the wrong direction.'"[8]

We have already contemplated Suzuki Roshi's wise advice in connection with the essence of the Welcoming Exercise: "To give your sheep or cow a large spacious meadow" is the best form of control. Note that in this context of considering "best practices" for controlling ourselves and others, this statement expresses strong confidence in the original nature of all beings. "All beings are basically good," as it says in a text from the lineage of spiritual warriors. In contrast, the command-and-control paradigm enacts doubt about the pervasiveness of wakefulness. From that limited perspective, intelligent compassion and good-heartedness are scarce commodities, rarely encountered in the "real world." Taking scarcity as a given, command-and-control approaches proceed with the forceful practice of doubt. Only those at the top really know what's best for all. In contrast, trust is the practice of strong confidence in the originally awake nature of all. This trust is expressed in our willingness to listen to each other, particularly when we disagree. Mindful communication is key here—listening without grasping, speaking without pushing to prove our point. As writer Sarah Nir writes in *Horse Crazy*, "Taming a horse, gentling it, or, crudely, breaking it, involves messaging more than anything."[9]

MIND WEEDS AND MIND WAVES

Let's look toward engaging in another round of the Welcoming Exercise informed by this spacious meadow approach. From this generous, accommodating perspective, thoughts and emotions that arise in the space are not difficult "wild" forces to be forcefully controlled, but vivid and rich upsurges to be included and appreciated. Here, taming is not struggling to tamp these energies down. Taming is welcoming.

In a chapter called "Mind Weeds," Suzuki Roshi reminds us of the necessity for embodying this approach to living through practice. It's not enough to enjoy this as philosophical or psychological insight, he warns: "We must have the actual experience of how our weeds change into nourishment."[10] In some Buddhist traditions this process is called "transmuting." As in ancient practices of alchemy, heavy lead can become shining gold. Challenging emotions—anger, passion, pride, jealousy, fear—all contain innate wisdom that can be released from within, not imposed or imported from outside.

There is a similar teaching in the songs of Tibet's great Buddhist yogin Milarepa, a devoted practitioner and enlightened teacher of the eleventh century. In his collected Hundred Thousand Songs, Milarepa sings in response to a question from Lady Paldarbum. She tells him that in meditation, she can easily experience her mind like the sky or the ocean, but she doesn't know what to do about clouds or waves: "What about all these thoughts, Milarepa? I don't know what to do with all my mental agitation in meditation." Milarepa sings his dharma response to her, rendered in rhyme (and set to music) by dharma teacher Winfield Shaw Clark:

If the sky's as easy as you say,
Clouds are just the sky's play.
Let your mind stay
Within the sky.
. . .
If the sea's as easy as you say,
Waves are just the sea's play.
Let your mind stay
Within the sea.
. . .

If your mind's as easy as you say,
Thoughts are just the mind's play.
Let your mind stay
Within your mind.[11]

The pith instruction here is to welcome the play of the mind as a vivid display. It is the dynamic expression of the flow of life in and around us. We would not want to tamp this life-force energy down or restrict it too much. Wouldn't it surely rebel and run off to the swamp for relief? We would not wish to get rid of our feelings and sensations, as that would be approaching meditation as an anti-life project. Sometimes there is a false yet persistently lingering notion that enlightenment is like becoming a stone-carved Buddha sitting for days without moving in the desert. Not likely. We human beings laugh and cry and are moved as expressions of our fundamental human-heartedness. Emotions aren't problems to be solved or illnesses to be cured. The biomedical model applied to human spirituality has its limits.

The practice chapter before "Mind Weeds" is titled "Mind Waves." Our Welcoming Exercise allows some direct experience of the ocean-like qualities of basic awareness, free from struggling or seeking, vast and originally at peace. Yet again, the basic peacefulness of welcoming emerges as inseparably joined with movement and activity. Dispelling our dualistic delusions, Suzuki Roshi clarifies, "Actually water always has waves. Waves are the practice of water. To speak of waves apart from water or water apart from waves is delusion. Water and waves are one. Big mind and small mind are one. . . . A mind with waves in it is not a disturbed mind but an amplified one."[12]

WELCOMING AND INQUIRING

When taming is accomplished by leading with appreciation and the gentleness of ox whispering, it marks a decisive shift in view or approach. The awake qualities hidden within our fears and angers, desires and jealousies, bloated pride and wounded insecurity—all are welcomed and allowed to unfold peacefully, without the aggression that frames them as inherently problematic: "Something is wrong with this ox's nature. I have to hurry up and whip it into shape. Then it will obey my command." The alternative approach does not mean acting on every passing feeling of attraction or repulsion. The basic Buddhist ethical guidelines of first not causing harm and then compassionately helping others are more within reach when we begin with welcoming rather than rejecting ourselves. The seeds of basic nature flower in this spacious meadow. We welcome ourselves as a first step toward welcoming others.

The next step is unleashing our innate curiosity through inquiring. This is the basic innocence that genuinely wonders, when desire arises, "What is this?" Of course, we already know what it's called—we know to name it "desire"—but what is it really? I'm not the same as my name, and neither are you. All names are conventional designations: Cousin Barbara, Uncle Roy, Sister Alicia, Mother Teresa. Feelings of warmth, passion, lust, affection, and love are also conventional designations with a family resemblance. Leaving the names aside for a moment of contemplation, when we ask and "look" at desire, what do we see?

Asking "What is this?" in a spirit of genuine inquiry feels very different from asking "How can I fix this? How will I cure my attachment disorder? What about my problematic tendencies toward codependence?" These are all sophisticated questions, common in our contemporary societies where therapeutic approaches to understanding ourselves are widespread. Basic innocence asks simpler questions, without the assumption that we already know what passion is. What we "know" is based on past experiences and thoughts, downloaded memories of something similar. Leaving those aside for a moment, what is this really now? What does it feel like? Where do you feel it in the body? What is its texture, shape, and dynamic pattern? If there were a one-word haiku for this desire in this moment, what would it be? Consider some possible first thoughts using images from nature: river, sky, valley, volcano, meadow, mountain, tree, leaves of grass, spring flowers, rain, rainbow, waterfall, ocean, or lake? Whatever arises as an answer to your inquiry, cradle that thought with gratefulness, rest for a moment, and then look again, gently inquiring, "What is this so-called 'river of passion'?" Let go of the words for a moment so as to taste and see for yourself, trusting your own experience more than anyone's names for it. There may have been thousands of brilliant psychological insights about passion, but not one of them is the same as direct experience. Pause for a moment to contemplate this sentence from Don DeLillo's novel *Point Omega*: "The true life is not reducible to words spoken or written, not by anyone, ever."[13]

Spaciousness is always the initial gesture of taming, and welcoming is its first and primary step. Welcoming is allowing spaciousness to encourage taming. Inquiring is the second step, expressing genuine interest, as with our surprised questions on seeing an old friend at the local shopping mall: "How are you these days? How's the family?" Note that the friendliness of this concerned inquiry differs from the intense scrutiny of a police investigation: "Tell us again where you were between the hours of nine and eleven on the night of July 25, and what's your real nature? Never mind your various official identification cards; who are you really?" No wonder the ox runs back into the woods.

It is possible to let inquiring have the same flavor as welcoming. Ask with gentleness, and then ask again with patience and appreciation. This second contemplative step of inquiring is more active and engaged, involving the effort to ask and then to look and see. (This is an insight contemplation aiming to see clearly.) Welcoming tends toward effortlessness. At this fertile stage of our journey, we are joining non-effort with effort. Our aim is the union of the effortlessness of welcoming and the effort of inquiring. They both have something to teach and learn from each other. Non-effort teaches effort about patience and gentleness. Effort reminds non-effort that true spaciousness is not limp passivity or flaccid indulgence. Open space is also inquisitive, interested, concerned, caring, and freely engaged, even intimately involved, in direct action.

WELCOME, INQUIRE, REST (REPEAT)

Let's continue our experiential inquiry based in welcoming by adding a few questions. Questions are like food for innate knowing, our ability to see clearly and precisely. Our natural capacity for intimate understanding develops and grows stronger through questions. Our perceptions are often generic, broad brushstrokes with few specifics: "If you've seen one, . . ." Contemplative questions are like a stone used to sharpen the cutting edge of our discernment. The question we have been using so far is asking, in the face of whatever arises, "What is this?" If sweet memories arise, let them linger, asking, "What is this?" If the image of a deceased family member comes to mind as we sit for a moment doing nothing, "What is this?" If we feel anxious about health or money or current events in our country or anywhere on this planet, "What is this?" Again and again, we are welcoming and inquiring, welcoming and inquiring. Remember to rest naturally for a few moments in between these cycles.

Contemporary Zen teacher Joan Sutherland Roshi writes, "The basic inquiry is *What is this?* And it's a way back to what we're trying to avoid. . . . We inquire into whatever *What is this?* evokes—thoughts, feelings, sensations, images, memories. The unexpected and surprising are particularly valuable, because they come from somewhere other than what we usually imagine."[14]

This form of contemplative inquiry may begin with this phrase, these words, but eventually it becomes less specific, just an open questioning, almost like a single question mark: Desire arises, "?" Boredom arises, "?" Anger arises, "?" Love arises, "?" Let questioning arise playfully as the expression of basic innocence, the beginner's mind of not-knowing. Youthful innocence wants to know.

Then, in a second step, welcome whatever arises in the wake of your questioning. Whether it comes as words or an image or a felt-sense, welcome that "answer." Let's say that, as you sit welcoming, anxiety arises. Ask, looking to see, "What is this anxiety?" What does it feel like? Underneath the names for it, what is the raw, rugged experience really? Maybe the next thought is, "Right now, anxiety is a tensing in my stomach." Pause, welcome this thought, grateful that something arose in response to your question. Then, after that appreciative pause, ask again, "What is this that we call 'stomach tension'? What is its texture or quality? Is it only tension in the area of the stomach? Does it change or stay the same as I feel it?" Look, and then look again to see. Remember, "Seeing is forgetting the name of what one sees." This is the cycle of inquiring and resting, welcoming and asking, a cycle of appreciative inquiry.

The gesture of inquiry is always inviting more intimate feeling. The aim is never a distanced conceptual knowing, "I (the meditator over here) know the true nature of these emotions (over there)." For all the profundity of ancient spiritual books and classic dharma teachings, the answers are not to be found there. Responding to these questions by spouting dharma jargon about "emptiness," "luminosity," or "buddha nature" is worse than useless here. The truth of our experience is never reducible to any of our concepts about it.

WELCOMING AND INQUIRING

Let's pause for a few minutes to engage in these welcoming and inquiring contemplations. Please sit for three minutes, hands in your lap with your eyes open, doing nothing. This is simply revisiting the Welcoming Exercise on its own.

Next, sit for three more minutes, this time inquiring into whatever arises in your experience: "What is . . . ?" . . . "?" . . . "?"

Finally, conclude this little session by returning to simply welcoming for three minutes. The entire session might take about ten minutes. Time yourself, and allow yourself to be gentle and brave in alternating engaging and resting, inquiring and welcoming.

MINDFULNESS OF EFFORT

As we have seen, one of the main challenges in taming our ox is effort. How much effort is too much, crossing over into aggression? Our experience will teach us that applying too much force backfires. But then, how much effort is too little, covering over the dynamic, energized qualities of true nature with entrenched habits of laziness? Again, the resulting experience of dullness instructs us.

In a series of talks on the four foundations of mindfulness, Trungpa Rinpoche taught about mindfulness of effort: "The style of right effort, as taught by the Buddha, is serious but not too serious. It takes advantage of the natural flow of instinct to bring the wandering mind constantly back to the mindfulness of breathing." [15] This wandering mind sounds a lot like our repeatedly straying ox. We need the rope of mindful attention to bring it back from the swamp of distraction.

Before introducing a wordless effort he called "abstract effort," or "sudden jerk," Trungpa Rinpoche corrected some prevalent misunderstandings. In the wrong view, we approach effort as deliberate and elaborate, telling ourselves about a slow, laborious process of coming back to the body and breathing. According to Rinpoche, "The crucial point in the bringing-back process is that it is not necessary to go through deliberate stages: first preparing to do it, then getting a hold on one's attention, then finally dragging it back to the breathing as if we were trying to drag a naughty child back from doing something terrible." This sounds like unskillful attempts to tame the ox using too much effort. We call this approach "unskillful" because it does not work. Our minds resist and rebel against aggressively enforced concentration practices. As Tibetan Buddhist meditation master Dilgo Khyentse Rinpoche taught, "We can never understand the nature of the mind through intense effort but only by relaxing, just as breaking a wild horse requires that one approach it gently and treat it kindly rather than running after it and trying to use force. So do not try to catch hold of the nature of the mind, just leave it as it is."[16]

Let's linger for a moment to contemplate Trungpa Rinpoche's striking phrase: "the natural flow of instinct." Our ox, like all animals, has instincts—unlearned, patterned behaviors. Think of any newborn. Birds, fish, bears, human beings—we are all born with innate capacities. "Unlearned" means natural, in our own nature, or "hardwired" as we say nowadays. This approach to taming as gentling relies on a particular inborn impulse in human beings (and many other creatures) to cooperate, to live and work together. Without this natural tendency, no community or society, no gathering or association, would be possible at all.

Let's consider some examples of evidence for an innately compassionate tendency. In 2010, Berkeley professor Dacher Keltner and colleagues at the Greater Good Science Center published a collection of articles as The Compassionate Instinct, part of the center's mission of presenting the new science of human goodness. Similarly, Stanford professor Thupten Jinpa, translator for the Dalai Lama, titled a section of the former's book A Fearless Heart, "Where the Research Is Taking Us." There, he writes, "What all of these findings suggest is this: Our capacity for empathy, compassion, kindness, and altruistic behavior is inborn, rather than acquired through socialization or cultural exposure. Only later, through socialization, do we begin to differentiate between those who are worthy of our kindness and those who are not. So, to some extent, Rousseau was right when he spoke of society having a corrupting influence on an infant's pure instinct for kindness."[17] Historian Barbara Taylor and psychoanalyst Adam Phillips share similar historical insights in their book On

Kindness: "An image of the self has been created that is utterly lacking in natural generosity. . . . Most people appear to believe that deep down they (and other people) are mad, bad and dangerous to know; that as a species—apparently unlike other species of animal—we are deeply and fundamentally antagonistic to each other, that our motives are utterly self-seeking and that our sympathies are forms of self-protection."[18] What if, they ask, to the contrary, "the kind life—the life lived in instinctive sympathetic identification with the vulnerabilities and attractions of others—is the life we are more inclined to live, and indeed is the one we are often living without letting ourselves know that this is what we are doing?"

This expansive perspective, grounded in extensive research findings, suggests that our basic nature enjoys compassionate action. Being generous fulfills an innate desire, our inmost request. We do not have to be threatened and cajoled into kindness. Mindful presence and loving-kindness are natural qualities that can be encouraged and developed. The ox can be persuaded—not forced—to carry the oxherder home.

Now we see some of the ironies in calling the ox "wild" in a pejorative sense of that word. This is, after all, our description based on the powerful will to domesticate, to render beings tame and docile as quickly as possible. "Wild" is one translation of the French sauvage, closely related to the English word "savage." Passing through remembrance of the terrifying historical violence of worldwide European colonialism, we arrive at Rousseau's notion of "noble savages." As Professor Zakiyyah Iman Jackson reminds us, "Repudiation of the 'the animal' has historically been essential to producing classes of abject humans."[19]

Similarly, what we describe as "human nature" is often the product of being trained—to shop, to acquire, to control, to efficiently micromanage our unruly emotions and sometimes turbulent inner lives. These are practices common in our culture. Greed would not seem to be a necessary part of our natural state. Materialistic outlooks and practices are actively cultivated in many contemporary cultures. What might a community or society based on cultivating innate kindness and compassion look like?

COMMITMENTS AND VOWS

Trungpa Rinpoche concludes his presentation of mindfulness of effort by emphasizing the need for "a sense of commitment."[20] Commitment opens the way. In making a spiritual journey, commitment arises naturally. Once we've tasted genuineness, we feel strongly attracted to it, not as the peak experience of a weekend workshop but as a complete way of life. Vows of commitment to waking up are part of the unfolding of true nature, not externally imposed requirements. Daoist teacher Liu Ming emphasized the naturalness of our "spiritual appetite."

In the chapter of *Zen Mind, Beginner's Mind* called "Bowing," Suzuki Roshi discusses four Buddhist vows: "Although sentient beings are innumerable, we vow to save them. Although our evil desires are limitless, we vow to be rid of them. Although the teaching is limitless, we vow to learn it all. Although Buddhism is unattainable, we vow to attain it."[21] Commenting on the first of these vows, Zoketsu Norman Fischer Roshi writes, "This is a vow of compassion. It expresses that at the heart of our practice we cherish the wish to practice with a radical unselfishness—for and with others. And we vow not to rest, not to feel as if our practice is complete, until all sentient beings, infinite in number, are saved—which in this case means saved not only from oppression and outward forms of bondage, but also saved inwardly, from bondage to self."[22] Contemplating these vows, we remind ourselves that compassion is at the heart of all our practices. This awakened heart of compassion is true nature. It is true nature that welcomes and tames our self-centered delusions, returning us to the reality of our deep connectedness to all beings in a living world.

In many Buddhist traditions, practitioners take vows of commitment to the Three Jewels, resolving to follow the example of the Buddha, the path of the dharma, and the community (the sangha) journeying together on a path of awakening. This is the ceremony called "taking the Refuge Vow." There are also Mahayana vows of commitment to the awakened heart of compassion (similar to the four vows chanted in Zen). Trungpa Rinpoche connects vows with "a sense of commitment to relating with things as they actually are." Naturalness is not opposed to training but is the basis of our discipline. Training is the fulfillment of innate wakefulness. "It is not enough just to hope that a flash will come to us. . . . We have to prepare a general atmosphere. There must be a background of discipline which sets the tone of the sitting practice."[23] The tone both ox and oxherder hear is the simple melody of nonaggressive welcoming. In this atmosphere of loving-kindness, practice and everyday life are both expressions of basic appreciation, the unconditional gratefulness of being alive. As is said in many traditions of compassionate bravery, "We are speaking here of the basic goodness of being alive."[24]

What is truly natural requires no effort. Like the color of our eyes, true nature is not commercially produced. (Manufacturing eyes remains, as yet, a future scenario from Blade Runner.) Training and discipline require effort. These two provide the atmosphere in which the seed of natural instinct sprouts and grows, matures and manifests. Here we see the nonduality of effort and effortlessness, training and nature working together seamlessly as though they are one. Are they? What needs to be tamed is the impulse toward separation and aggression. The two rivers of nature and training flow into the same ocean of compassion.

This union of nature and training returns us to basic cooperation, cocreating with others. In the sixth image, we see the ox carrying the oxherder home, which expresses this harmony in difference. Ox and oxherder are not one and the same. Ox is ox; oxherder is oxherder. Probably the oxherder is not strong enough to lift and carry a one-ton ox. They are also not-two. Freed from the aggressive impulse to control and the reactive response of rebellion, these two are natural allies.

六騎牛歸家

6 | RIDING THE OX

The sixth image shows our oxherder riding the ox while playing a flute. At last, the rousing music of expansive celebration resounds around us. All of us—all beings without exception—are invited to make a joyful noise, to join in the great dance. After our frustrated seeking, glimpsing the tantalizing footprints of the ox, the first partial sightings, and our initial hands-on contact, we have also experienced the power of gentle taming. Our ox is now tamed and gentle enough to carry us all the way home. We enjoy renewed and increasing appreciation for the quiet strength of nonaggression. Ox and oxherder are now good companions, both enjoying the freedom of welcoming space. They are journeying together in harmonious synchrony.

RIDING SUGGESTS A sense of ease, discovering an expansiveness that includes daily challenges. Perhaps this is a stage on the path where fearlessness welcomes fear. Daido Roshi points to "a state of relaxation amidst difficulties."[1] This is further experiential confirmation of mind weeds as fertilizing and nourishing our practice. Here we develop even more confidence in mind waves as the expressive play of a vast ocean of wisdom. Waves and water are not-two. Each of the five classic conflicting emotions—passion, aggression, ignorance, jealousy, and pride—is a temporarily frozen form of our fluid innate wisdom. The open warmth of compassion gradually melts the solid dualistic ideas that lead to grasping, clinging, or prejudiced rejecting. How many love relationships begin with passionate attraction and move on to desperate attachment, only to end in angry denunciations: "You did *what*?" Left to themselves in the basic space of welcoming, these entangled energies gradually emerge into brilliant wakefulness, like a snake uncoiling itself in the sun. This is not just an idea, a concept some believe and others doubt. The truth of this teaching can only be found in direct experience. What does it feel like to move from struggling to riding?

Here in the sixth stage, we're riding spaciousness, and spaciousness is riding us. Who's on top? Earlier, there may have been some lingering fear of absence, impermanence, or insubstantiality. When we first notice the ceaselessly changing flow of our experience, it can feel startlingly abrupt. It's as though we were asleep, happily sleepwalking, and suddenly we've been tossed into a mighty, rushing river. We wake to discover a simple truth: everything changes. Change and nonsolidity are constant threats to the deadly serious empire-building strategies of ego. Now, emptiness is our friend, a welcome companion. There is buoyancy in the lack of solidity, because at last we are liberated from the heavy desperation of "toxic seriousness."[2] As Martine Batchelor comments, "We begin to take ourselves less seriously and enjoy life so much more as we open to its changing and ever-fluctuating nature. We dance and sing with life. We have become friends with our body and mind."[3] Making friends with ourselves as we are and extending simple kindness to others—maybe that was the point all along?

To ride the ox is both to move and to be moved. Something beyond individual effort is carrying us, moving us along the path. Now our movement is propelled by a great motive force. Earlier, as Daido Roshi explains, "the strength of our spiritual intent largely depended on our individual personality and predispositions: our desires, needs, motives, and effort."[4] Now, a larger transpersonal drive catches us and carries us along. We feel the force of a great wind at our backs. This big wind gently lifts us out of the prison of self-preoccupation into limitless loving-kindness, boundless compassion.

Further evidence is surfacing that we have caught the highly contagious Mahayana fever to awaken for the benefit of all beings. This is our strongest desire, our inmost request. We take vows of commitment, making the choiceless choice to act from care for the needs of others. Daido Roshi calls this phase of our journey "a stage of no return. It's hard to turn back. Almost impossible."[5] Some of the traditional names for the ten stages (bhumis) on the brave bodhisattva's path evoke similarly irrevocable qualities: "Gone Long Way" and "Immoveable." In a chapter called "Single-minded Way," Suzuki Roshi tells us that "even if the sun were to rise in the west, the bodhisattva has only one way."[6] In the midst of the roller-coaster ride of impermanence, right down here in the thick of things, the direction of this universal, compassionate way does not change.

Guo-an also comments on this sixth stage: "Onward I go, no matter who may wish to call me back."[7] Are there voices within us that might wish to call us back? If so, good. Let's listen to those voices, welcoming them while allowing the way to continue to unfold. Is there really a choice here? In the groundless space of uncertainty, riding continues. It feels as though the path unfolds beneath our feet, moving us swiftly along as with automated walkways in airports.

Here, much of the experience involves a shift from tiresome individual effort to the joyful, untiring exertion of the bodhisattva. Rather than seeking what is nowhere to be found, and rather than exhausting ourselves in the effort to tame our wild minds and unruly hearts, effort comes to us. Innate nature invites the energy of compassion, opening our hearts to its natural boundlessness. We uncover deep hidden wellsprings of natural exertion.

What differentiates this joyful exertion from our usual effort of seeking? The motivated action of karmic life always seeks *something else*, constantly searching for some new, better alternative to what is. We never feel we have arrived. It's as though we are constantly wondering and asking, "What comes next, what comes next?" In contrast, the exertion flowing freely from the great motivation arrives with each step. This exertion is *always* arriving. The Sanskrit word *paramita* (as in *virya paramita* or "transcendent exertion") literally means "arriving at the other shore." As Aitken Roshi explained, "The idea that once you reach the other shore the raft can be discarded is ultimately not true. The raft is the shore. Your koan, each point in your breath-counting sequence, your inhalation, then your exhalation—there is the shore itself." This is striving inseparable from arriving, an effort that constantly arrives with itself. It is perfected by being perfectly what it is. Unlike the desperate road-runner effort that quickly exhausts itself, this exertion is supremely sustainable. Joyful exertion reigns.

The image of the oxherder riding and playing a flute suggests relaxation mixed with keen delight. Hearing the music of celebration signals great joy united with great sadness—so much suffering, so much spacious freedom, *at the same time.* This is sad-joy. The space of emptiness sometimes sounds cold and unfeeling, until we remember that it was the gentle bodhisattva of compassion, Guan Yin herself, who first expounded the wisdom teaching that form is empty of concepts. Less conceptual buffering between us and our experience, between us and others in our world, means more empathy, more heartfelt sense of the suffering around us. We find ourselves pierced by singular events, such as the death of a loved one or eruptions of the widespread, senseless brutality of our time. Beyond artificially constructed dualistic barriers, compassionate responses arise as natural expressions of instinctual caring. The light of insight shows us the need for systemic change.

Daido Roshi says, "This effortless activity emerges in our daily encounters."[8] This is welcoming in everyday life. We may first invite all sentient beings as our guests in vow ceremonies and rituals of commitment. We send out invitations to all beings (no RSVP needed), and we receive thousands of responses. We remind ourselves of the strong aspiration to be of benefit to others through daily formal practices of arousing the limitless heart of wakefulness (bodhichitta). These contemplative wishes are further fulfilled in actual acts of generosity and patience, skillful care and wise encouragement. The practice of a bodhisattva is on-the-job training.

Nature is all around and within each of these stages. Even at the first stage, when the exhausted herder cannot find the ox, Guo-an's perky verse invites us to listen to "the locusts chirping through the forest at night."[9] Daido Roshi evokes the despair and loneliness when we cannot find the ox, with sympathetic Nature singing the blues all around us: "There is only the gentle rustle of maple leaves and the cicadas' evening song."[10] True nature as our original home has been with us all along as the surrounding matrix of our journey.

As we ride, the musical ups and downs of the flute are magnetizing, and Guo-an says, "Whoever hears this melody will join me."[11] Similarly, elegant, peaceful statues of bodhisattva Guan Yin in zendos and meditation halls show us the magnetizing spirit of compassion gathering us into communities of courage. From the perspective of Buddhist tantra, Trungpa Rinpoche suggests that the direct perception of a vivid phenomenal world—Nature's brilliant colors and ringing sounds—"becomes the music which leads the ox home."[12] Bartok Roshi also notes the developmental sequence in which the spacious gentling of the fifth stage glides into the celebration of the sixth: "Here we can begin to loosen our grips on our minds, on our stories of how we and the world are or should be, and even on the tools of the dharma. We play freely on the iron flute of no holes."[13]

To ride the ox is a state of unwavering confidence. Ordinarily, our confidence is based on receiving praise or validating confirmation from others. Our confidence waxes and wanes based on conditional feedback: "Are others agreeing or disagreeing? Do they like me and what I'm offering or not? Am I being admired or blamed?" In contrast, here ox and oxherder enjoy unconditional confidence and well-being. There is an unwavering, indestructible quality to their deep determination to liberate all sentient beings. The Sanskrit word *vajra* is often translated as "indestructible." Our vajra nature, not based on causes and conditions, cannot be destroyed. This innate wakefulness is without beginning or end. Yet this indestructible power and strength are all the more vulnerable and tender for being unconditional and spontaneously arising. Not being basically needy, the bodhisattva can be unstintingly generous. As the wise Mahayana slogan advises, "Don't expect applause." This is transcendent giving, beyond the mere accumulation of likes on social media.

RIDING THE OX AND MINDFULNESS MEDITATION

Trungpa Rinpoche connected the unfolding path of mindfulness meditation with the development of a "sense of being" and "unconditional well-being," similar to the confidence we have just been contemplating.[14] Mindfulness of body involves synchronizing body and mind, developing embodied presence. When mind and body are in the same place and the same time (nowness), he says there is a "sense of being." First, let's look closely at his meditation instructions, walking slowly like a turtle. Then, we can reflect on our practice, mixing the meaning of the words with our own experience. Since words don't cook rice, after reading and contemplating the recipe, we need to cook and taste the soup for ourselves. As Cajun musician Michael Doucet once gently reminded me, "In the end, everything depends on the gumbo."

Listen now to this teaching from Trungpa Rinpoche's 1973 seminar, the first extended presentation to his students of the traditional four foundations of mindfulness: "There are several levels of mindfulness one can achieve. It is like the images shown in the oxherding pictures of the Zen tradition. (1) First, there is a sense of watching yourself. And then, (2) there is a sense that you don't actually have to watch yourself, because you can feel your own footprint; that is a level of how confident you are with yourself. And then, as you go along, (3) you begin to feel that you are very much in control of everything. The sense of being is always present there. You could ride on yourself and complete the accomplishment of experiencing proper being, total being. And then, (4) as you go along beyond that, you can ride on yourself, and play a flute as you ride on yourself. The sense of well-being is so solid, so definite."[15]

Let's walk through each of the steps along the path outlined here. We begin the practice of mindfulness-awareness meditation monitoring ourselves, closely watching for distractions (fear) and signs of progress (hope): "Am I getting better at this? Have I improved even slightly? Aren't there even more thoughts today than last week? Uh oh." Then the sense of watching ourselves falls away occasionally, maybe just for a few moments initially. After a few moments of abstracted distraction, suddenly we feel our own footprints during walking meditation. Walking is still walking, nothing special, but this bare simplicity is enjoyable. There is a carefree dignity in just walking. Occasionally, during sitting meditation, our hardworking inner critics and judges take a well-earned coffee break together, allowing us to discover that we can simply sit and breathe without so much verbal commentary. As we sit, what's that? We hear birdsong floating in through the open window. We realize that, as the Ordinary Mind Zen teacher Elihu Genmyo Smith confidently proclaims, "You lack nothing. You lack nothing of the wisdom and perfection of the Buddha, right at this moment. Hearing, breathing, you don't differ even one drop from hearing, breathing Buddha. Not even a hair's breadth."[16]

Trungpa Rinpoche's description of "being in control of everything" is a puzzling phrase, unless we understand it in Suzuki Roshi's sense of "control in the widest sense." When thoughts and images arise during sitting, Roshi advised, "Let them come, and let them go. Then they will be under control. But this policy is not so easy. It sounds easy, but it requires some special effort. How to make this kind of effort is the secret of practice."[17] Once again, the more trust we have in the innately spacious capacity of mind, the lighter the touch of our effort. Like a sugar cube melting in hot tea, effort dissolves into effortlessness.

Then the unfolding of our meditation practice on a cushion or chair is less marked by hope and fear. We can sit with fewer gaining ideas. Contemporary Zen teacher Jakusho Kwong Roshi, transmitting the wisdom of many Zen ancestors, once described sitting meditation as "actively participating in loss." The irony is that lessening the tight grip of anxious control—loosening the reins—allows the flow of experience to carry us. Lo and behold, maybe there really is no need to push the river. Again, it's as though the road under our feet is supporting us, moving us along. We're discovering how things actually are. It's only in our fearful imaginations that each step we take needs to *create* new ground beneath to support us. Earth and foot find themselves together.

This is riding, and the further celebration of this sense of being and inner well-being is like playing a flute as we ride. Trungpa Rinpoche, bowing toward the wisdom of nondual experience, says we are "riding on ourselves." Ox and oxherder are not-two, and both seem to enjoy the music. This joy, called "great joy" (*mahasukha*) in the traditions of tantric Buddhism, is the experience of inner freedom.

In short, the sequence outlined here begins with us watching ourselves and gradually moves to less monitoring and checking back, until eventually we become so confident that we don't have to watch ourselves. Mindfulness is often misunderstood as the effort to constantly watch ourselves in meditation or everyday life, to be "conscious" of every moment. Not so. The progression in these stages of mindfulness moves beyond intention or being conscious, always doing things with a clear sense of purpose. Intention and attending consciously to activities like sitting and walking and cooking are surely part of a beginning stage. Yet musicians and athletes and artists and performers and cooks of all kinds move to levels of action that are not "conscious" or done with deliberate intention. Not needing to watch and correct oneself is one sign of great skill. Hearing a skilled musician play their instrument, we sense that adding intention or self-consciousness would only interfere with the flow of the music. Yes, interrupting unconscious patterns is helpful. Adding intention, being conscious and deliberate, is important at the beginning of learning a new activity. Confidence, on the other hand, arrives when we can let go of closely monitoring every movement or thought pattern. Someone calls out to us ("A little help, please!"), and we stand and walk across a room to assist them. This is ordinary wakefulness, spontaneous compassion.

RIDING AS WELCOMING: LEVEL ZERO

Now, let's again consider the Welcoming Exercise, which we'll soon practice once more, engaging it from this independent yet caring perspective. Welcoming allows the play of our experience free from anxious monitoring for signs of progress or success. We can ride on into steadiness, free from the ups and downs of closely counting victories and failures. Welcome with the quiet strength that allows experience to roam freely, just as, in everyday life, our first open gesture is welcoming others.

Commenting on this sixth image, Trungpa Rinpoche writes, "There is no longer any question of search."[18] This comment illuminates an essential aspect of riding: it is not seeking. Seeking is trying to reach something not present, something to be found somewhere else at some other time. Seeking is like walking up a mountain in anticipation of a magnificent experience at the peak. When we finally reach the top, sometimes we turn around and walk back down in deep disappointment. Turns out that a moment of being at the peak is just another temporary flash, as impermanent as any and all of our experiences. On the long walk down the mountain, more hopeful, seeking thoughts arise: Maybe try a higher mountain? Maybe try climbing alone, with fewer distractions? Maybe next time invite friends and family, bring a tent, and camp out near the peak? Maybe try hang gliding for a change? All of this is seeking.

Riding, on the other hand, is not seeking. It is finding what has never been lost. We may ask ourselves, "Is this truly discovering anything?" It is discovering our human birthright—something that has never left us and never will, something we cannot throw away even if we try flinging it with all our strength. What is this?

"There is no longer any question of searching." This is also a key instruction for the Welcoming Exercise. Once, over a long weekend in Los Angeles, I joined a small group of meditators exploring our experience of the exercises in this book. After a few cycles of welcoming, a woman named Angela raised her hand to comment, "I really don't like this Welcoming Exercise. I feel like I need to put on one of those happy, smiley faces to greet every experience that arises: 'Hi! I'm Angela. Welcome to my spacious meadow.'" We all laughed. We were all familiar with the habitual impulse to achieve the imagined state of best welcomer. Isn't that one popular narrative suggesting the path to a meaningful, happy life—try harder to become the best something or other?

Eventually, after listening for a while to each other's descriptions of our diverse experiences, someone in the group suggested we reframe welcoming as a "Level Zero" activity—or better yet, nonactivity. We were meeting in a bright, spacious room where a secular meditation program called Shambhala Training—which includes weekends progressing from Level One though Level Five—had been held for many years. Angela's comic comment clarified a crucial point for all of us. Level Zero is not doing anything to attain or achieve something, not even trying to become a happy welcomer. Level Zero is just nothing. Level Zero is doing nothing, being nothing in particular, becoming nothing outstanding or extraordinary in any way. According to Zen tradition, when Buddha silently held up an ordinary flower, Mahakashyapa smiled. This was a direct transmission beyond words.

THE WELCOMING EXERCISE AS LEVEL ZERO

Please pause now for a three-minute session of Welcoming as Level Zero. Some traditions suggest we engage in short sessions many times over the course of a day. In this case, we will do a single short session. In that spirit, for the next three minutes, let welcoming welcome.

RADIATION WITHOUT A RADIATOR

This sixth image signals our discovery of the ox as awareness. When we were busy seeking, it was awareness that allowed us to look, then to see the footprints, and eventually to glimpse, touch, and tame the ox. Awareness has been with us all along—without awareness, there is no path and no journey. Riding signifies trust and confidence in the innate power of awareness. We do not require an outside agitator to make awareness more aware. We are not talking about an awareness that needs to be improved or perfected through profound practices. This is our ordinary, garden-variety awareness—it's not mystical or otherworldly at all.

Trungpa Rinpoche often spoke of awareness as "radiation without a radiator." I hear this phrase with emphasis on the final syllable—"without a radiator." The grammar of our language suggests that the verb *radiate* needs a subject, an agent called the "radiator," the one who is *doing* the radiating. Not so. "Radiation can only exist if there is no radiator. . . . Awareness takes place and that awareness is 100 percent all by itself. There is no need for you to watch your awareness as a careful speculator or instigator. If you are just being aware, that is openness, a welcoming gesture."[19] This open awareness is welcoming.

We sometimes imagine that there must be a solid "doer" to efficiently accomplish all that needs to be done in a day. One teacher calls this "the Mussolini fantasy"—the trains will only run on time if there is a fascist dictator in charge of making things happen punctually. Ironically, the heavy hand of ego-controlling often interferes with a group's self-organizing process and flow, backfiring into confusion and inefficiency. We blame some as "too slow," praise and reward others for aggressive speed. Welcoming suggests an inclusiveness where we can all move together at differing speeds.

This imagined one-who-radiates (the meditative radiator) sounds like a cousin of the one who welcomes (the overzealous welcomer). There is some family resemblance here to our identity as a seeker, a searcher, someone on the spiritual path. We identify as seekers, beings who lack wisdom and compassion and set out one fine day to find them. That's the core impulse of the spiritual search for many of us. Something is missing, and seeking is the way to find it. Welcoming is quietly letting go of this effort to find something else. Welcoming is not-seeking. Welcoming ceaselessly welcomes this and this and this. What is doing this?

Welcoming is the direct experience of awareness welcoming, without the need for an extra "aware-er," someone doing the awareness. If we are aware of this someone (a doer), then awareness knows the doer, not the other way around. Still, we may wonder, "If there is no welcomer, who or what is welcoming?" Clearly, from our own experience of the exercise, welcoming happens. Who is the primary agent?

There is a sense in which space itself welcomes whatever arises. Spaciousness is not created through practice or destroyed through nonpractice. Spaciousness is. If you have a memory of your grandparents, space welcomes that thought. If you hear the sound of a skateboard rolling on the sidewalk outside, space welcomes that hearing. If you feel an itch on your right arm, space welcomes that itch—as well as the movement to scratch it. Space welcomes; that is its nature.

Fundamentally, our experience arises in a creative flow without the need for outside interference to "get things going" initially or to "move things along" later. Riding is like being carried along by a powerful stream. "Things can only flow if the flow is the process that's happening rather than somebody instigating the flow," writes Trungpa Rinpoche.[20] Stage six involves emerging trust in our experience of being carried along. Daoists call this "trusting the flow of the Dao," the way of Nature.

WELCOMING AS RIDING

Let's briefly recall our contemplative exercise journey so far. Our engagement with the Welcoming Exercise was followed by Natural Noticing. First, in the original Natural Noticing Exercise, we paused to notice whatever was arising: sounds in the room or outside in the street, colors and shapes around us, thoughts and emotions inside us. These are generally considered objects of awareness of the six senses as understood by Buddhist psychology: sights, sounds, smells, tastes, tangibles, and mental phenomena. Without making any special effort, our six dualistic consciousnesses experience these aspects of the phenomenal world.

Then, with Natural Noticing 2, we turned our attention toward attention itself. This second contemplative inquiry considered the nature of awareness, regardless of the visual, auditory, or mental objects arising. Our focus shifted from the various contents of awareness—what we are naturally noticing—to ask, "What is this mirror of awareness itself?"

In the guided sequence of Natural Noticing contemplations, we shift our focus from the experiences arising to the container they're all arising in, the spacious meadow of awareness. There may be many sleepy cows and even a few playful sheep, but all are grazing in the same meadow. Doing these exercises is like being in a revolving door, turning from focusing on "that" to focusing on "this." This is revolutionary, a radical turnabout. During a meditation retreat some years ago, Tsoknyi Rinpoche gently invited us to "look hither." This is a direct introduction of awareness to awareness, like two old friends delighted to meet after years of separation: "Is it really you again?"

If you wish to refresh your momentary experience of unentangled awareness, turn back to pages 60–64, and explore this inner terrain for yourself. Be careful not to try to repeat any previous experience. We are looking and asking and seeing in a fresh way—in the spirit of basic innocence. We are not trying to reproduce a "good" result from last time. The best result will be no result, or as the eleventh-century Tibetan yogini Machik Ladron said, "When you look at mind, there is nothing to be seen." Then she helpfully explained, "In this very not seeing, you see the definitive meaning" (nitartha).[21]

Now that we've noticed awareness—and even though it's ever present, it often goes unnoticed—we may inquire whether awareness is aware of itself. It does not seem plausible that something *else* is noticing awareness. What would that noticing be? Awareness cannot be an object for anything else. As Suzuki Roshi says, "The big mind in which we must have confidence is not something which you can experience objectively. It is something which is always with you, always on your side."[22] Similarly, awareness is always on our side, never an object of something else knowing it. There is no separate watcher or witness here, like a carefully observing babysitter or monitoring supervisor. Awareness takes care of itself. It does its job quite well, thank you. Awareness is self-aware. Is that why self-awareness is said to be joyful?

Where does this awareness come from? Sometimes, in the Zen tradition, this question is approached via the famous koan request "Show me your original face before you were born." We were born from the union of our parents. We are produced and cultivated in our family of origin and culture. What produces awareness? If awareness were a product, produced by external causes and conditions, it would not be self-reliant. Like a spy secretly working on behalf of a foreign government, it would not be trustworthy. Awareness-as-product would be dependent on a powerful other, something outside itself. Mahatma Gandhi taught a way to nonviolent decolonization through self-rule (swaraj). Similarly, awareness is sovereign and rules itself. "Attention comes from nowhere," writes the Zen teacher Toni Packer. "It has no cause. It belongs to no one. When it functions effortlessly, there is no duality."[23]

The key point of welcoming as riding is that we do not make something called "welcoming" happen. Welcoming is not caused or produced by any effort. It happens by and of itself, without any outside intervention. We are the only possible interveners here, and welcoming gently suggests we all take early retirement from that job.

We experience riding when we feel carried along by our own innate power, the strength of natural wakefulness. In our time of turbulence and chaos, the ox symbolizes rich inner resources available to meet the ten thousand challenges facing us, our families, communities, nations, global humanity, all living beings. This is the contemporary relevance of these ancient teachings for our fragmented and fearfully violent societies. The profound peacefulness of the ox is not fragile and is not found by ignoring or spiritually bypassing the state of our world. This is a strong peace grounded in unconditional confidence itself. This confidence is sourced in nature. There are no advanced spiritual teachings needed to acquire this original not-knowing. No circumstances overwhelm it. It's ready to meet, equally, life's easeful and difficult moments.

WELCOMING UPSETTING NEWS

Let's pause for a moment to engage in the Welcoming Exercise again, but this time begin by deliberately calling to mind some of the most upsetting news accounts you've heard or read recently. Be gentle with yourself, but also be brave enough to feel into the challenge of being alive now. This is the path where fear finds fearlessness in our hearts. This is the innate power of the lion's roar inviting order and chaos, turbulence and peace, from all four directions.

INVITE ALL BEINGS TO RIDE

The Zen tradition traces its lineage back to the great ancestor Bodhidharma, who brought the practice from India to China. In Tibet, the revered "lotus-born teacher" Padmasambhava played a similar role, firmly planting the tantric Buddhist tradition in the Land of Snow. Centuries later in East Tibet, a great saint called the Madman of Tsang told this story: "When I was a young student and a very devout Buddhist, full of faith, I used to want my body to become one with Padmasambhava's body. I did countless recitations, thousands and millions of mantras and invocations. I used to shout myself half to death reciting mantras. . . . I called and called and called to Padmasambhava, trying to make my body one with his. But then suddenly I realized: I am—my body is—Padmasambhava. . . . So I decided not to call on him any more. Then I found that Padmasambhava was calling on me."[24] This is a vivid recollection of a moment of turnabout, a radical reversal from seeking and lack to fullness and abundance. This is the revolutionary insight of beginner's mind: "it is wisdom which is seeking wisdom."[25]

From stages one through five, we have been searching for the ox in various ways. Motivated by a deep sense of something missing, of basic neediness, we've been making a spiritual journey that culminates in touching, catching, and taming our own nature. Now, with the sixth stage, our motivation flips over. Discovering innate awareness is experiencing natural fullness. Instead of searching for wakefulness, we find wakefulness coming toward us. We are—the whole body and mind—this wakefulness. The whole of existence and all phenomena are this wakefulness, this one bright pearl. All along this wakefulness has been propelling us, seducing us, beckoning us, playing with us, carrying us. Who knew?

This is our experience of the great motivation of the way of compassion. Now, instead of seeking to overcome scarcity, we are moved by the impulse to share an inner fullness. Out of this sense of innate richness, our natural response is generosity. We let go of the concepts of a fixed giver, a needy recipient, and heavy-handed giving ("Don't you see how generous I'm being to you?"). When we engage in disciplined activity to benefit others, it's without ulterior motives of gaining merit or approval through virtuous action. Instead, recognizing our own nature, we continue centuries of transcendent actions of the family of bodhisattvas.

Trungpa Rinpoche calls this approach "the open way," the path based on the fundamental openness of original nature: "The action of the bodhisattva is like the moon shining on one hundred bowls of water, so that there are one hundred moons, one in each bowl. This is not the moon's design nor was it designed by anyone else. . . . Openness means this kind of absolute trust and self-confidence."[26] Riding is only possible with trust and confidence in being carried.

When we look at the image of oxherder and ox journeying together, we usually identify (human-centered beings that we are) with the rider. Yet the poster child of compassionate exertion here may be the ox, ever willing to carry others. In Shantideva's classic guide to the way of the bodhisattva, he aspires to sustain and care for all beings: "As earth and the other elements, together with space, eternally provide sustenance in many ways for countless sentient beings, so may I become sustenance in every way for sentient beings."[27] Beings dedicated to the awakening heart of compassion are willing to be a universal bridge for weary travelers, a supreme medicine for the world's sickness, a tree providing rest and shade, a sun or moon illuminating the way—whatever is needed. These brave beings are willing to transform themselves in order to carry beings across turbulent realms of confusion. Taking vows of limitless compassion, we commit to carrying all beings. Like the ox, we are willing to lift and transport beings beyond suffering by any means necessary. All these compassionate actions express vast trust in the resourcefulness of original nature.

WELCOMING IN ACTION EXERCISE

Since welcoming does not depend on sitting on a cushion, following our breathing, or contemplating a particular teaching, trying the Welcoming Exercise outside comes next. Find a park or area in Nature where you can walk for five minutes in silence. Allow Nature to welcome you. Nature and your true nature are secret kin, quietly working together anonymously and seamlessly. Allow welcoming to mix with the trees, grass, leaves, clouds, and sky. As with welcoming while sitting still, simply allow whatever arises to arise, whatever leaves to leave. Birds fly by overhead, and water rushes on. Clouds form and dissolve. In the distance there are sounds of children playing.

This is an exercise in not-doing while walking around instead of while sitting still. Let go of the expectation that your experience will be the same as during sitting; conversely, let go of the expectation that it will be shockingly different. Begin with curiosity, continue with unforced and unfocused interest, conclude with appreciation for whatever occurs. This open, naturally curious appreciation is the essence of welcoming.

忘牛 七
弄人

7 | FORGETTING THE OX

The seventh image shows the oxherder resting peacefully at home. The awesome ox—and our long, painful seeking for that lost, wild animal— are both forgotten. As in the first stage, there's no ox to be seen anywhere, yet now there's no sense of lack. As Zen teacher Bartok Roshi asks, "Who can even remember what that search was for?"[1] Anxious seeking gives way to restful confidence. Here, we enjoy the freedom of nonstruggle, abandoning the rope and the whip. There is no need for the concept of taming an unruly other. There is no other. At the seventh stage, a delightful possibility quietly dawns in the night: maybe we are the ones we've been searching for. Oxen are us.

PEACE IS THE courageous heart of this journey. Here, peace means original peace, the peace of our original nature. Sometimes peace arrives as a difficult achievement, the result of a series of hard-fought, bloody battles. Eventually one side emerges victorious— until the other side regroups and launches another attack. To conquer through war is to live in the constant shadow of violent retribution. Original peace has no shadow. It's all-illuminating, like a brilliant sun that shines everywhere, all the time, on everyone. This is nonaggression as the essence of all paths, echoing the wise saying "There is no way to peace; peace is the way."

We first explored this experiential way in the Welcoming Exercise, raising a white flag of surrender to whatever arose as we sat still, doing nothing. We engaged this exercise in allowing welcoming to be all-welcoming. As it says in "On Trust in the Heart," an ancient Zen text, "In its essence the Great Way is all-embracing."[2] Welcoming is the modest expression, not the heroic attainment, of our fundamentally peaceful nature.

When we welcome experience, all our experience, just as it is, however it is, we find ourselves in intimate connection with ourselves and others around us. This intimacy was first suggested in the image of touching the ox at the fourth stage. Our oxherding journey continues in the direction of direct experience by shedding layer after layer of conceptual buffering. We let go of the idea of a goal of "awakening" to be gained in the future. This suggests a subtle shift in our relationship to experience both on and off the meditation cushion, one result of the experiential inquiry we began in the last chapter and will continue here. If we welcome others, even those we sometimes find irritating or annoying, we become the expansive hosts of our lives.

The practice of the tea ceremony (chado) elegantly expresses this attitude of open generosity. The host prepares the environment and then graciously invites us into a space of simplicity and warmth. Beyond words, the atmosphere itself seems like a silent invitation: "You are welcome, just as you are. Please enjoy some tea." Tea is a formal example of an attitude and practice for our everyday life. Welcoming is a gentle springboard into a life of inviting all living beings to be our guests. We carry a sense of home and belonging into our world, sharing it with all we meet. The title of filmmaker Miranda July's collection of short stories says it well: No One Belongs Here More Than You. Likewise, mindfulness meditation teacher Sebene Selassie explores the basic belonging of our fundamental interconnectedness in her book, You Belong: A Call for Connection.

Welcoming lessens separation. Feelings of separation can lead to various forms of painful alienation and estrangement from each other. First, welcoming brings oxherder and ox closer together in a harmony that includes their differences. Then, gradually, our experience becomes so direct, so empty of dualistic gaining ideas that "ox" as an external goal disappears. Neither the carrot nor the stick approaches to discipline apply here. We're not trying to grasp the golden carrot of "enlightenment," and all whips have been cast aside. Fundamentally, there is no possible distance from what we always already are. World and practitioners in the world are not-two. We have never been separate. We all emerged from the many causes and conditions we now know as parents, family, friends, community, and culture. All of us came into being human in a matrix and network of care. Though each of us is singular and unique, we have never been independent, solitary beings arising in self-sufficient isolation. We breathe air, drink water, and are nourished through the exertion of many beings from infancy till this very moment.

True nature is not outside us. There is no ox "out there." As we have seen, even our wondering and wandering about as we search for true nature are expressions of true nature. What motivates our spiritual search? What else do we use in our seeking? Rather than a special state we need to reach for and desperately hold on to somehow, true nature is something we could not throw away, even if we tried. Our true nature is deeply inseparable from us, the essence of who we always already are. Pause and consider for a moment this fundamental teaching as a possibility. Is this possible? Is it true? Does it resonate with your experience of daily life or meditation practice? What difference would it make to live this truth of inalienable nature—at home, in your neighborhood or bioregion, at work?

NO OX

This lack of separation from our true nature is radical nonduality. There is no extraordinary state we're trying to attain. Suzuki Roshi writes, "There is no need to try to attain some special state. When you try to attain something, your mind starts to wander about somewhere else. . . . A Zen master would say, 'Kill the Buddha!' Kill the Buddha if the Buddha exists somewhere else. Kill the Buddha, because you should resume your own buddha nature."[3] Here, Suzuki Roshi is describing the journey of deepening confidence in original nature. There is no ox elsewhere. Just this.

The phrase "no ox" echoes the famous Mahayana Buddhist Perfection of Wisdom *Heart Sutra* (*Prajnaparamita Hridaya Sutra*). This sutra, chanted daily during Zen Buddhist ceremonies all over the world, is a fearless proclamation, a lion's roar: "Form is emptiness, and emptiness is form. . . . There are no eyes, no ears, no nose, no tongue, no body or mind." (Occasionally someone will wonder what we're chanting with if there really is "no tongue.") Suzuki Roshi comments, "In the Prajna Paramita Sutra the most important point, of course, is the idea of emptiness. . . . Emptiness is nothing but the practice of zazen."[4] The sound of this "big no" of emptiness resounds throughout centuries of Zen tradition: no appearance, no sound, no smell, no taste, no touch. "No ox" could mean that the ox is empty of all our concepts and ideas of what "ox" is. Zoketsu Norman Fischer, former coabbot of the San Francisco Zen Center, writes, "Zen practice helps you to live your actual life, not your descriptions of it."[5] When we hold on to our descriptions of life, of others, of ourselves, grasping after them with toxic seriousness, it's as though we were eating recipes, chewing on menus, feasting on familiar falsehoods, rather than enjoying the genuine nourishment of real foods.

"Form is empty of our preconceptions, empty of our judgments," says Trungpa Rinpoche.[6] We judge the ox of buddha nature as an ultimate good, something to be attained at all costs, through striving over many lifetimes (if it takes that long). According to tradition, bodhisattvas are those awakening beings dedicated to attaining compassionate enlightenment by any skillful means necessary. Still, from time to time we wonder, freed of these positive preconceptions, what this ox is. If the ox is our true nature and also the true nature of everything and everyone around us, what is it really? Aside from the ten thousand names and descriptions (sister, mother, daughter, cousin, teacher, doctor, liar, saint), who are we *really*?

Many helpful hints have been handed down in Buddhist tradition for the inner meaning of the emptiness of the ox. "If we do not evaluate and categorize the maple leaf falling and landing in the stream as opposed to the garbage heap in New York, then they are *there*, what is," says Trungpa Rinpoche. "They are empty of preconception. They are precisely what they are, of course! Garbage is garbage, a maple leaf is a maple leaf, 'what is' is 'what is.' Form is empty if we see it in the absence of our own personal interpretations of it."[7] Here, pausing on the peaceful plateau of the seventh stage, we see the true ox as "no ox," beyond all our ideas. This suggests direct experience as the only way to know true nature. Through intimate practice, we resume our own nature.

Often, resuming our own nature is taught in Zen tradition as a matter of giving up goals or at least being less goal-oriented. Practicing with no gaining idea could apply to how we lead our everyday lives as well. With constant inner struggle to get to a better life, we might miss the basic goodness of the lives we are living. (Are these also the lives that are living us?)

Historian Jill Lepore questions our pervasive contemporary descriptions of burnout as the human condition: "You can suffer from marriage burnout and parent burnout and pandemic burnout partly because, although burnout is supposed to be mainly about working too much, people now talk about all sorts of things that aren't work as if they were: you have to work on your marriage, work in your garden, work out, work harder on raising your kids, work on your relationship with God. ('Are You at Risk for Christian Burnout?' one Web site asks. You'll know you are if you're driving yourself too hard to become 'an excellent Christian.') Even getting a massage is 'bodywork.'"[8] I am persuaded by this insight into patterns of contemporary society. Lepore's suggestion here is that ours is a culture in which life itself is increasingly framed as "working" to attain something ("the good life"?), not only through better time management and workplace habits, but also through better parenting, better marriages, better bodies and abs and minds. (We could also probably use some deep inner work on our emotions as well.) Certainly, speaking personally for a moment, there is room for improvement in all these areas of my life. (We are perfect as we are, and we could use some improvement.) The oxherding images suggest a question for us to contemplate: beyond the risk of pervasive feelings of burnout, what's lost in narrowly approaching our lives this way as ceaseless work? What if this constant searching and reaching leads us past a simple appreciation of what's already here?

Leadership teacher Jay Ogilvy writes similarly in *Living without a Goal*, "If goodness is not some Goal that awaits us after we jump through all the hoops of some long linear journey, but is instead a perpetually elusive feature of the path itself, then we can no more be expelled from goodness than we can reach it once and for all."[9] The phrase "basic goodness" suggests that experiencing goodness may not be exclusively reserved for a special few but is instead commonly available to us all.

In the embodied learning tradition of the Alexander Technique, practitioners teach physical movement without "end-gaining." One Greek word for "end" is *telos*, so some teachings are described as teleological, taught with a definite end, goal, or final purpose. In teleological practices, we are constantly moving toward reaching a higher ground. "No ox" suggests a different spiritual path, making a journey without a goal. That's the title of a book on tantric Buddhism (*Journey without Goal*), and it has a sister book on basic meditation with a related title, *The Path Is the Goal*. What's really meant here by "goal-lessness"? How might that feel?

If there is no endpoint to be achieved that will make it all worth it, a final peak experience that justifies all our hardships and exertion, then what? Having no final goal may sound liberating and fulfilling, but diverse possibilities for disappointment loom large. Here, I'm thinking about my own experience of walking the spiritual path: What does it feel like when the ox suddenly disappears? First, I thought I was getting closer, mostly walking with a few glimpses of riding, definitely moving with a community of friends dedicated to reaching that higher ground (for the benefit of all beings, of course). What does it feel like when, one fine day, belief in the ground and the goal both disappear, suddenly puncturing your expanding balloon of hope? It feels empty, not the higher emptiness of the sutras but the emptiness of grief and despair, a dragging sense of futility, being flattened into purposelessness. Now what? All that effort and, in the end, what do you have to show for it? "I walked the path for many years and awoke one day empty-handed." Writing that sentence in my journal, I remembered the title of one of Trungpa Rinpoche's early seminars in North America: "Buddhadharma without Credentials." Similarly, contemporary Zen teacher Ed Brown writes, "A gentle rain settles the dust. . . . The ancient sand castles are nowhere to be found."[10]

I am guessing that many practitioners, after extended periods of self-deception, experience similar moments of spiritual despair: "This is not what I thought it was going to be like, not at all. This is not the journey I thought I was signing up for. Where's the great bliss I've read about, the kensho and satori described in *The Three Pillars of Zen?*" We may have read in a spiritual classic that "disappointment is the best chariot to use on the path of dharma."[11] That sounded good in a textual, abstract sense, but when we are *personally* disappointed, we think, "Surely they didn't mean *this?*"

In a series of mystical poems, sixteenth-century Spanish priest San Juan de la Cruz described various stages of a "dark night of the soul." Sometimes practitioners in intensive meditation retreats experience day after day of blank boredom—nothing, absolutely nothing interesting or entertaining seems to be happening. One practitioner described watching an ant making its slow, solitary way across the floor of the meditation hall as the dramatic highlight of the day. Trungpa Rinpoche spoke of both "hot boredom" and "cool boredom," but the keyword here is *boredom*. When was the last time we read that word in the exciting ads for another life-changing weekend meditation retreat? Novelist Jonathan Franzen, reviewing Professor Sherry Turkle's book on life in our digital age, states, "Boredom is the condition that smartphones have taught us most to fear."[12]

"No ox" means no external target for our practice, nothing we're aiming toward. We may feel lost without a sense of greater purpose to achieve, a target and destination we're steadily moving toward. Now I'm remembering a story about Kobun Chino Roshi at a Zen archery range, aiming his bow and shooting arrow after arrow into the sky, shouting, "Target everywhere!" This crazy-wise demonstration suggests another important perceptual twist. When we sit with the aim of hitting a single bull's-eye somewhere out there, then everything around that target diminishes and fades, appearing as, at best, a means to be used to get to our goal and then discarded. Concentrating on getting to *that* obscures our vision and appreciation of *this*. Conversely, abandoning a narrow focus on the goal allows the value of all that surrounds us (and the target) to shine. Welcoming is making friends with our experience, all our experience, not just a few special, targeted moments.

The Welcoming Exercise invites us into an experience of this natural state. If there's no target or focused attention during welcoming, then whatever arises is the natural state: welcoming everywhere. Here, "natural" means arising without deliberate cultivation, like wildflowers popping up in a summer meadow or wind moving over the ocean. "No ox" suggests no effort to produce awareness or successfully manipulate our minds into awakening. Trungpa Rinpoche commented about the seventh image, "You totally abandon the ambition to manipulate."[13]

NO MOTIVATED EFFORT

Awareness is spontaneously present without motivated effort. Let's pause a moment to consider the psychology of motivated activity. In the teachings that were collected in the Abhidharma (one of the three canonical "baskets" of early Buddhist teachings, and the one most focused on psychological analysis), "karmic action" means anything done within the cycle of causes and effects. The experience of karmic seeds and results is a circle of confusion swirling around and around, seemingly without end. Tired from a difficult day at work, we lose our temper in an argument over dinner with our partner and let fly some harsh words. Ouch! In addition to the immediate harm wrong speech can cause, it also strengthens our karmic patterning to lash out the next time we feel frustration, disappointment, or the looming threat of loneliness. In this way, harshly expressing anger is simultaneously planting a seed of aggression *and* watering previous seeds that are already sprouting.

One classic Tibetan Buddhist text describes the psychology of the karmic process as involving "motivation and motivatedness." First, we feel pleasure or pain or indifference as we walk into a gathering of friends. Then, a somewhat vague *impulse* to grasp or push away or ignore arises, and the dynamic force of that energy results in a fully formed *state* of being motivated to act: "How do I keep the pleasant moments happening, the jokes and smiles flowing, and how do I avoid that person who always reminds me of something embarrassing I'd really rather forget ever happened?" In a rapidly cascading series of effects, like a pinball bouncing here and there, we find ourselves acting from neediness, jealousy, greed for attention, anger at being slightly snubbed, or general insensitivity to the feelings of others. Motivation and motivatedness are like potter's clay being shaped into a cup or pot. Once the clay is fired and hardens, the shape tends to endure. Repetition of the feeling of wanting a certain result (to attract or repel or remain slightly numb) gives birth to familiar psychological attitudes, habitual tendencies toward enacting passion, aggression, or ignoring. Occasionally we indulge in the samsaric trifecta of all three at once. Buddhist scholar Steven Goodman cites an ancient Buddhist text describing karmic habits in relation to three basic personality types: a greed type, a hate type, and an ignorance type.[14]

Suzuki Roshi describes the traditional Buddhist understanding of neurotic confusion this way: "Our egoistic ideas are delusion, covering our buddha nature. We are always creating and following them, and in repeating this process over and over again, our life becomes completely occupied by ego-centered ideas. This is called karmic life or karma. . . . The purpose of our practice is to cut off the karmic spinning mind. If you are trying to attain enlightenment, that is a part of karma, you are creating and being driven by karma, and you are wasting your time on your black cushion. According to Bodhidharma's understanding, practice based on any gaining idea is just a repetition of your karma."[15]

"No ox" means an interruption, a gap, in the cyclic process of motivated effort toward achieving a spiritual goal. We are, much of the time, exerting ourselves to move toward or away from something, someone, or some inner state or mood. And now for something completely different: motivated effort is not needed to produce the ox. In fact, the effort to create an ox of awakenment moves past the riches already present. In a misguided attempt to get to imagined spiritual goodies over there, we miss the mark of what's already here. Remember Tulku Urgyen's koan-like question "How far must your fingers go to touch space?" Do we miss the ox by overreaching? Maybe letting go of that imputed goal allows a different kind of discovery. Welcoming is an invitation to see for ourselves.

WELCOMING AS A NOT-DOING EXERCISE

What is welcoming as an exercise in non-effort? Sometimes I remind myself not to make not-doing a kind of subtle doing. Karmic propensities can turn anything into more of an ego game of being one-up, becoming the best welcomer ever. Welcoming is not an esoteric practice only available to those who've completed thousands of preliminaries. Welcoming is just welcoming, completely ordinary, nothing special.

In his afterword to the fortieth anniversary edition of *Zen Mind, Beginner's Mind*, David Chadwick, longtime Zen student and Suzuki Roshi's biographer, tells a story that relates to this crucial step of forgetting the ox: "One of Shunryu Suzuki's closest disciples, Silas Hoadley, remembers Suzuki saying in the early sixties, 'I've come to destroy your mind.' Silas realized that the mind targeted for annihilation was the ego, the small mind, a delusion to begin with, but he said it was still a chilling statement. Suzuki recalled how he and his fellow disciples were losing their beginner's mind in their teens—through innocently seeing Zen as good, special, a means to gain something. He warned about the perils of being attached to any idea, including that of beginner's mind."[16] So, this stage of ox-forgetting includes destroying the idea of welcoming, destroying all our notions of experiencing "enlightenment," destroying our concepts of a special ox to be tamed and ridden. Such a move also includes destroying spiritual goals such as "being present" and "being aware." Here there is letting go and disowning even that "letting go" as a motivated action.

FORGETTING AND REMEMBERING

Many years ago, I trained with a Daoist priest who instructed us in a meditation called "sitting-forgetting" (*zuowang*). He speculated that this simple practice may have been a spiritual ancestor to sitting meditation (zazen) in Chinese, Korean, and Japanese Buddhist traditions. *Forgetting* is a keyword here. The word *forget* has roots in ideas of not having, not possessing, not getting something. Maybe this ordinary, familiar English word contains clues for practicing meditation with no gaining idea?

At the seventh stage, our precious ox is forgotten. As it says in a treasure text from the Tibetan practice lineage, "Hopes and fears of achieving and abstaining are all used up." We forget the goal and enjoy the way. There are momentary glimpses of such forgetting all the time. We don't usually drink a cup of tea just to get to finish it. Who lives life as a race to get to the finish line? "Be moved aside to who you are and what is really happening," writes the late Zen teacher Philip Whalen. "In the life of Zen practice, you shouldn't come out alive."[17]

One of the great master Dogen Zenji's famous phrases is "dropping off body and mind." It derives from the story of Dogen's awakening, which occurred while he was studying and practicing in thirteenth-century China. His teacher, Rujing, yelled at the student sitting next to Dogen, "Drop off body and mind!" According to tradition, Dogen attained great enlightenment upon hearing these words and immediately went to offer incense in his teacher's room. Rujing confirmed the awakening with the words "Body and mind dropped off."

As contemporary Zen teacher and Dogen scholar Taigen Dan Leighton explains, "In some sense, 'body and mind dropped off' refers to the letting go of our ancient, twisted karmic attachment to this limited body and mind. We are conditioned to try to acquire objects to embellish, enhance, or improve this body and mind. So just dropping off body and mind is to abandon that effort of acquisitiveness."[18] This acquisitiveness is also known as "spiritual materialism." What does it feel like to let go of some of the habitual acquisitiveness of spiritual materialism? When we experience the frailties and strengths of our ordinary bodies and minds—momentarily freed from cultural pressure to transform them into better, special, new and improved body-minds—they can be let go, left to themselves, released into space.

Many centuries after Dogen recorded "body and mind dropped off" as the koan of his awakening, Maezumi Roshi wrote a capping verse: "The thought-cluttered bucket's bottom broken; neither water nor moon remains." Daido Roshi, after receiving this verse in Los Angeles, commented, "The thought-cluttered bucket's bottom broken. The bucket is the container, the bag of skin, the illusion, the thing that we think we are. It's the thing that's in a constant state of becoming and change, the thing that we cling to, put our armor around, and try to protect so desperately. It's the illusion that separates us from everything else, from everything that we need and from everything that we love. The illusion. When the thought-cluttered bucket's bottom is broken, the body and mind fall away. The illusion falls away. Neither water nor moon remains. The water—mind. The moon—enlightenment. Both gone."[19] This commentary connects the "falling away" of forgetting to the ancient sutra teachings of "Gone, gone, gone beyond."

———

Forgetting has a dance partner called "remembering." Our word "mindfulness" is a translation of two words from ancient Indian languages, sati and smrti. These words can also be translated as "recollecting" or "remembering." As in the title of Bhikku Mangalo's practical guidebook, mindfulness is "the practice of recollection." Mindfulness involves training the attention to stay stably in the present. When our mindfulness wanders, like that stubbornly rebellious ox, we notice and return bare attention to the body breathing. What is it that knows the mind is with the breathing, has wandered, and now has returned to the breath? Awareness. Without this even, nonjudgmental, inner knowing, it would not be possible to train in mindfulness, remembering again and again to come back.

Forgetting is letting go of deliberate mindfulness. Mindfulness training begins as a motivated activity ("Now I'm going to do this practice in order to get that"), but awareness is discovered in non-effort. Awareness is born fully developed, spontaneously complete. Awareness does not require our careful shepherding of it along various stages of development, as deep training in the samadhi of mindfulness meditation certainly does. Awareness quietly suggests that one of the most helpful things we might do is "forgettaboutit."

The two-step dance here combines effort and non-effort, then effort and non-effort. Deliberate, intentional, conscious effort dissolves into non-effort. We are diligently doing something, an activity called "meditating"—within a spacious atmosphere of not-doing, nonaggression. With each step on the path, we arrive. If there is no ox at the end of the road, then journeying itself is the goal.

There is another sense in which the ox disappears on the mindfulness journey. Initially, we place our attention on the body or the body breathing with a sense that this (over here) watches that (over there). Becoming more and more familiar with gently training attention in this way, eventually we apply this discipline to all our activities: mindful walking, mindful cooking, mindful eating, mindful speaking. Then nonduality dawns. We are not observing the body breathing, we are body-breathing-mind as one. We are not watching ourselves walk or eat or speak, we *are* this walking, this eating, this speaking. Consciousness and body are moving together, like a hand fitting snugly in a glove. In a 1974 seminar called "Techniques of Mindfulness," Trungpa Rinpoche described a similar process: "We could have a somewhat dualistic attitude at the beginning, before we get into real mindfulness. . . . But then we just do the thing, we just do it. It is like the famous Zen saying 'When I eat, I eat; when I sleep, I sleep.' You just do it, with absolutely no implication behind what you are doing, not even of mindfulness."[20]

In other words, we may well begin with placing our attention on the ox, and as we go along (as we have seen), there is an emergent synergism, ox and rider journeying together with a coordinated sense of mutual well-being. The ox disappears, is forgotten, when we completely identify with the breath in meditation, realizing that we *are* this process of breathing in and breathing out. Bartok Roshi describes the Zen meditation practice of "just sitting" (*shikantaza*) this way: "In shikantaza we use body-breath-mind-universe to receive the entirety of body-breath-mind-universe. But don't imagine this is accomplished by 'you' alone, and don't imagine it is accomplished by 'mind' alone. This receiving is only ever accomplished with body, breath, mind, and universe together."[21]

Some kindred suggestions are found in a guided meditation instruction from Trungpa Rinpoche's time living and teaching in the United Kingdom: "First, let the mind follow the in-and-out rhythm of the breath until it becomes calm and tranquil; then rest the mind more and more on the breath until one's whole being seems to be identified with it."[22] This identification with the breath suggests a nondual relationship of such intimacy that there is no "me" over here following something called "breath" over there. With direct experience, there is no more ox.

―――――――――

Let's move now toward bringing the Welcoming Exercise out into our world. It's time for a coming-out party celebrating welcoming in everyday life. Rather than a contemplative exercise done while sitting still on a cushion or chair, from time to time remember welcoming in the midst of everyday life—over breakfast or at an online meeting or traveling to work. What does welcoming in everyday life feel like? To begin with, it's probably just an attitude of inclusiveness, simple openness without an agenda. For a moment, I'm not trying to gain something from this conversation with my colleague or win the debate about annual budget allocations. Just for a moment—this need not become a belabored or elaborate process—just for a moment, welcome. You're welcome, they're welcome, we're all welcome here. Everyone belongs. If this seems like a tall order, we might begin our exploration of welcoming in the world at home. As in the seventh oxherding image, when the ox is forgotten, the oxherder rests peacefully at home.

WELCOMING IN EVERYDAY LIFE

Here's a suggested sequence for experiential inquiry. First, sit for two or three minutes on your cushion or chair allowing welcoming to happen. If something unwelcome arises—worry or fear or judging yourself or others, welcome that as well. Remember Pema Chödrön's book title: *Welcoming the Unwelcome*. If a pleasant sensation or memory or anticipation arises, allow welcoming to welcome that ordinary happiness. Body, emotions, thoughts, sense perceptions—all welcome. Everything belongs.

Then, rise from your seat and walk around your apartment or house for a few moments, taking your time going from room to room, welcoming the sights, sounds, smells, and atmosphere of your home. If you appreciate the spacious and uncluttered feeling, let appreciation arise. If you feel anxious looking around this space, seeing the need to clear clutter and clean surfaces, let those feelings arise but continue to just walk and welcome for two or three minutes. Then, finally, return to your seat and let welcoming welcome for another brief period. Welcome home.

One suggestion for engaging in welcoming at home and in everyday life is experientially exploring no-separation. This is a silent form of inquiry, as though, stepping outside in the morning, we wordlessly wonder, "What is this?" The challenges of family and work life are not separate from awareness itself. How could they be? Who's kidding who here? Who's *really* on first? These challenges are arising in *our* lives. We are the hosts of our lives.

Zen teacher Martine Batchelor emphasizes nonseparation, nondual meditation in action in her comments on the seventh image: "Until now there was this idea that there was something to do, something to practice. There was a separation between ourselves and the practice. There was a dualism between what was spiritual and not spiritual, what was Zen and not Zen. At this stage we become united with the practice. It is not special anymore. It does not happen just when we sit on a cushion in a special room. Everything becomes meditation."[23] Reading this description, at first I experienced it as a liberating message: practice everywhere! Then I felt the weight and burden: now I have to practice all the time, 24/7, every minute, every hour of every day? The mistake here is regarding welcoming or mindfulness or awareness as something we need to *do*—radiance with a radiator. It's only when some of that urge toward heavy-handed mental managing begins to fade that we notice the natural wakefulness already shining. In Martine Batchelor's capping comment, she says, "Awareness becomes as natural as breathing."

I'm also wondering if our focus on an ox to be captured and tamed and ridden is part of constructing ourselves as the central agent in a life story. Seeking suggests a self, identified as the spiritual seeker. Even in traditions proudly proclaiming selflessness, this motivated activity could be part of practicing a life of self-centeredness. Consider Sojun Mel Weitsman Roshi's description of Suzuki Roshi's practice of shikantaza as an example of awareness in action: "Suzuki Roshi's simple day-to-day activities—the way he would sit down and stand up, eat his dinner, walk, put on his sandals—this was his expression of shikantaza. Everyday activity with no selfishness—just doing the thing for the thing—that was his shikantaza. We usually say that shikantaza means 'just sitting.' And that's true. Just putting on your shoes too. But this 'just' has a special meaning. It means 'without going any further' or 'without adding anything extra.'"[24]

What is this absence of excess, of adding something extra, going too far? Maybe it's also a kind of forgetting. There is less separation between welcoming and practice, between meditation and everyday life, when we forget to draw a line dividing them. Ordinarily we not only draw lines of separation but also underline and highlight, reinforcing these imagined divisions. What if we forgot to make that dualistic distinction? Forgetting the ox suggests that, from time to time, we might even forget to construct a self. And that is the eighth image—forgetting both the ox and the oxherder.

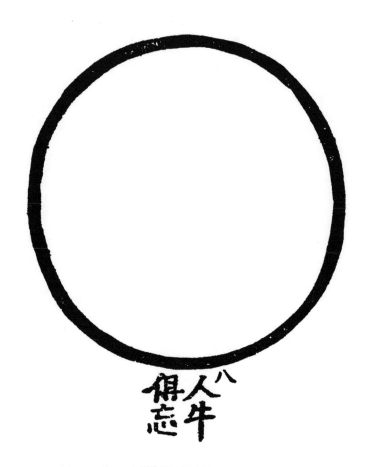

八
人牛
俱忘

8 | FORGETTING OX AND OXHERDER

Most versions of the eighth oxherding image show an empty circle: no ox and no oxherder. Poet Lewis Hyde translates Guo-an's original verse as "Whip and rope, person and ox: all are empty."[1] In the spiritual art practice of Japanese calligraphy, meditatively drawing this circular form is called making an enso. This is meditation in action. It is a moment of unconcerned movement. Ox and oxherder both forgotten, drawing in one stroke the open image of emptiness—that's it.

IT SEEMS THAT the seventh and eighth oxherding images are intimately connected, perhaps even life partners. First, at the seventh stage, there is no projected enlightenment. Then, at the eighth, there is no one aware of this absence of projection, no projector. In the clear light of daybreak, flimsy mists of object and subject dissolve together. Guo-an says of this stage, "I seek no state of enlightenment," adding, "Neither do I remain where no enlightenment exists."[2] Here we fall beyond the spell of the dualistic sophistries of "samsara" and "nirvana." According to Trungpa Rinpoche, "This is the absence of both striving and non-striving."[3]

Throughout our journey together in this book, we have been engaging in an effortless exercise called welcoming. Is the pregnant space of the eighth stage the absence of both effort and non-effort?

In the broken circle of emptiness, beyond struggle and nonstruggle, open space presents itself as limitless possibility. As we have heard, "In the beginner's mind there are many possibilities." Thank you, Suzuki Roshi, for this endlessly great gift.

Circles are archetypal forms, sometimes closed, suggesting completion, sometimes deliberately left open and incomplete. Sometimes, gazing at this fertile absence configured as an empty circle, I feel grateful, appreciating what has been handed down to us: inspiring stories of ancestral exemplars, teachings, practices, communities. At other times, looking again and again at this vacant image, I feel as though I'm slowly falling through space. The groundless quality of vast emptiness gently ushers in a spiritual identity crisis. If there's no ox and no oxherder, who am I? Who are we? Where's my community? I love the subtitle of Buddhist meditation teacher Kate Johnson's book *Radical Friendship*, offering ways to "find your people in an unjust world." Still, looking into the mirror of this open circle, I sometimes wonder where we are in this picture? If there's no ox and no virtuous action of oxherding, what are we doing?

We can welcome the unsettling quality of not knowing what we are doing, but we can't predetermine whether we'll find our experience frustrating. Frustration is a felt personal experience. Sometimes the more I try to relax, the more self-conscious I become about my lack of relaxation, despairing at my failure to rest evenly. Sometimes the more awareness I have of body and mind, the more I feel the tension within and between them. The more I mistake shooting arrows as just a means of hitting a target out there, the less insight I have into the nature of archery itself. Eventually, listening for a message in all this frustration, we pause to wonder, Who is the archer here? Will the real oxherder please stand up and be counted? Trungpa Rinpoche describes a similar moment when "the individual's self-conscious search is surrendered to the selflessness of the bodhisattva way." This is the way of compassionate action, "compassion being the act of radiation of intense warmth, radiation without a radiator."[4]

In a radical reversal, at the eighth stage we find ourselves turned around from looking for an imagined (internal or external) attainment to exploring and examining this seeking itself. We experience a quiet inner revolution. Something seems to welcome all our searching. What is that? Who or what is welcoming? This means who is doing what we call "welcoming"? Who was it who went looking here and there for the lost ox? What is it that clearly sees confusion? As we saw in our earlier discussion of Level Zero, we let go of even the notion of deliberate welcoming, of emanating warmth from a heavy-handed radiator. There may be glimpses of the eighth stage through inquiring into the nature of the welcoming person, quietly asking, "Who is this welcomer?" as well as, "What is this that we've been calling 'welcoming'? If it's not a thing, not a process or practice, then what is it?"

The answer to all our questions, the end of all our seeking, is this empty Zen circle. Recalling Eliot's poem "Little Gidding" again, "We shall not cease from exploration / and the end of all our exploring / will be to arrive where we started / and know the place for the first time."[5] The empty circle of the eighth image is this original place.

This experience of falling off the cliff of a fixed sense of self and other is basic to the entire buddhadharma, the Buddha's radical and revolutionary teaching of no-self. As the Zen teacher Robert Meikyo Rosenbaum reminds us, "The emphasis mindfulness places on the contents of the awareness of mind can inculcate a sense of an 'I' being mindful of an 'it' and in doing so reinforce the very ego the practice is meant to shake up."[6] One might begin with a dualistic sense of "this" being mindful of "that," but the meditative journey burns this solid sense of a doer in the fire and immediacy of direct experience. Practitioner and the object of mindful focus become one and then both dissolve in open spaciousness.

Indo-Tibetan Buddhist traditions teach twofold egolessness: the emptiness of a personal "this" and the absence of a solidified "that." Dogen's famous essay "Manifesting Suchness" (Genjokoan) outlines the steps of this gradual, contemplative journey: "To study the Way is to study the self. To study the self is to forget the self. To forget the self is to be enlightened by the ten thousand things."[7] Clearly this is an image of great enlightenment. As Trungpa Rinpoche says of this eighth stage, "It is the naked image of the primordial buddha principle."[8] Here, primordial means common, basic to all, not a rare peak experience of the fully awakened few. Consider the anti-spiritual materialist title of Jiyu Kennett Roshi's book on Zen training Selling Water by the River.

THREE BODIES OF ENLIGHTENMENT

Mahayana texts such as the Lotus Sutra transmit an important teaching known as the trikaya, the inseparable "three bodies" of buddhahood. These grounding principles, also called the "three bodies of enlightenment," are the basis of our entire journey of awakenment:

1. The physical embodiment of wakefulness (nirmanakaya)
2. The limitlessly radiant, energetic body of wakefulness (sambhogakaya)
3. The truth body of enlightenment (dharmakaya)

In Sanskrit, the full name of this third universal buddha wisdom is jnanadharmakaya—literally "wisdom-truth-body." Of course, this cosmic body includes—but is not limited to—the famous North Indian person of color known as Shakyamuni, the Awakened One. Ultimately, dharmakaya buddha is a universal principle, the enlightened reality of everything.

In his commentary on the oxherding images, Trungpa Rinpoche connects this eighth image of open space with dharmakaya, the warmth and fullness of the ninth image with the sambhogakaya, and the final image of return with nirmanakaya, "the fully awakened state of being in the world."[9]

Let's linger with this contemplation of the trikaya teaching as it relates to the oxherding stages. The open spaciousness of this eighth image (dharmakaya) is inseparable from the dancing, energetic play of the ninth, the "body of complete enjoyment" of all sights, sounds, colors, and tastes (sambhogakaya). These two are inseparable from the tangible embodiment of the tenth image, of all forms as sacred world and beings-in-a-world (nirmanakaya). Altogether these three are the mind, speech, and body of enlightenment. As with our ordinary body, speech, and mind, they are *inseparable* aspects of awakenment.

So what? Why does this ancient teaching matter for us modern oxherders? What is its contemporary relevance? Sometimes the three bodies of enlightenment are presented as the crowning culmination of the spiritual path. At the end of a long journey lasting, perhaps, many lifetimes, we attain complete realization of buddha's body, buddha's speech, buddha's mind. Here, we are considering a different approach: the possibility that these three bodies are primordial—present from the beginningless beginning, before practice, during practice, all along the way. This is a discontinuous continuity: not solid, yet without beginning or end. In this second approach, the trikaya is glimpsed, experienced, and realized as an all-pervading *ground* of commingling rather than an isolated *peak* experience. The trikaya is there when we're seeking, it's there when we contact the ox, it's there as we engage in gentle taming, and so on. These qualities of intelligent seeking, gentleness, exertion, and curiosity are all expressions of innate wisdom. Since the trikaya is the awake aspect of all there is, it's there with the lonely oxherder and the wandering ox, and now, in these three stages, it moves to the foreground as basic openness, energy, and manifestation.

APPROACHING FROM THE GROUND
OF COMPASSION

Let's consider again, in the light of compassionate engagement with suffering, the classic teaching of the six transcendent actions (paramitas) of an awakening being (bodhisattva): generosity, discipline, patience, exertion, meditation, and intuitive knowing. Suzuki Roshi calls these the six ways of true living. Are these a continuous way of life? In the case of transcendent generosity (dana paramita), the action is a giving freed from the concepts of a solid giver, a heavy-handed sense of giving, and a perpetually needy recipient. These three absences—no giver, no giving, no receiver—are called "threefold purity." As in the open circle of enso, this is the simultaneous and complete emptiness of self, other, and interaction. Activity can be fluid and appropriate, flowing yet precise, suffused with caring, yet free from clinging. Each of the paramitas is called a "transcendent" action because it goes beyond our customary concepts of an actor, an action, and the acted upon. Conventional generosity is dualistic, karmically entangled and entangling. Actions are called "paramitas" if they spring forth from the openness of spacious yet energized possibility. These compassionate actions are spontaneous expressions of the ground of the three bodies of awakenment: open, energetic, tangible.

In this approach, we are not being generous and patient *because* we will be rewarded someday with the prize of perfect enlightenment. (In a nontheistic tradition, it's not clear who hands out such rewards or withholds them as punishment. Poet William Blake wrote derisively of an old "Nobodaddy" in the sky.[10]) Generosity and patience are not means to an end. Bodhisattva activity is free from the domination of instrumental reason, where the transactional bottom line is often, "If I do this for you, what's in it for me?" Our actions can join insight and skillful means to interrupt systems causing suffering on this planet. The discipline of bodhisattvas aspires to and enacts the liberation of all beings. These actions are the direct expression of our innate qualities of wisdom and compassion. Paramita action is the expression of all our innate enlightened qualities, the ground of our being alive.

When we are seeking the ox, it is basic sanity that illuminates and guides our search. "It is wisdom which is seeking wisdom," teaches Suzuki Roshi.[11] Delusion deviously seeks to avoid wisdom so that confusion may endlessly proliferate. When we are seeking the way, this is our first taste of what Dogen Zenji called "the way-seeking mind." "If you wish to pursue the buddha way (but-sudo), then you must first cultivate the way-seeking mind (dōshin)."[12] This way-seeking mind is itself the jewel we seek.

In a talk during the 1969 winter practice period at Tassajara Zen Mountain Center in California, Suzuki Roshi clarified some of the important nuances here: "Our way-seeking mind is buddha-mind.... Usually, when we say the way-seeking mind or dōshin—dō is dao, and shin is mind—it also means bodhisattva-mind: not only to help ourselves but also to save or to help others. Strong nuance of this kind is always there when we say dōshin."[13] This way-seeking mind has been with us all along the way and will continue driving us until all beings are liberated from suffering. This is the motive force driving our initial interest in the way, our innate spiritual appetite. It is the energy to persevere on the path. It is the fruition, the end that was here where we began. It is beginner's mind. How could it be otherwise? This is the great continuity. Broken or unbroken, the circle continues.

EMPTY CIRCLE WELCOMING

The Welcoming Exercise expresses the openness, appreciation, and vividness of true nature. As we have heard, another name for this ground nature is trikaya, the inseparable three bodies of enlightenment. Is welcoming the ongoing practice of these three? Sometimes

I hesitate to say "practicing" welcoming as that suggests intentional activities like meditating or chanting or prayer. Those all involve more effort than is recommended in this little exercise. Welcoming is tiny, perhaps almost insignificant, so ordinary and easily ignored. As Buddhist teacher Sherab Chödzin Kohn once said, in another context, "It's not nothing, but it's almost nothing."

As we have seen, welcoming awareness does not occur in the usual way of a time-bound event. It's here as you read and welcome these words, just as it was here when you washed your face this morning, just as it will be here as you fall asleep tonight. Perhaps it will be here with each of us as we are dying. Welcoming is the natural openness of all our experience. Any experience partakes of this open dimension, since without this fundamental accommodation, there would be no room for the arising of laughter or tears, happiness or sadness. Welcoming is everywhere, all the time, always with us, and in this sense is beyond any particular experience. The mahamudra teacher Traleg Rinpoche spoke of "a sense of well-being irrespective of what we are experiencing."[14]

There is a sense, then, in which welcoming never occurs as a discrete process, a deliberate practice, or a specific experience. Welcoming is not an activity we start and then stop. Welcoming has no beginning or end. Welcoming has no instigator, no karmic agent with a hidden agenda to get somewhere or attain something else. One of the main points of the Welcoming Exercise is that, from the beginning, it's free from all such compulsive acting and reacting. If these erupt into the space of welcoming from time to time, so what? Let them play. Let them roam like deer on a mountainside.

This primordial openness or freedom includes natural, spontaneous appreciation. If these topics seem elusive or obscure, just pause for a moment. Feel into your experience of whatever is arising. Initially, our experiences often seem like objects appearing in the clear mirror of awareness. Move closer in the spirit of intimate practice. Find a place to walk outside and look at the green leaves of a sycamore tree. Yes, there is the word *green* that names a color of the leaves on what is called a "sycamore tree." Yes, so far, so good. Now, look more closely at the actual experience of seeing, letting go of the names and conceptual labels for a moment. What is this experience we call "seeing the green leaves of a sycamore tree"? What is our experience of green, green leaves, green leaves of a tree? Poet Federico Garcia Lorca wrote, "*Verde, te que quiero verde.*" (Green, how I want you green.)[15] Someone told me that their Buddhist teacher said, "No eye, no ear, no nose," and so forth in the famous *Heart Sutra* might mean, "I love my eye, I love my ear, I love my nose," and so on.

One could approach this more intimate knowing with any of the sense perceptions. This is mindfulness, yes, but also something more immediate and encompassing than a deliberate practice of directed and concentrated bare attention. Right now, I'm hearing what we call a car rolling along on the road near our home. What is that sound? Where is it? What is the sound we call "birdsong"? What is the blue of the sky—no names or descriptions but the raw, direct experience itself? Look, asking yourself, "What is that?" Then look to see directly. You could even engage in this inquiry while eating: "What is the taste of tomato soup or sauerkraut, cheddar cheese or broccoli?"

We can also apply this form of inquiry to inner emotional phenomena. What is desire, longing, love, passion? What is anger, jealousy, wounded pride? In some traditions one deliberately arouses a conflicted emotion and then feels into its texture, its energy, its rhythm. This requires courage. After a period of inquiring, let go of any deliberate looking and seeing. As Machik Ladron reminded us, no-seeing is the best seeing.

Guo-an suggests that the actual space of heaven is so vast that nothing can actually stain it. Kazuaki Tanahashi and Daido Roshi translate the lines this way: "Vast blue sky cannot be reached by ideas."[16] This is the open dimension of sky-like awareness itself, always inseparable from vivid colors, sounds, and tastes. This dimension is ordinary yet immeasurable, uncountable. As poet-theorist Fred Moten says, "You can't count how much we owe one another. It's not countable. It doesn't even work that way."[17]

This inseparability is sometimes expressed as a union, the root meaning of the word *yoga*. The ten oxherding images picture stages in an increasingly direct union, an intimate practice of life. As Daido Roshi writes of the eighth image, "Whip, tether, self, and ox all have merged."[18] Sometimes this merging is called "becoming one," yet we might also inquire into our experience of "oneness." In other words, "one" is also a concept, yet another attempt at verbal description. Look up from the book now, and without using any words, answer the question "What is this?"

———

We'll engage in the Welcoming Exercise again in a minute, so let's remember now that its key point is complete naturalness. Welcoming is our natural wakefulness. Here are some synonyms for the word *natural*—innate, instinctual, spontaneous, self-existing, unborn, unoriginated, not manufactured, genuine. The felt-sense of welcoming is open and inviting, a kind of basic warmth of friendly accommodation. If we invited friends over to our home and then rushed to meet them at the door, saying, "Go away now! Get outta here!" that would not be considered welcoming. In the Welcoming Exercise, we invite and allow and embrace all our experiences of body, emotion, mental discursiveness, and sense perceptions as they arrive in the primordial meadow of open space. This does not require any effort. Welcoming is not a deliberate, conscious, intentional, motivated action. Trying to welcome obscures what is already taking place.

Welcoming is inviting, not fixated, yet vulnerable. As human-hearted beings, we feel as an innate and intimate aspect of being alive. We are alive with gratitude, alive with grief, alive with jealousy, alive with love. We join all living beings in this natural state. In a fearless song of sad-joy, Roshi Joan Sutherland, a contemporary Zen teacher, writes, "Grief is a buddha. Not something to learn lessons from but the way it is sometimes, the spirit and body of a season in the world, a season of the heart-mind. Grief is a buddha, joy is a buddha, anger is a buddha, peace is a buddha. In the koans, we're meant to become intimate with all the buddhas— to climb into them, let them climb into us, burn them for warmth, make love with them, kill them, find one sitting in the center of the house. You're not meant to cure the grief buddha, nor it you. You're meant to find out what it is to be part of a season of your heart-mind, a season in the world, that has been stained and dyed by grief, made holy by grief."[19]

EXPLORING WELCOMING, TASTING UNWELCOMING

Please pause for three minutes to allow and enjoy this openness that neither rejects nor clings to whatever appears ("Let's keep this one going; it's juicy." "Let's swerve away from that one; it's an embarrassing memory."). Welcome the changing seasons of the sacred world.

Now, as a contemplative exercise, let's explore unwelcoming by momentarily reversing these three aspects. Instead of extending an open, friendly invitation, let's deliberately judge and reject our experience. Instead of not fixating, we will deliberately hold on, cultivating stubborn attachment. Instead of being vulnerable, we will deliberately cloak our caring nature in insensitivity and numbness. Let's walk through each of these as a brief exercise in antiwelcoming and noninclusiveness.

1. Sit for a minute or so, then energetically activate the voice of your inner critic. Whatever arises, mentally say to yourself something like, "Not this again! May this soon go away." Judge whatever arises as inappropriate, ugly, or simply wrong. Further, judge yourself as a hopelessly neurotic person for even having such thoughts or feelings. "Still crazy after all these years? Really?" The keynote here is aggression

toward all your experience and toward yourself. Notice how this exercise feels in your body and mind. Is this a familiar sensation or something new? Now pause for another minute or so, allowing this deliberate effort to fade into the not-doing of this reverse contemplation.

2. Next, move on to explore clinging. Call to mind pleasurable memories and try to hold on to them. Make them last as long as you can, milking them for all they're worth. Stick close to them, and if they slip away, bring them around again and again and again. Think of what you like and would like more of today, tomorrow, forever. Here the keynotes are passion, desire, and fixation. Notice how this feels in your body and mind. After lingering in attachment, drop the whole thing for a minute of not-doing. Refresh. As meditation teacher Rashid Hughes suggests, rest.

3. Finally, take a minute to actively ignore whatever is arising in your body, mind, or environment (sights, sounds). Whatever it is, just distract yourself with an avalanche of thoughts about doing something else. (Research studies suggest that most of our thoughts are about something in the future or the past.) Keep busy by occupying yourself with a chatty, inner monologue: "What about *this*? Then, again, what about *that*?" Take a break from this busyness to settle into a self-snug, inner comfort zone of "What, me worry? Doesn't bother me, not one bit. I'm spiritual." Linger in emotional numbness, not feeling your human-heartedness or anyone else's. If this insensitivity feels like something, notice that, but conclude these three reverse contemplations by letting them all go. Again, rest.

Return to the Welcoming Exercise as three minutes of not-doing—not deliberately practicing passion, aggression, or ignoring. If any of these flavors continue to arise, welcome them. Possibly they are mind weeds that, as Suzuki Roshi suggests, we can experience as nourishing our practice. If loving-kindness and joy arise, welcome them. Whatever arises, welcome. Notice that welcoming is not sowing the seeds of causing harm through the extra exertion of grasping, repelling, or ignoring. Confusion arises as chronic busyness. Notice that welcoming is natural, effortless, unforced, and gentle, the direct expression of an instinct for openness. What else do you notice?

EXPERIENCE, NO EXPERIENCE, CONTINUITY

There is no ox in the open circle of the eighth oxherding image. There is no "experience" of anything special—nothing. That's the negative way of saying it. In the positive phrasing, *anything* we experience during welcoming is included. We're not trying to be present or insightful or mindful or intentionally positive, uplifted, wise or woke or right. To not try to be any of these things is probably a rare moment for many of us. Our modern times of pervasive burnout are marked by standards and criteria and measures of efficiency in moving from A to B. What's the quick path? In contrast, there is no evolution here. We are not progressively moving into an integral state. Whatever arises, arises. Whatever dissolves, dissolves. So what? There is no implication that we're getting better at welcoming or becoming more resilient. The playing field begins and remains level. As it says in a Tibetan Buddhist practice text, "Here there is no hierarchy, and the mind returns to its naked state."[20]

In the popular television show, *The Simpsons*, Bart would often say, "Don't have a cow, man." This slang expression dates back to the 1950s, meaning, "Don't get so agitated or worked up (about something)." Our approach to the spacious meadow is often flavored by an anxious concern for what is appearing in the meadow. It's as though there is a persistent question that keeps fearfully popping its head up: "Are we having the right cow?" We wonder, "Is my sheep or this ox the one the great wisdom books are talking about?" Maybe. What's sometimes overlooked in this questing after the right experience is the meadow itself.

Cows and sheep and oxen come and go. We humans, as contingent beings, are also necessarily impermanent. The meadow, on the other hand, does not arise in one moment and dissolve in the next. It's not an "event" in that sense. It's not an experience. It's the accommodating space in which all events arise, dwell, and cease. This "space" is also not a thing to be acquired or lost. What is space?

Welcoming cannot be the product of our effort, the effect of our deliberate intention. All intentions and efforts start and stop. The great open space of the eighth image is not something we create, as in the suggestion of some meditation instructions to "create some space." (Whatever it is we're doing by such "creating" there is not this. This is not that.) This is not a very special bovine or super-ox moment. This is not a rare and exquisite peak experience to be cherished above all else. What is it?

Welcoming continues—on the cushion, off the cushion, at the office, at the dinner table, in the bedroom, in the kitchen, inside, outside, on subways and bicycles, online and in shared cyberspaces, walking in wilderness areas. This is sometimes called the "great continuity." I think that means that it lasts and lasts, that it's not a thing to be bought and sold, subject to planned obsolescence and in need of continual upgrades. I'm not sure how to fully monetize welcoming. (All suggestions gratefully accepted at www.welcoming .com) While we wait for some clever person to figure that out, there is the ongoing great matter of this very life and death.

The empty circle that is the eighth oxherding image is not really empty. This space suggests the open dimension of all our experience. Whatever we see, hear, taste, touch, think, or feel is not fixed. This openness includes the changing nature of our bodies, feelings, and thoughts; all our communities in the midst of changing seasons and changing times; meteor showers and constellations moving across the night sky. All of these are welcoming.

The great Mahayana Buddhist teacher Asanga, a fourth-century monk and founder of the Yogacara school, contributed to the Third Turning of the buddhadharma with eloquent writings on emptiness and buddha nature. Asanga's texts describe emptiness as filled with the awakened qualities of compassion, skillfulness, energetic power, and inspiration. This is an emptiness, these texts say, "fully endowed," just as the night sky includes brilliant constellations of stars, the moon, and visible and invisible planets. Open space arrives replete with regalia and retinue. Sometimes the open circle of the dharmakaya principle is mistakenly imagined as an empty void of complete negation, a nothingness lacking all qualities. (It does lack all *solid* qualities, but that's not the same thing.) In light of that popular misconception, Zenshin Tim Buckley's fulsome description in *Wind Bell*, the magazine of the San Francisco Zen Center, is all the more striking: "The dharmakaya buddha, beyond all conceptualization, represents the highest spiritual quality embodying all perfections, all processes, *all manifestations* [emphasis added]."[21] This is not a transcendent, unmanifest reality behind or underneath everything, but an everyday aspect of all we see and hear and feel and experience, the open dimension of all there is. This openness is invisible yet always vividly presencing. "The invisible is what one cannot cease to see; it is the incessant making itself seen," writes French philosopher Maurice Blanchot.[22] The open-circle emptiness of the eighth oxherding image is inseparable from the fullness of the ninth, a naturally abundant source.

返本
還源

9 | ENJOYING THE SOURCE

The ninth oxherding image presents a serene scene in Nature. As with the open circle of the eighth image, ox and oxherder have disappeared. All seeking and taming are long forgotten. The image here shows the trunk and willowy branches of a tree with a few leaves gently falling. Birds are flying around in the space. A river flows toward then away from the base of the tree. Guo-an's verse commentary says, "The endless river flows tranquilly on."[1] Perhaps this peaceful, natural setting recalls early Daoist prefigurations of these images, before Ch'an Buddhists began adapting them in eleventh-century China. As in Daoist teachings and the spare, spacious beauty of Chinese landscape paintings, Nature is basically good.

LOOKING AT THIS image now, I'm wondering if our entire oxherding journey might be about the human relationship to Nature. The basically peaceful background of a natural setting is highlighted here, but Nature has been in play throughout, implicit in all the images. The embodied presence of earlier stages requires direct contact with the most intimate aspect of Nature for us all—our own bodies. Even the ox as a living being is a domesticated form of Nature.

Our default focus has been the human being in the pictures, how they're doing, what their psychological state might be. Are they feeling tired or inspired, confident or anxious? These questions are certainly central to our concerns, the inner journey aspect, as in the old wilderness retreats slogan "Outward bound is an inward journey." Yet, in the cosmology suggested in these images, what we call "matter" or "the physical world" is not really separate from what we call "spirit" and the journey of awakening. What is the relationship of Nature and the nature of mind? Were these originally not-two? Are they still in a nondual relationship? Many years ago, a friend of mine went for a meditation interview with the venerable Tibetan lama Dilgo Khyentse Rinpoche, a renowned teacher of teachers. He asked her, "When you experience the nature of mind, do you feel your body?" According to the contemporary Zen teacher Zenki Christian Dillo Roshi, "In Zen, conceptual understanding is never enough; transformation needs to manifest in, through, and as the body."[2] In the nondual context of our oxherding journey, perhaps transformation is embodying what we always already are?

The ninth oxherding image shows a return to origins. Guo-an and Trungpa Rinpoche both title this stage "reaching the source." Daido Roshi calls it "returning to the source." Martine Batchelor says it's "returning to the original place."[3] Some might wonder how we left this primordial source-place. When we wandered, where did we go? What is the route and means of return? Others ask how such a departure from the ground of our being is even possible. Where else is there to be? Is there another there, there? After all, it's only from the perspective of having lost touch with an ever-present source that we need to search, find an origin, and return there. Where?

Seeking and finding the ox occur on the same ground as all our experiences. After engaging a mindfulness of body practice, returning to feeling the earth underneath our feet, we say, "I feel more grounded." Yet, in Tibetan Buddhist teachings, the source-place alluded to by the ninth oxherding image is called the "ground of all" (Tibetan: kunzhi). What does it mean to be "more grounded" while standing on the "ground of all"?

Looking back now, we see the open circle of the eighth image as this basic ground also. The eighth stage offers an openness that includes everything, welcoming all the way down and all the way out. In this ground, writes Trungpa Rinpoche, "there is already such space and openness and the total absence of fear."[4] Fear motivates our reactive response of shutting down, fighting, or fleeing. Fear is the impulse behind all our habits of unwelcoming. Let us pause to contemplate the word and the contemporary social reality of xenophobia. Welcoming suggests an alternative approach, a path to bravery, including directly relating to our fear as an expression of basic fearlessness.

The blossoming, buzzing fullness of this ninth image invites appreciation of the richness of Nature. Welcoming is like stepping outside in the morning to feel the cool air on your face, to listen and see what comes next. In the image, sights (a grounded and branching tree) and sounds (flowing water, singing birds) are all part of a vast celebration, delighting in the play of the senses. Now we see the complete openness of the eighth stage and the natural enjoyment of the ninth are two aspects of the same ground.

Let's pause for a moment to appreciate the many dharmic reminders that the dimensions depicted sequentially in the eighth, ninth, and tenth oxherding stages are the simultaneously *inseparable* three bodies of buddha (trikaya). Asked whether the trikaya comes into being by our coming to awakening, the early eighteenth-century Rinzai master and artist Hakuin Zenji responded, "Although the three bodies . . . are originally inherent and complete in everyone, unless they are brought to light, they cannot be realized." As Zen teacher Albert Low commented, these three bodies are "different ways our fundamental, true nature manifests. . . . An analogy would be the plan, [showing] side elevation, front elevation, and three-quarter elevation of a building. . . . Each of these refers to the same building, but seen from different viewpoints."[5] Enlightenment in the house from the very beginning? The eighth stage is the open dimension of being, while the ninth is being's ceaseless, energetic, colorful display, and the tenth shows the compassionate activity of this fundamentally spacious and lively ground. Nondual wisdom, playful richness, and skillful manifestation are all aspects of basic nature commingling with Nature.

Our English word *source* comes from Old French and Latin roots meaning "to rise, spring forth, begin." Of course, as Thinley Norbu Rinpoche reminded us, this is a realm of beginningless beginnings. Is this a groundless ground, an empty source? *Source* also shares roots with the word *surge*, to rise up, as with water in a geyser or the dancing display of a plaza's fountain.

Trungpa Rinpoche clarifies this: "It is the source in the sense of being an inexhaustible treasury of buddha-activity. This is, then, the sambhogakaya."[6] Let's linger a moment over these two sentences. They remind us again of the inseparable bodying forth of basic richness as compassionate action. This means the ninth oxherding image shows the ground nature of sambhogakaya as infinite treasury, limitless resource for skillfully manifesting. It also suggests that this, as in this place, wherever we are right now, and this duration of time, whenever it is, comprise a body of enlightenment. For the time being, this is the sambhogakaya.

"Just this" might also mean that no external empowerment is required to make it so. Suchness is already just so. Just as it is, the whole of existence is a nourishing and tasty cosmic soup, no transcendental additives needed. To be sure, some of the flavors of this soup are also terrifying. I'm thinking of earthquakes, hurricanes, tsunamis, and raging wildfires, as well as the thousands of ways we human beings terrorize each other and kill other living beings. Suchness is always already richness; a superabundance; an unimaginable, unmanageable plenitude. Our ordinary, mundane situation and the entire world—the everyday environment and its inhabitants—are fully endowed with power, brilliance, tenderness, and beauty. As in the title of Karen and Jeremy Hayward's book, this is the experience of "sacred world." Life and the world, our life world, may seem too much for us, over the top, filled with small acts of kindness and violent brutalities. The fullness of life exceeds our understanding of it. Think of the cosmic, awesome terror evoked in the biblical book of Job or the title of Thelonious Monk's jazz waltz composition "Ugly Beauty."

The sambhogakaya is "a source of energy which need not be sought."[7] As we have seen, certain misguided ways of seeking can lead to missing this source, this "first" place. First place, best place, fullest place? We can easily mistake original fullness for lack, primordial presence for absence. When we narrow our focus, desperately searching for that which we might gain or attain in the future, we miss the multitude of expansive possibilities arising now.

This basic richness is not the same as conventional understandings of wealth. As Trungpa Rinpoche generously explains, "It is that you are rich rather than being enriched by something else."[8] Overturning the dominant outlook of materialism, this teaching fearlessly proclaims a natural wealth that *cannot* be acquired or lost. Suzuki Roshi, in the prologue to *Zen Mind, Beginner's Mind*, says, "Our 'original mind' includes everything within itself. It is always rich and sufficient within itself."[9] There are practical, economic, and environmental implications to these teachings of basic richness. Excellent examples can be found in Professor Juliet Schor's book, *Plenitude: The New Economics of True Wealth*. We will turn to some of those in considering the tenth image.

DISMANTLING THE MENTALITY OF SCARCITY

Poet and translator David Hinton suggests that the central "adventure" of Ch'an Buddhism in ancient China was to "dismantle all our human conceptual constructions, all of the explanations and assumptions that structure consciousness and orient us and define us as centers of identity." And, he adds, "to do that not in the abstract, but at the level of immediate experience." Reading his book *China Root*, I find myself lingering over the mention of this linchpin of "identity-centers." This slightly unfamiliar phrase names an all-too-familiar experience. Hinton then gently asks a series of provocative questions about the effects of Ch'an and Zen's complete and thorough dismantling, including: "What would that leave us? . . . And what would it mean about the texture of everyday experience?"[10]

Is there a related dismantling implied in the trikaya's expansive teaching of basic richness? Here I'm remembering translator Jules Levinson's rendering of the Tibetan for *sambhogakaya* as "body of abundance." What dissolves and what arises with an experiential glimpse of life's fundamental fullness? As Hinton hints, "[I]n the end, Ch'an dismantles all of our answers, including its own, to leave a new way of being."[11] To expedite this clearing of the ground as an exercise in expedient means, we might inquire, "What was the basis of the old way of being?"

My life, and perhaps yours as well, can be accurately (and admittedly, partially) described as a series of struggles with various senses of lack. I borrow this term from David Loy's *A Buddhist History of the West: Studies in Lack*. At times I have felt that the key to "a good life" might be found in (1) romantic fulfillment—perhaps leading to marriage and a loving family; (2) academic achievement—maybe a step toward a successful career; (3) politically engaged helping by working alongside others toward a more just, compassionate, and sustainable society; (4) cultivating an art practice to a level of moderate proficiency; or (5) spiritual experiences—perhaps eventually bearing fruit in glimpses of realization. Sometimes some combination of these or even "all of the above" have felt important. Regardless of the solution—and there are too many other possibilities to list them all here—the basic premise was always a variation on the basic theme of lack: something vitally important is missing from my life and, seemingly, from all our lives. Until I find it, a quiet desperation will live on underneath a noisy clamoring for something more, something else. Who knows what will feed the beast? Did I glimpse it once when my first dharma teacher was still alive and teaching, showing us the way? Was it somewhere down the path of one of the many roads not traveled? Was it in this workplace or that other one, with that group of friends and colleagues or this one? Was it there in my childhood feeling of being quietly held in beloved community? All along the way, I didn't know, and I still don't know.

What is clear is that this feeling of something important being missing, even in the midst of relative material comfort and privilege, covers over the fundamental richness proclaimed in sambhogakaya and similar teachings. How is it that many of us have come to experience the ninth stage's basic space of natural abundance as vacant, lacking, insufficient, or never enough? Years ago, diagnosing a widespread, chronic malaise in contemporary culture, Christopher Lasch wrote of a "void within,"[12] which seems to describe this feeling well.

Perhaps our experience is similar to a moment of simple misrecognition. Crossing the street on my way to work, I glimpse someone moving toward me in the crosswalk as if to initiate a conversation. Feeling hurried and not wanting to engage with a stranger, I lower my head and try to move quickly around them. But then the person calls my name, and lo and behold, it is the very colleague I'm on my way to meet.

Our misrecognition of basic nature is similar. It's here, coming toward us all the time, yet we think it's someone else and somewhere else. One way we misrecognize this fullness is in thinking it's to be found in an object. This feeling of "if I only had *that*" is cultivated as part of the daily practice of getting and spending in consumerist cultures. As we know, entire industries are devoted to producing and then finding an inner sense of lack while connecting it with a possible outer fulfillment. Some of the most meaningful aspects of being alive are not objects. Love is not a thing; compassion is not a thing; wisdom is not a commodity that can be bought and sold. Note that our misrecognition is both a personal felt-sense and collectively produced. We've learned—and we reteach and remind ourselves regularly—that this is not enough, that is not enough, nothing is ever enough. Our next contemplation will be the Not Enough Exercise.

American Zen teacher Zenkei Blanche Hartman Roshi shares this memory: "The first time I heard Suzuki Roshi speak, he said, 'You are perfect just as you are.' I thought, 'He doesn't know me. I'm new here.' But again and again he would keep pointing in that direction, saying, 'You have everything you need.' 'You are already complete.' 'Just to be alive is enough.' I finally had to assume that I was not the sole exception to these assertions, but I was still dubious." Again, note that our self-doubts arise in a social field. As Hartman Roshi explains, "As I continued to practice and to talk with other students of the buddhadharma, I found that many people share the conditioning that leads us to think there's something wrong with us. If we could only *get*, *do*, or *be* something more, then we would be all right."[13] What would it take for us to be, to feel that we are, fundamentally all right?

A similar misrecognition hovers over all our relationships. Who will make us happy? When will we be loved, admired, appreciated enough? How many "likes" do we really need? The transfer of this addictive approach to the realm of spirituality is spiritual materialism, plain and simple. Which advanced practice or profound teacher (roshi, lama, or monastic) will bring lasting inner satisfaction? Will this next intensive meditation retreat finally get us there?

Part of our confusion circles around the meaning of "joy" in this context. Translated literally, *sambhogakaya* means "body of complete joy." The complete enjoyment of basic nature isn't the same as a moment of pleasure or happiness. One difference is that the pleasure of eating even the world's largest chocolate bar begins and ends, whereas this joyful fullness is here before, during, and after consuming anything. Experiencing this great fullness is sometimes called "equal taste," a basic equality. "At this point," writes Trungpa Rinpoche, "the pain and pleasure that derive from practice are regarded as absolutely equal. It is not as if getting some pleasurable experience is a sign of one's development and feeling painful experiences is regarded as a regression. That approach does not apply anymore. Everything is on equal terms. Pain and pleasure are the south and north poles of one world."[14] This one world is our world.

Many of us grew up in spiritual or religious traditions where "worldliness" was usually suspect, a bit too close to sinfulness. The world, this world, our world—all were regarded as "fallen" places. My beloved maternal grandmother frowned on dancing as part of the world's many devilish seductions. Imagine my surprise and delight doing fieldwork in West Africa where people *danced* their experience of sacredness. Some of us inherit deeply negative feelings about our bodies, emotions, and sexuality. Redemptive fullness is, from this point of view, something that needs to be conferred by someone else, a powerful being who can remove our basic sense of inadequacy or inferiority. Dissolving this rigid attitude of lack, direct experiences of sacredness embrace our world and all living beings as inherently worthy, valuable, meaningful, dynamic, and potent beyond belief. Now, let's explore this realm experientially by doing the Not Enough Exercise.

THE NOT ENOUGH EXERCISE

The Not Enough Exercise begins with a brief return visit with our old friend, Welcoming. Sit for a minute or two with your eyes open and your hands folded in your lap, without any deliberate effort to meditate or contemplate. This includes not trying to be present or mindful. If presence spontaneously happens, welcome it. If distractedness shows up, welcome it. As we have noticed, even though we aren't deliberately cultivating anything, various experiences continue to arise. These are all signs that you're still alive, so welcome them. You may feel shifting physical sensations, a twitch in an elbow, an ankle, or a knee. You may feel subtle movements in and around your face or chest. You may feel moments of fleeting emotion or what feel like long-term inner weather patterns ("Here comes that storm again."). Your busy thoughts may flicker, flitting from past to future and back again. Whatever arises, let welcoming welcome it.

After a few minutes of welcoming, silently say to whatever is present, "Not enough." Greet each experience that arises—a sensation, a sound, a sight, a feeling, a thought, a memory—with these two words: "Not enough." Do this for two or three minutes, perhaps concluding by changing from mentally saying, "Not enough" to "Never enough." Of course, there's never enough time to perfect this exercise, but at the end, return for a moment to the silent nondoing of welcoming.

A DIALOGUE ABOUT THE NOT ENOUGH EXERCISE

KAY: I'm somewhat unclear about the point of this particular exercise. How is saying, "Not enough," to all our experience related to the theme of underlying, basic fullness we were exploring?

JOE: Yeah, that's what I wondered about as well. I felt like practicing some kind of contemplative affirmation, maybe saying, "This is complete," or "This is enough," to whatever arises would have been more helpful, more to the point.

GUIDE: Yes, that does sound like a more direct approach. The Not Enough Exercise is deliberately nonaffirming and somewhat indirect.

Bear with me for a moment while we consider some echoes of this approach in the teachings of buddhadharma. Just as the true emptiness spoken about in the sutras is beyond all our concepts of "empty" and "full," this basic richness cannot be experienced within the realm of concept. We cannot find it there. We might find lots of pale copies but not this abundance itself. This is a very important point: it's not an idea to believe in. The great Indian Buddhist teacher Nagarjuna's most famous text, *Fundamental Verses of the Middle Way*, states, "All phenomena are devoid of inherent existence and are empty."[15] Yet Acharya Nagarjuna also says, "Those who believe in emptiness are incurably ill."[16] We're left with a question: What's underneath the conceptual overlay of our familiar ideas of "is" and "is not," "enough" and "not enough"? If we say, as an answer to this question, "Absolutely nothing," that's a concept. If we say, "Something brilliant, luminous," that's also a concept.

KAY: That makes some sense, but the exercise isn't really non-conceptual. Instead, it uses the words and concept "not enough." What's that about?

GUIDE: Yes, that's exactly right, Kay. This little exercise first explores our habit of seeking something *else* based on an underlying feeling that what's *here* is insufficient. For many of us, this feeling of "not enough" is so familiar that it often goes unnoticed. This feeling lives and breathes with us; we are co-conspirators in searching for what's missing. Sometimes we even project this idea as a human universal: Doesn't everyone, everywhere, in all times and places feel this way? (Maybe, but maybe not in the same way, given cultural and historical differences.) This ongoing sense of lack is like an invisible elephant in the room. We adjust our steps and quietly tiptoe around it all the time without consciously acknowledging its monumental presence. Does that make sense?

JOE: Maybe. If our denial is really as strong and ingrained as you suggest, it's hard to know for sure, right? There were times in the exercise when I felt moments of recognition, not quite "Oh, I'm doing this all the time, silently saying or feeling, 'Not enough, not enough,'" but something unpleasantly familiar for sure. Some spiritual psychologists I've worked with suggest that we often walk around with a feeling of gaping "holes" in our psyche. From that point of view, most of our activities are attempts to fill these gaps and spaces of insecurity.

KAY: Yes, I've heard similar teachings here and there, like in Ernest Becker's book *Denial of Death*. But, again, that's my question: what's the point of making this explicit, this idea, this concept and feeling of "something missing" in our experience? Why not, like Joe said, contemplate something positive using affirmations like "This is complete, this is enough, there's nothing missing"?

GUIDE: Yes, uh . . . maybe. You both raise key issues for us to examine together. It might be more to the point to explore, at least for a moment, what actually happened in our experience, rather than projecting what should have happened. What was your experience of, first, welcoming, and then saying to each new arrival, "Not enough"?

KAY: My first thought was noticing the contrast. Saying "Not enough" felt so unwelcoming.

JOE: Yeah, I noticed that as well.

GUIDE: Yes, I hear you both acknowledging the different flavor there is in opening the door with welcoming ("Yes, it's good that you're here. Please come in.") and then greeting whoever walked in with, "No, not enough. Not you again." What else happened? What else did you notice?

KAY: Disbelief. There were moments when I definitely didn't believe the little inner voice repeatedly saying, "Not enough, not enough, never enough." I could see out the window to a building painted green across the way. I wondered, what does it even mean to say that seeing this green is "not enough"? I love green. It seemed absurd, this tiny commentator judging everything, all that's actually happening, as "insufficient."

JOE: Yep, definitely something silly about this busy, voice-over judging of everything. At one point I thought, "Not enough" according to whose standards and criteria?

KAY: Yes, at moments, there was almost a little giggle or smile, a sense of transparency to these thoughts and ideas. Sure, they were arising, but why take them so seriously? Sometimes it's like we can see right through them, they're so flimsy compared to the vividness of what is.

JOE: Yes, sometimes I felt something like that, but also sometimes I felt slightly sad, reflecting on my own insecurities and persistent feelings that, whatever happens, it's never good enough, I'm not good enough, the world's not good enough. So, what's the point of it all?

[Silence for a few moments as Joe's question hangs in the air]

JOE: Thank you both for allowing some space for me to feel into that question. I just remembered something from Rilke where it says something like, eventually we care for the questions, not just the answers.

GUIDE: Good, good. Thank you both for heartfelt engagement, for your comments and insights. Your questions are challenging me to reflect more on this mode of inquiry. What is the view embedded in this exercise? I need to find time to write about that, but lately it feels like time is one of those things there's never enough of.

UNBORN RICHNESS

The view from the ninth oxherding stage, or the sambhogakaya, suggests that it's not necessary to *produce* unconditional or basic fullness. (It's probably a good thing that it's not necessary, since it's not possible.) After all, one of the fundamental teachings of Buddha Shakyamuni was that everything that is produced will, eventually, fall apart. Looking around us, this seems true of our bodies, emotions, minds, relationships, families, communities, and societies. Things fall apart because of their composite nature, which is to say, because they have been put together. This suggests that if, as the Buddha taught, enlightenment is something that does not fall apart, it *cannot* be produced through effort and practices. Therefore, Buddha Shakyamuni spoke often to the early Buddhist community of an "unborn." Basic richness is, similarly, unborn and unceasing.

It cannot be manufactured through affirmations, mantras, meditation, mindfulness, or prayer. Even though it cannot be produced, it can be *realized* by many skillful means. Realization means awakening to the reality of what is already here, waking up for real.

Instead of attempting to produce richness, inventing a target we try, try, and try again to successfully hit, this Not Enough Exercise invites us into a few moments of contemplating the feeling of insufficiency. This sense perception of seeing or hearing, smelling or tasting? Not enough. This emotional weather and feeling? Not enough. This thought or thought pattern? Definitely not enough. What is our experience of lack, of something missing, of inadequacy, feeling one-down instead of one-up? What is our experience of feeling stupid? What happens during times of illness, whether our own or those of others? During painful divorces or deaths? When things fall apart? How about when there's a sense of inferiority, of feeling not quite as good or competent or kind as others? When and where were we taught to constantly seek more power, more strength, more confidence, more of something sorely lacking? The materialistic outlook and practice seem to be everywhere.

This exercise invites us into a more intimate experience of lack. It's not an analytical exploration of the history of the heightened production of scarcity in modern times. That's a worthy endeavor for historical scholars, but this exploration begins personally, with our own felt-sense. No one else can tell us what this feels like for us. Strangely enough, it's both deeply personal and as commonly shared as being human. As Kay's comment suggests, we can all become more familiar with these voices of negativity, hearing them but perhaps not quite believing them. Here, the arising of doubt is salutary, like taking a vaccine to inoculate against a spreading disease. (Do we suffer collectively from this pervasive dis-ease of lack? What are the signs and symptoms?) In some Buddhist meditation traditions, there is a saying "Small doubt, small enlightenment; great doubt, great enlightenment." We often have fierce loyalty and strong belief in our thoughts. What would it feel like to doubt them? Genuine doubt of "never enough" might be healing, opening onto a larger field of possibility.

The Not Enough Exercise encourages an awareness of the qualities of our perceiving as it's happening. Sometimes we notice scarcity-seeing, scarcity-feeling, and scarcity-thinking as a process of narrowing and fixating. It's as though we are momentarily locked into seeing small parts of clearly larger systems. We see the bark on the tree, but not the forest, the forest but not the surrounding bioregion. Both Kay and Joe noticed a panoramic, oceanic fullness in which many tiny thoughts of basic insufficiency arose. Nowadays we speak of ecosystems, economic systems, the criminal justice system, systemic racism, family systems, global communication systems. The pioneering, practical insights of systems theorists such as Donella Meadows, Gregory Bateson, Joanna Macy, Peter Senge, Fritjof Capra, Margaret Wheatley, Francisco Varela, Otto Scharmer, and others demonstrate that we can approach any problem or challenge in its larger, more holistic setting. In our complex late modern culture, many of us have come to doubt the ability of any single, narrow perspective to fully comprehend the movement and complexity of whole systems. Systems teachings encourage a panoramic view. Systems approaches, then, are also ways of appreciating basic richness.

COSMIC BUDDHA AND THE ANTISCARCITY MOVEMENT

At the beginning of the fall 1968 practice period at Zenshinji, Tassajara Zen Mountain Center, Suzuki Roshi gave six lectures on the profound and provocative Mahayana teaching of the three bodies of enlightenment (trikaya). Practitioners at Tassajara were concurrently studying the famous *Saddharma-Pundarika Sutra* (*Sutra of the White Lotus of True Dharma*). Roshi's talks were subsequently transcribed and edited, appearing in the spring of 1969 as a complete issue of *Wind Bell*, the center's magazine. Zenshin Tim Buckley, the editor for that issue, wrote that these talks "indicate Suzuki Roshi's emphasis on intellectual study to deepen and focus *zazen* practice."[17] Many years later, editor Dairyu Michael Wenger placed these talks as the first chapter of the anthology *Wind Bell: Teachings from the San Francisco Zen Center 1968–2001*. Please join me now in nine bows of gratitude to all who worked to transmit these liberating teachings to us.

This sutra, Suzuki Roshi explained, "was supposed to have been told by Buddha himself, but actually it appeared about seven hundred years after Buddha passed away."[18] A key question then, as Wenger asks in an introductory note, is "Who or What is Buddha?" The *Lotus Sutra* was not spoken by the historical Buddha Shakyamuni but by the sambhogakaya buddha. So, who or what is that? According to Roshi, "Some people may be disappointed to hear that the *Lotus Sutra* is not a sutra which was told by the historical buddha, but this is characteristic of Buddhism. Buddhism had a long history before a complete understanding of the historical buddha came about." It is this complete understanding that concerns us here.

The person of Shakyamuni is called the "nirmanakaya buddha," a "delineated form-body" manifesting formless wisdom. In the ox-herding images, this is the tenth, being in the world. If we narrowly fixate on the embodied human being who was born and died in North India some twenty-five hundred years ago, we may miss the larger richness and dynamic power of wakefulness itself. As Roshi warns, "If we arrive at the concept of just the nirmanakaya buddha, we have already lost Buddha himself. . . . That Buddha was so great because he had a limitless background, a limitless practice." This limitlessly open dimension of a buddha's being is called, as we saw in chapter 8, the "wisdom body of wakefulness" (jnanadharmakaya). This teaching reminds us that the world-famous, exemplary human being of great compassion was inseparably wise, spacious, loving, caring, and therefore deeply engaged in liberating all beings from suffering. To emphasize this essential unity, the inseparability of the three bodies of enlightenment is sometimes given a further name, the "essential-nature body" (*svabhavikakaya*). Just as our minds and bodies are not-two, so the trikaya is not-three.

We might call this larger dimension of wakefulness "Cosmic Buddha." The historical person known as Shakyamuni was, of course, part of this primordial wisdom display, but so are we and everyone and everything around us all at once. This is the vastness that is the inner meaning of the small word *buddha*. Perhaps one aspect of the Great Vehicle known as Mahayana is this greater vision of wakefulness. The arising of Mahayana teachings and practices two thousand years ago was, then, part of an antiscarcity movement, a fearless proclamation of basic richness.

This richness manifests in thousands of ways—not exclusively in any single individual or group, doctrine or practice. It is ultimately nonsectarian. The main message is that all living beings are potentially awakened ones, completely enlightened buddhas. Many compassionate spiritual teachers speak the encouraging news that we all have "enlightened genes." In the *Prajnaparamita Hridaya Sutra* (*Heart Sutra*), the members of the family dedicated to complete awakening and the liberation of all beings are called "daughters and sons of noble family." This dedication and commitment arise from true nature. It is our inmost request.

This intimate family connection is expressed in some Japanese (Shingon) and Tibetan Buddhist lineages as the five families of wakefulness (*pancha buddha-kula*). Basic richness appears in five flavors, styles, directions, textures, and colors. As with the dispersion of light passing through a triangular prism, all the colors of the rainbow appear. As Trungpa Rinpoche, an early exponent of this approach in North America, explained, "As well as describing people's styles, the buddha families are also associated with colors, elements, landscapes, directions, seasons—with any aspect of the phenomenal world."[19] Let's briefly consider these five wisdom families in two related dimensions: as they arise in nature and in human social settings.

NATURAL RICHNESS

Appreciating the sacredness of Nature is a guiding principle in all indigenous cultures. Nature is supernatural. Australian aboriginal traditions, Native American rituals, African earth-based ceremonies, European pagan lineages such as the ancient Celts—all express deep respect for the immanent powers of this world. Similarly, in Asia, Daoist, Shinto, and Bonpo spiritualities recognize earth, water, mountains, and fire as living presences. Many of the peoples of Turtle Island (North America) transmit a wisdom called the Medicine Wheel of four directions. From the Cherokee to the Lakota to the Ojibwe Anishinabe, North American tribes have carefully braided diverse teachings around this common theme.

In each tradition, various colors, elements, seasons, and times of day are associated with the cardinal points of east, south, west, and north. Each direction embodies a guardian spirit that protects, supports, teaches, encourages, and challenges. Offerings are made to the four directions to affirm our fundamental interdependence. Collective ceremonies celebrate the intimacy of our human relationship to Nature. As descendants of the union of spacious heaven and practical earth, we are Nature as well.

In the tantric Buddhist lineages transmitted from India to Tibet, there is a similar ordering principle called "mandala," four directions arranged around a center. Sacred arrangements of mandalas are present in the body, in society, and in the natural world.

The richness of the east is called "indestructible" (*vajra*), reminding us that we are still moving in the realm of the unborn. Any quality or thing that is produced can also be destroyed; causes and conditions rule. The eastern direction is associated with dawn, the "place of first permission." It is connected with the color white, the precision of winter, and the elemental reflectiveness of water.

The richness of the south is called "jewel" (*ratna*), another image of self-existing abundance. There is no someone or something needed to make the jewel wealthy; true jewels are already rich. The color is golden yellow, the element is fertile earth, and the season is autumn. The time of day is midmorning, when the southern sun reaches toward full ripeness.

The richness of the west is called "lotus" (*padma*), an image of pristine beauty. The color is red, the season is early spring, and the time of day is late afternoon. Who can resist the seductions of afternoon delight? The primal element here is dancing fire, ceaselessly attracting our gaze and demanding our attention. Fire!

The richness of the north is called "activity" (*karma*). The season is summer, the time of Nature's maximum activity. The associated color is green, growing abundantly like leaves of grass. The time of day is dusk. The element is the swiftly moving wind.

In the center is the richness of spaciousness, the all-accommodating nature of awakened wisdom itself (*buddha*). Perhaps the Welcoming Exercise is a member of this family—a distant cousin at least? The associated color is the dark blue of midnight, the luminous darkness of the dead of night.

NATURAL RICHNESS EXERCISE

Now that we've received a conceptual layout of the traditional map, we need to explore this territory experientially. This next exercise may take about a half hour. Please shorten or lengthen the time as your schedule and inclination suggest.

First, go to a spot in a city park or nearby wilderness area where you can walk about freely and undisturbed. Walk in silence for five minutes with the general attitude of welcoming—noticing sounds and colors, the light and clouds, the temperature of the air, the texture of the local terrain. Include awareness of the "inner" terrain as well: how does it feel to be in Nature? Allow the richness of place to be your companion.

Afterward, review the description of the five elemental directions, and choose one that stands out for you now. Write a three-line poem that praises one of the five flavors. Alternatively, sing a song or make a gesture or utter a single syllable that expresses the energy of the season, the time of day, or the energetic rhythm you experienced in your chosen natural setting. Remember that *sambhogakaya* means "body of complete enjoyment." Here are some lines from a timely poem appreciating the richness of summer and winter:

SUMMER
As the thunder gathers rain,
Flowers drink water;
Arrogant greenery has no hesitation.
Summer provides festivity,
and life is worth living.

WINTER
Constrictions and rigidity of your martial law do not frighten me,
You give me chills and shivers;
But the way you decorate the mountains—
I admire your extravaganza.[20]

FEELING THE BASIC RICHNESS OF RELATIONSHIP

As a species, we human beings are unique in the time it takes us to become self-sustaining organisms. All other species reach functional maturity more quickly than our newborns, who would die without long-term attention and care from older humans. From birth, we are all deeply "dependently related" beings. Evolutionary psychologists suggest this as the biological basis of our human longing for connection and our appreciation of kinship and kindness.

Spiritual enlightenment, on the other hand, is sometimes approached as a quest for absolute independence, complete self-reliance, not being attached to others. Consider that the historical roots of all Buddhist traditions are monastic. Originally, we were a sangha of monks and nuns one-pointedly dedicated, above all else, to the noble path of awakening. Siddhartha Gautama, bodhisattva and future buddha, left his family to become a wandering ascetic. He named his first child Rahula, meaning "fetter," suggesting that complete freedom from samsaric confusion could only be found outside the confines of family life.

Is it mere coincidence that, looking back over two thousand years, we see the arising of the compassionate teachings of a lay (nonmonastic) figure like bodhisattva Vimalakirti (in the sutra that bears his name) in the same era as the proclamation of the dharma of sambhogakaya fullness as richly displayed in the extravagant beauty of the *Lotus Sutra*? As Sutherland Roshi explains, "Vimalakirti lives the life of a householder and is deeply committed to spiritual practice without seeing them as separate, let alone mutually exclusive."[21] Married and a father, Vimalakirti—as his name suggests—is "unstained" while remaining fully engaged in the world. Here, social engagement is an expression of vast compassion.

Having experienced the abundance of Nature, we move now to contemplate the riches of relationships, our connections with family and friends; coworkers and colleagues; coaches and teammates; advisors, classmates, and mentors; allies in PTA meetings, demonstrations, rallies, protests, affinity groups, and communities. How is it that this potential source of richness has often gone unrecognized, been devalued, and left underappreciated? The Harvard professor Robert Putnam documented the postwar fraying of social ties in the United States in his monumental research study, *Bowling Alone:*

The Collapse and Revival of Community (2000). In *Plenitude*, the economist Juliet Schor comments on his findings: "Not only were Americans less likely to join clubs and social organizations, but they became less likely to trust one another, got together less. . . . While there has been debate about whether we're really bowling alone or whether we just stopped bowling and started book clubs, a broader change in social connection is well documented."[22] In the wake of the events of 9/11, Putnam and colleagues, including civic activist Lewis Feldstein, visited communities all across the country where social ties were being reinvigorated and strengthened. Inspiring examples of this social reweaving appear in a volume and on a website called *Better Together*, documenting cocreative community work in Philadelphia and the Rio Grande Valley; in Tupelo, Mississippi, and Chicago and Los Angeles; and in a small town in Wisconsin and Portland, Oregon.

Many meditators have told me they continue practicing, in part, because of strong connections with their dharma sisters and brothers on the path. Over decades of journeying together, in joy and in sadness, in bitter and sweet times, we find ourselves in spiritual communities. As the Buddhist teacher Larry Yang reminds us in *Awakening Together: The Spiritual Practice of Inclusivity and Community*, it's a mistaken belief that "we should be able to awaken on our own, that we would awaken on our own given the right conditions, and that if we do not awaken on our own, something is wrong or broken with the teachings, the teacher, or ourselves."[23] This is the narrow fixation of "rugged individualism," ignoring the vitally nourishing richness of relatedness. As in the words of many Native American prayers, let us gratefully bow to "all our relations." Yang welcomes us back into this great assembly with his wise elder words: "[T]he teachings of community and sangha invite us into the experience that not only are we not supposed to do this alone, but actually we cannot do this alone. We can only awaken within the compassionate arms of our communities together, in solidarity."

APPRECIATING RELATIONSHIP EXERCISE

To increase your appreciation of what is often taken for granted, please pause for a few minutes to contemplate one of your relationships. Think back over family members, living or departed, and a relationship you feel grateful for, whether with an ancestor or elder, a partner, a child or grandchild, or another type of relative. You might instead select a connection with a beloved advisor or mentor. Or perhaps you recall a friend or an ally, someone you've worked and practiced alongside, sitting shoulder to shoulder since the beginning of your path. You may also think of relationships with those you have counseled, taught, nurtured, and encouraged. Bring to mind one of these connections and say, "Appreciation." Name this feeling of mutual respect, care, love, kindness, and gratitude. If the mind wanders, bring the person to mind again, and say inwardly, "Appreciation." Repeat this for two or three minutes, then rest wordlessly in the feeling of appreciation. Conclude with a minute of not-doing, welcoming whatever arises or abides.

Then, in the spirit of cultivating limitless compassion, think of others you know and love and wish for them to have the joy you contemplated in that first relationship. This is cultivating limitless joy (*mudita*). You are rejoicing with others, basking in the warmth of relationship. Say to yourself, "May they experience the joy of connection with others. May they be happy. May they rejoice in the feeling of mutual respect and appreciation."

Then widen the circle of joy to include others you do not know, people you may have only glimpsed momentarily at the farmers' market or on a street corner. Spend a few moments wishing for their happiness in the fullness of relationship.

Finally, expand this contemplation to include all beings. Let it be as vast as the sky and as warm as the summer sun. Include those you do not like and those toward whom you currently feel anger. If this becomes too turbulent, move instead to previous groups for whom it was easier to feel appreciation and joy.

Once again, conclude with the Welcoming Exercise, allowing and inviting the presence of whatever presents itself in your experience. Sometimes it feels as though welcoming is also an expression of deep relatedness.

SO WHAT?

Appreciating some of the fullness represented in the ninth image of our oxherding journey has led us into a larger sense of the meaning of buddha, the richness of nature and our relationships. What might organizations founded on basic richness look like? How does the scarcity model limit our sense of future possibilities? Will there be a future? Are there implications of this view for practices of restorative justice? Does this approach bring new perspectives to the global environmental crisis? Sometimes this vision of basic healthiness is applied to the range of human psychology: neurotic, psychotic, and states of brilliant sanity. The energetic patterns of Buddhist psychology's five conflicting emotions (desire, anger, jealousy, pride and ignorance) each contain a corresponding awake-wisdom. Buddhist contemplative psychotherapy using this approach has been taught and practiced for decades at Naropa University. Might the diversity and inclusiveness of basic richness be good ground for interfaith and interreligious dialogue? Considering the realm of diverse practical applications leads us directly into the awakened heart of the tenth image, being in the world.

十
入鄽垂手

昭和辛卯夏
富吉郎
画並刻摺

10 | BEING IN THE WORLD

A smiling, portly figure enters the marketplace with, as Martine Batchelor says, "a sack full of goodies."[1] Sometimes this jolly person faces another smaller, younger figure, also carrying goods. In the midst of what seems an ordinary commercial exchange, these bulging sacks remind us of basic richness.

AS WE SAW when we contemplated the ninth image, the teachings of universal abundance fearlessly proclaim a sacredness available in all settings and situations. Accordingly, the different images that exist of the tenth stage show an awakened being engaging multiple, diverse contexts. Animating the scene by speaking for the central image, Guo-an writes, "I mingle with the people of the world."[2] Clearly this is wakefulness shining in ordinary, everyday life situations. All the images for being in the world show a wisdom figure engaging with others in spontaneous compassion. Poet Lewis Hyde translates a Chinese phrase for this image: "Entering the marketplace with helping hands." Hyde describes this free-flowing activity as, "In the wine shops and fish stalls, people are transformed into buddhas."[3] This might mean that, with radically changed perception, we see the awakened potential in ourselves and everyone around us. It might also mean that the radiance of effortlessly natural wisdom-presence awakens all to their innate wisdom.

I wonder about the ordinariness of this scene. After all, every day we encounter people busily engaging in commercial exchange: at a farmers' market, in a restaurant or coffee shop, at a bookstore. Some commentaries emphasize that the fully awakened oxherder appears ordinary, emanating a sense of nothing special. This is a bristling paradox that cannot be comfortably flattened into one side or the other: it's not that absolutely *nothing* has changed, and it's also not that such moments are *not* ordinary. As in Sojun Mel Weitsman Roshi's story from chapter 7, seeing Suzuki Roshi putting on his sandals was just seeing a person putting on sandals. And yet . . .

Some comments call this image a return, as though our wandering spiritual journey took us elsewhere and now, after a long trek, suddenly, "We're back!" In Japan, when entering the house, one calls out, "*Tadaima!* I'm home now." There are, however, other ways of viewing the tenth image besides this homecoming approach. Yes, it is depicted as "in the world," but so is the activity of the very first stage. When we are seeking, we search for our ox *in this world*. Some comments on the first stage note the surrounding sounds of the cicada's evening song and the rustle of maple leaves. These are the world signaling back at us, "Hello! We're here. Are you home yet?" Similarly, when we glimpse the ox's footprints in the second stage, those tracks are visible traces right there on the ground, definitely in the world as well. What about the eighth image, the famously empty Zen circle of enso? Is it out of this world? No—this open dimension of being is also with us every step of the way, a clearing in which everything appears. Where else are all these images arising if not within the spacious meadow of openness itself?

From this flattened, horizontal perspective, all ten images are versions of our ultimately indescribable situation of being in the world. We might call them "ten aspects of something ineffable," an unsayable, inexpressible event or happening. We can also wonder if there are endless ways of evoking this fullness, infinite descriptions and sayings. Isn't limitless possibility a salient aspect of sambhogakaya abundance? Aren't there always many possibilities in beginner's mind? Daisetz Teitaro Suzuki, in his *Manual of Zen Buddhism*, notes that Song dynasty China produced several versions of the oxherding journey, first showing five pictures (by Ching-chu) and then six (by Tzu-te Hui).[4] The meditation teacher and translator Shinzen Young says that some early Chinese versions stopped with the seventh image.[5] Perhaps someday there might again be five . . . or twenty-two.

The liberating skillful means of the great bodhisattvas are famously diverse, shifting and changing to awaken us from our temporary sleepwalking. Sometimes these great beings compassionately and fiercely shout, just as we're about to walk off a cliff, "Wake up!" Sometimes they gently whisper, "Please wake up now." I bow respectfully to the many genuine teachings and teachers. May all beings fully awaken through hearing the vast music of true dharma.

Borrowing from German philosophy, I have called the tenth stage "being in the world." This phrase emphasizes the environments that surround us from conception to the neonatal and infant stages through childhood, adolescence, young adulthood, maturity, middle age, and elderhood. As we have seen, when we narrowly focus too intently on this or that being, we miss the surrounding fullness without which there can be no individual beings at all. Helping sentient beings can take diverse forms, but offering panoramic spaciousness may be essential to all true generosity. Otherwise, we fix a given being (temporarily in need) in a rigidly confining box of always being "the needy one." Spaciousness allows us to see guest and host as exchangeable roles. Sometimes, bowing, I'm grateful for your warmth and hospitality. Other times, bowing, I offer silent encouragement to you. In the tenth oxherding image, maybe the younger, smaller figure occasionally offers fullness to the older one. No relation, nothing, is fixed.

Sometimes I worry that this borrowed phrase "being in the world" itself sounds fixed. Maybe the tenth image is more aptly called "continual becoming in the world." After all, we know that our bodies are changing (visibly and invisibly); our minds and emotions are in motion; and all our relationships are living and breathing, constantly dying and being reborn. This is impermanence, the original teaching of the Buddha. We are all more like processual events than static, permanent beings. Our world is also changing—politically, economically, culturally, technologically. Here in the Anthropocene, we're facing a multifaceted, global climate crisis and crying out for, even demanding, justice. "Nature is not the green stuff over there, something to either exploit or protect," writes Zenki Christian Dillo Roshi. "Nature and human behavior are an undivided activity."[6] It's a world in becoming. We are, all of us, becomings in a world of becoming. Philosopher Henri Bergson wrote, "Duration is the continuous progress of the past which gnaws into the future and which swells as it advances."[7]

What, then, is the Welcoming Exercise in relation to all this becoming? Welcoming is simply allowing all these becomings to become. We allow ourselves to be as we are, in body and mind, heart and soul, breath and spirit. Rising from our meditation seat, we follow the continuity of welcoming in action, allowing others to be as they are. We also allow our world to arise as it arises. The world invites us, teaches us, calls us, seduces us, challenges us, and provokes us into action.

Okay, then what? That's the inevitable next question because welcoming was never meant to be the end of the story, our only or final gesture in relating to life as it arises. Although I've highlighted welcoming in this book, I do not mean to suggest, "Just welcome, that's all there is." Such narrow dogmatism wouldn't be very welcoming or compassionate, would it? That would be more like an Exclude Everything Else exercise. Welcoming is a first step, an initial position. Our next steps might be affirming—engaging actions that say "yes" to what nurtures life—or negating—performing actions that say "no" to what harms living beings. Welcoming allows us to see clearly what is needed where and when. Trungpa Rinpoche describes the tenth stage as spontaneously compassionate action in which "you care for whatever needs your care" and "destroy what needs to be destroyed."[8]

Welcoming is attuning to the upsurges we are constantly surrounded by. It welcomes emergent properties, not insisting on knowing all possible outcomes beforehand. Welcoming allows becoming and becoming and becoming with no end or final goal in sight. No gaining ideas and no end-gaining are the flowing lifeblood of welcoming. Welcoming sees many possible destinations along the way and enjoys the unfolding journey. It is aligned with impermanence, flux, change, flow, and transformation. It adapts as shifting figures become grounds and vice versa, as margins move to the center and central figures move to the side. It allows space for new voices and startlingly fresh creativity.

What is it exactly that does all this? Who or what is it that welcomes? Not a thing. Welcoming arises in darkness, from not-knowing, nondoing. As the artist David Hammons says, "I decided a long time ago that the less I do, the more an artist I am."[9] Welcoming is not produced by an illuminator, a heroic "enlightener." Welcoming is space spaciously expressing inherent spaciousness. We are not the ones who "create" space. Instead, space welcomes us and all that arises. There's literally nothing for us to do in welcoming. We're not improving, fixing, processing, transforming, or integrating our experience. We're not healing, centering, or reconnecting. Nada, nothing, rien, bubkes, zero. Welcoming is not doing anything with or to our experience. Trungpa Rinpoche's comment on the seventh oxherding image—"You totally abandon the ambition to manipulate"—could be taken as the pith instruction for all welcoming. Welcoming happens regardless of our intention or motivation. You're always welcome.

THREE BODIES AS GROUND, PATH, AND FRUITION

These images of the tenth oxherding stage also remind us that the inseparable three bodies of enlightenment can appear in human form, such as an ordinary person exchanging goods in a market. The vast openness of the eighth image, the playful, abundant energies of the ninth, and the embodied human beings of the tenth are all present at once in this picture. The entire oxherding journey from the first stage through the ninth manifests in summary form in this concluding one. Here comes everybody!

In many classic Mahayana texts, the path of awakening bodhisattvas proceeds from a fundamental ground basis in buddha nature through ten stages (bhumi) to complete enlightenment, finally attaining or realizing the three bodies of buddhahood. This is the fruition of the path. Reaching the unobscured peak of meditative abiding in an indestructible "vajra-like samadhi," one awakens to the enlightened three bodies. In such teachings, one begins on the ground, walks the path, and eventually attains the result.

As we have seen, however, there is another perspective from which the trikaya is not exclusively an ultimate achievement but the ground under the entire journey as well. The three bodies are all here from the beginning as the basic nature of all. They are with us all along the path, and yes, they are fully revealed in the fruition. What is uncovered—like removing a tarp that temporarily covered the ground—has been here all the time. Using this alternative approach, we might say, "Trikaya is ground, trikaya is path, and trikaya is fruition." Please pause for a moment to contemplate the difference between these two approaches.

All three bodies are here at the first oxherding stage. It is our innate intelligence (dharmakaya nature) arising as sparks of dissatisfaction that motivate us to seek. In his most famous text, *Genjokoan*, Dogen Zenji writes, "To study the way of enlightenment is to study the self."[10] When we reflect on our own way-seeking hearts and minds, we discover that we are always seeking. This is suffering. The felt personal sense of ourselves as seekers looms so large that it's almost all we can see at the first stage. We experience keenly the dissatisfaction of seeking but not finding ("What's missing here? What is wrong with me and this situation?") Our inner questions resound so loudly that we cannot hear the cicadas or the rustling leaves.

In the second oxherding stage, the vast richness of the sambhogakaya appears as footprints, fresh impressions and conceptual traces of what is beyond all concepts. Hearing the teaching of suffering and its causes, contemplating the ancient system of twelve links of dependent arising, we discover the dharma of realization in our own experience. As it says in the rugged, realization songs of Kagyu Buddhist ancestors, "Rock meets bone in insight."

Ancestor Dogen says, "To study the self is to forget the self." This sounds like the realm of the eighth oxherding image, with its circle of emptiness, and the seventh in which ox and goals are forgotten. Forgetting and welcoming walk together hand in hand. We forget all descriptions and stories of what we are, who we are, where we've come from, where we're going. At the same time, this open emptiness is welcoming, inclusive of all our entangled and liberated histories, all our possible and impossible futures.

Then: "To forget the self is to be enlightened by ten thousand things." This is the fullness of being in the world. Earth and sky, trees and rivers and winds are manifest wisdom, awakening all beings. As with many indigenous traditions, Daoist teachers place great emphasis on Nature guiding us, teaching us, and illuminating the human relationship to Nature. Trungpa Rinpoche titles the tenth image "In the World" and says of it, "This state is dealing with the earth with ultimate simplicity."[11] And is the earth dealing with us as well? Dogen illuminates the dropping off of bodies and minds: "When enlightened by ten thousand things, the body and mind as well as the bodies and minds of others drop away." This is ultimate nonduality. Dogen concludes by erasing all possible dwelling in the "stink of awakening": "No trace of enlightenment remains, and this no-trace continues endlessly."

ALL THE WAY IS THE WAY

Here. contemplating the tenth and final image, we look back with expansive appreciation and humility, finally recognizing all ten images as pictures of awakening. As in the vast vision of the *Lotus Sutra*, all beings are on the way to becoming buddhas. The fourteenth-century mystic Saint Catherine of Siena said, "All the way to heaven is heaven."[12] Each step along the way is the way. Here is the feeling: even in making a thousand-mile journey, we arrive where we are with each step. How could it be otherwise? Seeking is the way, glimpsing the ox is the way, taming and riding and forgetting the ox are all equally the way. Yes, there are many steps and stages along the way, but wherever we are, the way is the way. Perhaps that is why it is the way, the Great Way that "does not pick and choose." As the third Ch'an ancestor Jianzhi Sengcan wrote, "In its essence the Great Way is all-embracing."[13] Dogen expresses it this way: "In birth there is nothing but birth, and in death there is nothing but death."[14] Each stage is complete in this moment. In some traditions, this is called "great completion."

The contrary approach (let's call it "walking the path as reaching the end someday") would persuade us that only the tenth stage is complete, full, and perfect. All the other stages are lacking. Only once we arrive at the "final" stage will we feel complete, satisfied, and meaningfully fulfilled. This may sound familiar as it's similar to the narrow perspective of the first stage, constantly searching for what can never be found or attained. Dogen explains it as, "When you first seek dharma, you imagine you are far away from its environs. At the moment when dharma is authentically transmitted, you are immediately your original self."[15] The word *environs* reminds us that we are always intimately connected to our world. Others and what we call "the world" are always dancing with us. This is true nature as being in the world.

Insisting again and again that welcoming is not something we do or accomplish or achieve, that it serves no purpose or function, I have written at times as though this nonmeditation, this not-doing, is *opposed* to all practices, techniques, and skillful means. Not so. I apologize for the, in my case, not-so-youthful folly of leaning toward that extreme. It's true that no one gets better or more accomplished at welcoming; it's always everyone's Level Zero. Yet welcoming also welcomes techniques and methods and practices for accomplishing personal and collective healing, reintegration, union, harmony, synchrony, and inner and outer peace. These are all worthy aims and purposes, and there are many effective skillful means for accomplishing them. Taming, pacifying, and rigorous training intensives may all be genuine expressions of our inmost request. Compassionate engagement in service to others is welcoming in action. Just as ox and oxherder eventually realize they are not-two, doing and not-doing are intimate partners. The democratic majesty of the welcoming spirit is quietly confident: "Let a thousand lotuses bloom."

The ancient Greeks used a word, *telos*, that may help us clarify what the tenth stage is and is not. The telos of an acorn is an oak tree, the culminating achievement all its organic development aims toward. Please be careful here: the tenth stage is *not* the telos of the oxherding journey. In the approach of this book, our oxherding path is nonteleological. The fundamental freedom of the tenth stage means that it may appear as a wise, awakening being entering a market, but it may also arise as a curious seeker at the first stage. Why not? Those in the tenth stage, as is said of great bodhisattvas, do not linger in samsara or dwell in nirvana. The tenth stage may manifest as a wild ox nature and a frustrated oxherder trying to tame it by stubbornly sitting through a long meditation session. It may seem to disappear entirely at the eighth stage or surge forth as the brilliant effulgence of the ninth. It may also manifest as the Level Zero of welcoming. The possibilities are literally limitless. The tenth stage invites us into limitless possibilities and runaway realizations.

OF MIMICRY AND IMMANENT GUIDANCE

Trungpa Rinpoche says of the tenth stage that it involves letting go of "following the example of anyone."[16] This key point is vitally important. When we mimic the behavior of others, we place the source of wisdom outside ourselves. We abandon the rich resources of our own inner nature. We seek a higher, more authoritative being to lean on, just as small children depend on their parents' protection. Perhaps such guidance is helpful and necessary at certain points in our journey. Perhaps there are also times when such "other-reliance" becomes a pernicious influence, toxic and dangerous for all concerned.

When we proceed by mimicking the speech or bravery, kindness or silence of others, we may inadvertently carry actions that are beneficial in one setting into another context where they don't quite fit. Splashing buckets of water is useful for extinguishing fire but a useless offering to a drowning person. In such decontextualized moments, we lapse into behaving like our idea of buddha rather than being the awakened genuineness we fundamentally are. What was nourishing kindness becomes saccharine imitation. What was acting with fearless confidence becomes insensitive aggression or macho posturing. Here we might remember the ancient Zen instruction to "kill the buddha." Suzuki Roshi commented, "A Zen master would say, 'Kill the buddha!' Kill the buddha if the buddha exists somewhere else. Kill the buddha because you should resume your own buddha nature."[17]

Many cues for accurate skillful means are present in our actual situation. There is no need for a transcendent counselor to direct our actions from above or outside our context. Yesterday someone said to me, "Will you please stop trying to help me?" This was clear and unmistakable feedback.

Systems theory and the dharma teachings of interdependence suggest that we all live enmeshed in nested loops of actions and responses, invitations and warnings, suggestions and cues. What is the blooming wildflower signaling to the honeybee? This is another image of being in the world as cocreating dialogues. This is the penetrating insight offered in Zen master Thich Nhat Hanh's brilliantly evocative term *interbeing*. From this perspective, living, for all of us, is a form of being-together-with. This being-together-with includes the entire natural world, perhaps our whole cosmos. As Ch'an teacher Hongzhi Zhengjie wrote, "The white clouds are fascinated with the green mountain's foundations."[18]

You may wonder, "So what? So what if this fundamental interconnectedness is an aspect of our situation? Are there any practical implications of this view? Even if it's true, so what?"

This basic resonance suggests responsiveness as our true nature as human beings. We feel the suffering of others and are moved to alleviate it. Ancient Confucian tradition praised and cultivated our innate "human-heartedness" (*jen*). Modern research scientists from diverse fields offer compelling evidence of a "compassionate instinct." Jewish and Christian religious traditions value love, kindness, and respect. Islam surrenders to the divine as "all-merciful." Secular humanists work to move us toward a more just and ethical culture. It seems that we humans are all hardwired for empathy, as though welcoming is our true nature.

If this is so, how is it that violence and aggression dominate in so many places and times? One of the meanings of the tenth image, with its awakening beings bravely entering the marketplace, is direct engagement with suffering. Wakefulness moves *into* rather than *away from* the turbulence of our times. This last oxherding image shows a reversal of spiritual bypassing, a radical turnabout in the deepest layer of consciousness. As Pema Chödrön describes it,

"On the journey of the warrior-bodhisattva, the path goes down, not up. . . . Instead of transcending the suffering of all creatures, we move toward turbulence and doubt however we can. We explore the reality and unpredictability of insecurity and pain, and we try not to push it away. . . . With us move millions of others, our companions in awakening from fear. At the bottom we discover water, the healing water of bodhichitta. Bodhichita is our heart—our wounded, softened heart. Right down there in the thick of things, we discover the love that will not die."[19] Well said. The tenth image shows this discovery, right down here in the thick of things.

LISTENING TO EACH OTHER

The great bodhisattva who embodies the principle of compassion has many names. In India, it's Avalokiteshvara; in China, Guan Yin; in Vietnam, Quan Am; in Korea, Kwanseum; and in Japan, Kannon. Some of these names are translated as "one who hears the cries of suffering beings." If we are entangled and enmeshed beings from birth to death and beyond, then hearing each other is an important source of guidance. I hear you and can respond to your voice asking for help: "Right now, this is what I need." Based on really hearing you, I can act accordingly. We hear each other's personal and collective stories, and through empathetic listening, we know and feel something of others' suffering. What are our family members, friends, coworkers, and communities asking of us? Consider the voices of other life-forms and the planet itself—what are they asking? Are we hearing the voices crying out in pain right now?

Let me speak personally for a moment. I sometimes find it difficult to hear clearly in the midst of the 24/7 thundering din of the digital world. When I spend too much time online, I find myself feeling more alienated, battered into numbness.

Here I will offer a few "unplugged" exercises, building on and extending the Welcoming Exercise approach, perhaps strengthening our capacity for listening so we can return to social media and global newscasts with responsiveness rather than fatigue. In chapter 9, we engaged in welcoming while in Nature, allowing true nature to feel into our relations to the sound of songbirds, the rushing of water, the whistling wind in the tall trees. As with Native American chants, we hear and feel into "all our relations." Taking our cue from the tenth image, we can begin by listening in the marketplace.

EXERCISES FOR THE MARKETPLACE

Take two or three minutes to gradually move from welcoming to listening in a market. What do you hear in a big supermarket in a shopping mall? Is it mostly Muzak? Anything else? The sound of any machines (cash registers, floor polishers) or of canned goods being stacked? What are the sounds bouncing around your local farmers' market? Sounds of children playing, chasing each other in slightly mad pursuit? Vendors calling out the virtues of their vegetables? What about those voices engaged in the call-and-response of greeting each other in the co-op on Saturday morning? These questions are not asking for conceptual answers but instead invite us into listening, hearing, *sensing* more deeply into where we are and what's around us. This is a first suggestion: let us be in the world by hearing it; let us listen ourselves into living.

Earlier I noted a line from Shakespeare: "I see it feelingly." What is it to hear feelingly, to listen from the heart? Sometimes I wonder if, in earlier times, our hearts were closer to the hearth. Practice listening at home for a few minutes. First, move through the space attending to what you hear and feel. This isn't diagnostic: you're not looking for a problem to be fixed in your household. You also aren't aiming to become a "superlistener," as in the latest superheroine movie. Just listen for a few moments, appreciating sounds and noises, silence and voices as you walk through. If you live in an apartment building, walk through the hallways. If your home has a yard, wander outside and then back inside. How does it sound? As poet Amiri Baraka asked, "How you sound?"[20]

Next bring this welcoming-listening into your workplace. When you first enter the office building, school, hospital, or bank, listen. What are the sounds offering themselves for hearing? Do it again at the end of the day as you leave your workplace, noticing the differences between morning and afternoon soundscapes.

Listening is a good first step in our ongoing dialogue with whatever and whoever surrounds us. Journalist Kate Murphy asks, "How can we reclaim the lost art of listening? In writing a book about listening, I asked people from Brooklyn to Beijing what it meant to be a good listener. The typical response was a blank stare. . . . The sad truth is that people have more experience being cut off, ignored, and misunderstood than heard."[21] Murphy titled her helpful book *You're Not Listening: What You're Missing and Why It Matters.*

Let's continue our contemplative exploration of listening, using her questions as part of our self-reflection: "When was the last time you listened to someone? Really listened, without thinking about what you wanted to say next, glancing down at your phone, or jumping in to offer your opinion?" Pause for a moment to think this over in an even, steady way, acknowledging and then letting go of inner critical or flattering voices. If there are few examples of really listening to contemplate, notice that. If there are many, notice that. Murphy now asks us to recall our experiences of feeling heard: "And when was the last time someone really listened to you? Was so attentive to what you were saying and whose response was so spot-on that you felt truly understood?"[22] Here we remind ourselves of the importance of listening and being heard in the world. Our shared humanity shows up in deep listening. The Zen teacher and writer Sallie Tisdale notes, "Few of us communicate really well. We think explaining ourselves is key, but listening is the most important part."[23]

The tenth oxerding picture is an image of being in dialogue, poised for generous exchange. By beginning with listening, we emphasize the passive aspect, first opening to receive what is given before offering something meaningful in turn. Note that we are taking our cues from the world as it moves and speaks to us now rather than relying on memories or fixed assumptions from the past. It's possible that the world beckons us forward, showing future possibilities as well. Sutherland Roshi asks us, "What becomes possible where the question is not *What do I need to do about this?* but *What wants to happen?*"[24]

Many artists speak of engaging their materials in this friendly, open-dialogue form. Sculptor Senga Nengudi says that when she looks at a piece of fabric, she asks again and again, "What do you want me to do with you?"[25] This is openness, listening, gentle curiosity, and reciprocity. Painter Ann Craven responded this way to an interviewer's question about working with oil paint: "This material—now what do I do with it. What *do* you do with it? And that's a question for every artist, I think." The interviewer agreed, "Exactly. The subject matter has to come out of the paint itself." Craven continued, "Yes! It has to come out of the paint, that's exactly right. Especially wet on wet—oil paint is so much easier for me than thinking about waiting for layers to dry. It's so immediate."[26] This immediate call-and-response rapport is a way of being, a way of living, a way of being alive.

Giving is a way of being in the world. In the bodhisattva way of life, generosity is primary. Bodhisattvas give all beings the opportunity to go first into enlightenment, understanding, as the Wisdom Sutras remind us again and again, that there are no truly existent sentient beings, bodhisattvas, or enlightenment. In some traditions, one gives material goods (food, clothing, shelter); psychological encouragement (the gift of fearlessness in a fearful time); and spiritual teachings (dharma). Many commentators mention that the awakened person in the tenth oxherding image enters the market with open hands of generosity. Martine Batchelor comments, "We naturally give to ourselves and others what is beneficial. We listen deeply, we observe unobtrusively and respond appropriately. When we give, we do not expect anything. We are not superior to others when we help them, on the contrary helping them is like helping ourselves, and we are grateful they give us the opportunity to extend ourselves."[27] True nature expresses itself to itself in flowing exchange.

Here is a Tibetan contemplative exercise, bringing attention to stickiness and stinginess, the fearful reluctance to let go and give. Take an object and place it in one of your hands. It could be a smooth stone or a silver ring, a cup or a leaf, anything at all that you consider valuable. Let one hand feel the weight of the object, then slowly pass it to the other hand. Feel the gesture all along the way (no end-gaining), then feel the weight of the object in the other hand. Let it rest there. Next, pass it from the second hand back to the first. Do this for a minute or two in silent awareness of giving, giving, giving, and receiving. Generosity arises from itself, gives to itself, returns to itself. Here there is no dualistic struggle leading to inner and outer warfare. The *Sutra of the Recollection of the Three Jewels* says, "Generosity is the virtue that produces peace."[28]

To conclude our exercises exploring listening and giving, offer something to someone. It could be as simple as a cup of tea or a meal you prepare and serve. It could be the invisible gift of embodied presence and silent encouragement. Give something to someone and let go of all complicated storylines about "giving" in the simple action itself: "See? I'm such a good giver, but what if I give too much? Will there still be enough for me?" Suzuki Roshi writes, "When you do something, you should burn yourself completely, like a good bonfire, leaving no trace of yourself."[29] As we have heard, this no-trace continues endlessly, giving again and again.

ARTFULNESS IN EVERYDAY LIFE

In 1938, the Japanese scholar Daisetz Teitaro Suzuki published a collection of essays in English titled *Zen Buddhism and Its Influence on*

Japanese Culture. There were chapters on tea ceremony, haiku, swordsmanship, and appreciating Nature. In 1959, this collection was revised and published as *Zen and Japanese Culture.* In the many years since, we find much appreciation and many criticisms of these pioneering essays. Bowing to Professor Suzuki, I call attention to his insight into the strong connection between Zen practice and the contemplative arts. In terms of our oxherding journey, the tenth image shows art-making as a meditative way of being in the world.

In 1973, Trungpa Rinpoche gave a talk called "Art in Everyday Life" to his students assembled for a three-month training program in Jackson Hole, Wyoming. He emphasized that the topic was not formal art for exhibition or performance. "The art we are talking about in this case, in terms of meditative experience, is, one might call it, genuine art," he said. "We begin to appreciate our surroundings in life, whatever it might be—it doesn't have to be good and beautiful and pleasurable necessarily at all. In other words, the definition of art from this point of view is to be able to see the uniqueness of everyday experience. Every moment we might be doing the same thing—we might be brushing our teeth every day, combing our hair every day, cooking our dinner every day. . . . Some kind of intimacies are happening with the daily habit that you go through, and the work of art that is involved in it. That's why it is art in everyday life."[30] This is a welcoming invitation into everyday wakefulness.

Bartok Roshi has this to say on the tenth oxherding image: "We partake and participate."[31] We are, every day and always already, participating in our world. The question is not *whether* we will engage but *how.* How are we being in our world? How is our world being with us? "Genuine art" suggests appreciation of the ordinary, meaning sensitivity to tastes, sounds, color, and shadow; small changes in the emotional tone of a loved one's voice; or large changes in the weather of our bioregion. Even an everyday action like washing a dish in the kitchen sink contains shifting textures, temperatures, and messages. The dish lets us know when it's clean; it does not lie to us about this. In an article titled "A Bite of the Universe," Sojun Mel Weitsman Roshi lists some simple instructions in the art of living from his teacher, Suzuki Roshi, including, "Don't scrape the chair across the floor. . . . Let the bluejay's squawk come right into your heart. . . . Your friend is more than just your friend—just step back and settle down in the center of it all for the sake of all beings."[32]

TRUE NATURE

Welcoming is our true nature—in the beginning, in the middle, and in the endless end of the journey. In the first image, true nature is with us, seeking itself. It is, as Suzuki Roshi says, "wisdom which is seeking wisdom."[33] Later, original nature carries us along the path, allowing us to ride on ourselves through genuineness in the sixth image. In the final image, world and living beings call and respond to each other in everyday, every-moment dialogues.

Sometimes true nature is called "buddha nature," or simply "buddha." This is the great continuity, an equality that pervades all experience, from the first stage to the tenth and around again and again, in any order, like the unpredictable play of a true dragon. In a 1968 talk at Tassajara Zen Mountain Center, Suzuki Roshi explained, "When your practice is not good, you are poor Buddha. When your practice is good, you are good Buddha. And poor and good are Buddhas themselves. Poor is Buddha and good is Buddha and you are Buddha also. Whatever you think or say every word becomes Buddha. I am Buddha. I is Buddha and am is Buddha and Buddha is Buddha. Buddha. Buddha. Buddha. Buddha. Whatever you say. . . . Everything is Buddha: sitting is Buddha, lying down is Buddha, each word is Buddha. If you say BuddhaBuddhaBuddhaBuddha, that is our way, that is shikantaza. When you practice zazen with this understanding, that is true zazen."[34]

POETRY IN THE WORLD

Teaching on the oxherding images, contemporary Japanese Zen teacher Shodo Harada Roshi tells us that, way back in the twelfth century, Ch'an teacher Guo-an wrote short poems for each of the ten stages. One of his students (also his grandson) drew a version of these pictures. What has been passed down to us, in Japan and now around the world, are simple images and verses together. What is it about poetry that fits this lively stream of teachings so well?

I'm wondering about the old kinship between Nature and poetry. Extending the tradition, Zen practitioner Gary Snyder has, for decades, expressed this deep, inner affinity in his poems and essays. Poet Lucille Clifton writes, "I think that we're beginning to remember that the first poets didn't come out of a classroom, that poetry began when somebody walked off of a savanna or out of a cave and looked up at the sky with wonder and said, 'Ahhh.' That was the first poem."[35]

Listening to Nature and speaking, acting naturally in response—this is our offering, our praise song. While living for the last year with these images of oxherding as daily companions, I was reminded by a good friend of the twelfth-century Ch'an teacher Hongzhi Zhengjie's great teaching of "Silent Illumination." Here, in a few poetic images, is a rich and vivid display of Hongzhi's intimate attunement to true nature: "The white clouds are fascinated with the green mountain's foundations. The bright moon cherishes being carried along with the flowing water. The clouds part and the mountain appears. The moon sets and the water is cool."[36]

Acknowledging Accusations in the Name of Love: How I Came to Write This Book

The truth is that I wanted the first sentences of what became *Welcoming Beginner's Mind* to say: "*Caveat lector.* Reader, beware. This is not a Zen book." (My guess was that no one in the editorial or marketing and publicity departments of the publisher would think this a good idea.) In the years when I was writing this book—while reading every Zen Buddhist commentary on the oxherding images in English I could find—I was often painfully aware that I am not a Zen practitioner nor a teacher of Zen. I never sat a single day of zazen—no *shikantaza*, no counting breaths, no engaging the koan of "mu." So how is it that I wrote a book on these classic Chinese and Japanese pictures?

The short answer is that what's written here is, mostly, comments unpacking the pithy commentary given by my "root teacher," the Venerable Chögyam Trungpa Rinpoche. His comments first appeared in a magazine called *Garuda: Tibetan Buddhism in America* (1971) and then were reprinted in his book *Mudra* (1972). Alongside edited talks from two 1974 seminars ("Zen and Tantra"), this commentary is now available in *The Teacup and the Skullcup: Where Zen and Tantra Meet* (2007) as well as in volume 9 of *The Collected Works of Chögyam Trungpa* (2017). I am grateful to the editors of all these publications, in particular Michael (Sherab Chödzin) Kohn, Judith L. Lief, Tensho David Schneider, and Carolyn Rose Gimian.

Still, there may be lingering questions about how a contemporary practitioner of Indo-Tibetan traditions (Kagyu and Nyingma) came to write about these ancient images from Sino-Japanese traditions. My first contact with literature about Zen was during my senior year in high school. I was a scholarship student at Phillips Exeter Academy, and I remember sitting in my dorm room, puzzling over the stories in Professor D. T. Suzuki's *Studies in Zen* (1955). Who were these provocative, crazy-wise figures doing outrageous things while compassionately suggesting that there is more to life than we might think?

I may have picked up that book by Suzuki because of his connection with Erich Fromm, whose popular book *The Art of Loving* (1956) I'd recently read. Fromm and Suzuki were part of a workshop on Zen Buddhism and psychoanalysis held in Cuernavaca, Mexico, in 1957.

I was also reading and enjoying the poetry of LeRoi Jones (Amiri Baraka), Diane DiPrima, Allen Ginsberg, and Jack Kerouac. The connection between Beat writers and Zen was important for me. I learned that the wedding ceremony of Jones and Hettie Cohen was in a Buddhist temple in New York City. I read that Ginsberg and Kerouac took the subway uptown to visit Professor Suzuki while he was teaching at Columbia University.

In my first year in college, I read Shunryu Suzuki Roshi's *Zen Mind, Beginner's Mind* (1970). This was the first book I'd encountered that focused on the essential importance of the practice of Zen meditation. Now it was clear—one had to engage the practice in order to taste any experiential realization. I remember reading that Zen lineage founder Bodhidharma practiced many years of "wall-gazing," so I sat for twenty minutes staring at the blank white wall in my college dorm room. Without any instruction in the practice of sitting meditation, my perceptions were mostly blurred and confused.

I received meditation instruction from Trungpa Rinpoche in the summer of 1973, after a seminar called "The Question of Reality," comparing Carlos Castañeda's teachings of Don Juan and Tibetan Tantra. In January and February 1974, I attended the seven talks of his extended seminar "Zen and Tantra," first at Tail of the Tiger Buddhist Meditation Center in Barnet, Vermont, and then in Boston, Massachusetts.

Twenty-eight years later, in the summer of 2002, I joined ninety participants in the first-ever African American Dharma Retreat at Spirit Rock Meditation Center in Woodacre, California. There were Buddhist practitioners from many lineages attending, including dharma teacher, prolific translator, and professor Jan Willis and Pulitzer Prize–winning author Alice Walker. Brilliant Black feminist writer bell hooks (who had dialogues with Zen teacher Thich Nhat Hanh) was scheduled to attend. This was a joyful first gathering that felt like it had been "a long time coming." Teachers and participants included Ruth King (*Healing Rage*), Konda Mason (cofounder of Jubilee Justice), Ralph Steele (*Tending the Fire*), and Rachel Bagby (*Divine Daughters*).

In particular, I remember meeting three dharma sisters from Zen lineages: Reverend angel Kyodo williams Sensei, Osho Zenju Earthlyn Manuel, and Ryumon Hilda Gutiérrez Baldoquin Sensei. Both Zenju Earthlyn and Ryumon Sensei studied with Zenkei Blanche Hartman Roshi at San Francisco Zen Center, founded by Suzuki Roshi and his students in 1962.

Ryumon Sensei generously invited me to contribute to the pioneering collection of essays she edited, *Dharma, Color, and Culture* (2004). As founder of the People of Color Sitting Group at San Francisco Zen Center, she also invited me to offer a talk on meditation to this group. On March 5, 2005, I gave the Saturday morning dharma talk at City Center, and I began by acknowledging Suzuki Roshi as an inspiring ancestor and close friend of Vidyadhara Chögyam Trungpa Rinpoche. After a public talk offered with co-abbot Ryushin Paul Haller Roshi, I also visited and spoke with Zen practitioners at Green Gulch Farm, where I met Jiko Eijun Linda Cutts Roshi.

Under the guidance of Shugen Arnold Roshi, Zen practitioners at Fire Lotus Temple in Brooklyn, New York, have invited me twice as guest teacher in the last decade. I have also taught alongside Zen teacher Barry Magid of Ordinary Mind Zendo.

I mention these connections and exchanges in order to express gratitude for these opportunities to engage in dharma dialogues, contemplatively inquiring together at the limits of our various received traditions. Nine bows. As Joseph Goldstein, author of *One Dharma: The Emerging Western Buddhism* (2003), says: "Many of us are practicing in several different traditions. It's not uncommon for people to list as their various teachers Tibetan rinpoches, Chinese, Korean, or Japanese Zen masters, Thai ajaans, Burmese sayadaws, and Western teachers of every school. We may have various opinions about whether or not this mixing is a good idea, but it is what is happening. And so our challenge is to understand it and craft it in such a way that it becomes a vehicle for awakening." Well said. I have been inspired by guided cultivating compassion sessions led by Tara Brach and Kate Johnson (both from Insight meditation traditions) that incorporate the practice of "sending and taking" (*tonglen*) from Tibetan lineages. Many of us have used Zoketsu Norman Fischer Roshi's helpful book on the Tibetan mind-training tradition, *Training in Compassion: Zen Teachings on the Practice of Lojong* (2013), in our courses on the bodhisattva way. Now this book, *Welcoming Beginner's Mind*, comprises some Tibetan Buddhist teachings on the Zen oxherding images.

———

I am grateful to the editors at Shambhala Publications, particularly Matt Zepelin and Samantha Ripley. Through your careful and insightful attention, you have made this a better book. In general, I appreciate the entire publishing team led by Nikko Odiseos with stellar contributions from Ivan Bercholz, Sara Bercholz, Tyler O'Malley, Mike Henton, and Laura Atchison. Tuttle Publishing kindly granted permission to use the oxherding images familiar to many since the publication of Paul Reps' pioneering collection, *Zen Flesh, Zen Bones* (1957).

Thank you to David Chadwick for contributing the foreword to this book—it was moving to read his first-person narrative of these two great ancestors, Suzuki Roshi and Trungpa Rinpoche.

Several friends, colleagues, and dharma sisters and brothers read early versions of some of these chapters. Thank you to Reed Bye, Holland Deane Hammond, Adam Seth Lobel, Liza Matthews, Jude Robison, Tensho David Schneider, Henry Shukman Roshi, and Charles Trageser.

Although I do not quote directly from them, I learned from the comments on beginner's mind by Zenju Earthlyn Manuel (*Lion's Roar* podcast), and on the oxherding images by poet Lewis Hyde ("Oxherding Poems," *Tricycle*), meditation teacher Shinzen Young, and Professor Bret W. Davis (*Real Zen for Real Life*, offered on The Great Courses).

I am inspired by the work of the Freedom Together BIPOC mindfulness teacher training collective. May all beings be liberated!

Some of *Welcoming Beginner's Mind* was written while on sabbatical leave from a core faculty teaching position at Naropa University. A warm Naropa bow of thanks for the continuing generosity of President Charles Gabriel Lief, faculty colleagues and administrators, and the librarian and staff of Allen Ginsberg Library. Thank you to Alan Wraye, manager of the Naropa Business Services Center.

I felt the loving encouragement of the entire "Gogo clan" while writing this book, the whole Hayashi-Gotesman-Teitelbaum-Hoops-Rebuza family, and particularly the rambunctious insights and wisdom of Opal, Beatrice, and Asher.

As always, ocean waves of gratitude for the inspiring example of Social Presencing Theater cofounder Arawana Ruth Hayashi. May you keep on keeping on. Let Big Milton have the last words of praise: "Grace in all her steps, in every gesture dignity and love."

—GAYLON FERGUSON
Boulder, Colorado
Hudson Valley, New York

Notes

INTRODUCTION: WHY WELCOME?

1. Shunryu Suzuki, *Zen Mind, Beginner's Mind: Informal Talks on Zen Meditation and Practice*, 50th Anniversary Edition (Boulder, CO: Shambhala Publications, 2020), 121.

2. Suzuki, *Zen Mind, Beginner's Mind*, 1.

3. Suzuki, *Zen Mind, Beginner's Mind*, 3.

4. Thinley Norbu, *Magic Dance: The Display of the Self-Nature of the Five Wisdom Dakinis* (Boulder, CO: Shambhala Publications, 1999), 129.

5. Chögyam Trungpa, *The Teacup and the Skullcup: Where Zen and Tantra Meet* (Boulder, CO: Shambhala Publications, 2015), 132.

6. Chögyam Trungpa, *Mudra: Early Poems and Songs* (Boulder, CO: Shambhala Publications, 2001). This collection of teachings was originally published by Shambhala in 1972 and was later included in *The Collected Works of Chögyam Trungpa*, vol. 1 (Shambhala, 2003). Trungpa's commentary on the oxherding images was also included in *The Teacup and the Skullcup* (see preceding note).

7. Tracee Stanley, *Radiant Rest: Yoga Nidra for Deep Relaxation and Clarity* (Boulder, CO: Shambhala Publications, 2021), 22.

8. Jenny Odell, *How to Do Nothing: Resisting the Attention Economy* (New York: Melville House Publishing, 2019), 1.

CHAPTER ONE: SEEKING THE OX

1. Shunryu Suzuki, *Zen Mind, Beginner's Mind: Informal Talks on Zen Meditation and Practice*, 50th Anniversary Edition (Boulder, CO: Shambhala Publications, 2020), 19.

2. Quoted in Charles Olson, *The Special View of History* (Berkeley: Oyez, 1970), 14.

3. Chögyam Trungpa, *Mudra: Early Poems and Songs* (Boulder, CO: Shambhala Publications, 2001), 74.

4. Karl Marx, "The Communist Manifesto," in Max Eastman, ed., *Capital, The Communist Manifesto, and other Writings of Karl Marx* (New York: Carlton House, 1932), 324, https://archive.org/details/in.ernet.dli.2015.59004/mode/2up.

5. David Loy, *Lack and Transcendence: The Problem of Death and Life in Psychotherapy, Existentialism, and Buddhism* (New Jersey: Humanities Press, 1996), 51.

6. Trungpa, *Mudra*, 74.

7. Trungpa, *Mudra*, 74.

8. Chögyam Trungpa, *The Collected Works of Chögyam Trungpa* (Boulder, CO: Shambhala Publications, 2004), 5:347.

9. Quoted in Peter Dockrill, "Consumers Have a Bigger Impact on the Environment Than Anything Else, Study Finds," *Science Alert*, February 25, 2016, www.sciencealert.com/consumers-have-a-bigger-impact-on-the-environment-than-anything-else-study-finds.

10. Martine Batchelor, "The Ten Oxherding Pictures," *Tricycle*, (Spring 2000), https://tricycle.org/magazine/ten-oxherding-pictures.

11. Quoted in Batchelor, "The Ten Oxherding Pictures."

12. *The Sadhana of Mahamudra*, excerpted in Trungpa, *Collected Works*, 5:344.

13. Batchelor, "The Ten Oxherding Pictures."

14. Chögyam Trungpa, *The Collected Works of Chögyam Trungpa* (Boulder, CO: Shambhala Publications, 2004), 3:13.

15. Josh Bartok and Chögyam Trungpa Rinpoche, "Searching for the Ox: The Path to Enlightenment in 10 Pictures," *Lion's Roar*, March 4, 2015, www.lionsroar.com/searching-for-the-ox-the-path-to-enlightenment-in-10-pictures.

16. "Milarepa's Dzogchen Song," *KeithDowman.net*, accessed April 27, 2023, http://keithdowman.net/dzogchen/milarepas-dzogchen-song.html.

17. Tsoknyi Rinpoche, *Carefree Dignity: Discourses on Training in the Nature of Mind* (Hong Kong: Rangjung Yeshe Publications, 1998), 87.

18. Excerpt from Charlotte Joko Beck, *Nothing Special: Living Zen* quoted in Kazuaki Tanahashi and Tensho David Schneider, *Essential Zen* (San Francisco: Harper, 1995), 8.

CHAPTER TWO: SEEING THE OX'S FOOTPRINTS

1. Chögyam Trungpa, *The Collected Works of Chögyam Trungpa* (Boulder: Shambhala Publications, 2004), 2:379–80.

2. Bayo Akomolafe (blog), "A Slower Urgency," accessed April 27, 2023, www.bayoakomolafe.net/post/a-slower-urgency.

3. "By the Book: Greg Iles," *The New York Times Sunday Book Review*, June 27, 2019, www.nytimes.com/2019/06/27/books/review/by-the-book-greg-iles.html.

4. In ordinary usage as found in most dictionaries, *mindfulness* and *awareness* are synonyms. In the Indo-Tibetan meditative tradition, they are carefully distinguished: mindfulness is *smrti*, or "bare attention"; awareness, or *sheshin* in Tibetan, is what notices where our attention is focused.

5. Chögyam Trungpa, *Mudra: Early Poems and Songs* (Boulder, CO: Shambhala Publications, 2001), 68.

6. Toni Morrison, *The Origin of Others* (Cambridge, MA: Harvard University Press, 2017), 36.

7. Kimiko de Freytas-Tamura, "Bastion of Anti-Vaccine Fervor: Progressive Waldorf Schools," *The New York Times*, June 13, 2019, www

.nytimes.com/2019/06/13/nyregion/measles-outbreak-new-york.html.

8. Trungpa, Mudra, 76.

9. John Daido Loori, Riding the Ox Home: Stages on the Path of Enlightenment (Boulder, CO: Shambhala Publications, 2002), 11.

10. Khenpo Tsultrim Gyamtso Rinpoche, Progressive Stages of Meditation on Emptiness (UK: Shrimala Trust, 2016), 16.

11. "Naropa's Roots," Naropa University (website), accessed April 27, 2023, www.naropa.edu/about-naropa/history-of-naropa/.

12. Shunryu Suzuki, Zen Mind, Beginner's Mind: Informal Talks on Zen Meditation and Practice, 50th Anniversary Edition (Boulder, CO: Shambhala Publications, 2020), 137.

CHAPTER THREE: GLIMPSING THE OX

1. John Daido Loori, Riding the Ox Home: Stages on the Path of Enlightenment (Boulder, CO: Shambhala Publications, 2002), 22.

2. Josh Bartok and Chögyam Trungpa Rinpoche, "Searching for the Ox: The Path to Enlightenment in 10 Pictures," Lion's Roar, March 4, 2015, www.lionsroar.com/searching-for-the-ox-the-path-to-enlightenment-in-10-pictures.

3. John M. Koller, "Ox-Herding: Stages of Zen Practice," ExEAS Teaching Unit, accessed May 30, 2023, www.columbia.edu/cu/weai/exeas/resources/oxherding.html.

4. Judith L. Lief, editor's introduction to Chögyam Trungpa, Glimpses of the Profound: Four Short Works (Boulder, CO: Shambhala, 2016), xiii.

5. Richard Baker, introduction to Shunryu Suzuki, Zen Mind, Beginner's Mind: Informal Talks on Zen Meditation and Practice, 50th Anniversary Edition (Boulder, CO: Shambhala Publications, 2020), 14.

6. Chögyam Trungpa, Mudra: Early Poems and Songs (Boulder, CO: Shambhala Publications, 2001), 78.

7. Loori, *Riding the Ox Home*, 1.

8. Suzuki, *Zen Mind, Beginner's Mind*, 92.

9. Bartok and Trungpa, "Searching for the Ox."

10. Zenju Earthlyn Manuel, *Sanctuary: A Meditation on Home, Homelessness, and Belonging* (Somerville, MA: Wisdom, 2018).

11. See Charles Belyea and Steven Tainer, *Dragon's Play: A New Taoist Transmission of the Complete Experience of Human Life* (Berkeley: Great Circle Lifeworks, 1991).

12. Suzuki, *Zen Mind, Beginner's Mind*, 134.

CHAPTER FOUR: TOUCHING THE OX

1. Chögyam Trungpa, Mudra: *Early Poems and Songs* (Boulder, CO: Shambhala Publications, 2001), 78.

2. Shunryu Suzuki, *Zen Mind, Beginner's Mind: Informal Talks on Zen Meditation and Practice*, 50th Anniversary Edition (Boulder, CO: Shambhala Publications, 2020), 51.

3. David Loy, "Wego: The Social Roots of Suffering," in *Mindful Politics: A Buddhist Guide to Making the World a Better Place* ed. Melvin McLeod (Somerville, MA: Wisdom, 2006), 45–56.

4. Arawana Hayashi, *Social Presencing Theater: The Art of Making a True Move* (Cambridge, MA: PI Press, 2021), 8.

5. Resmaa Menakem, *My Grandmother's Hands: Racialized Trauma and the Pathway to Mending Our Hearts and Bodies* (Las Vegas: Central Recovery Press, 2017), 12.

6. Suzuki, *Zen Mind, Beginner's Mind*, 26.

7. Chögyam Trungpa, *Shambhala: The Sacred Path of the Warrior* (Boulder, CO: Shambhala Publications, 1988), 37.

8. Erika Berlant, *Sitting: The Physical Art of Meditation* (Boulder, CO: Somatic Performers Press, 2017).

9. Denise Levertov, *O Taste and See* (New York: New Directions, 1964).

10. Suzuki, *Zen Mind, Beginner's Mind*, 60.

11. Philosopher Martin Heidegger's notion of "profound boredom" is discussed in Giorgio Agamben, *The Open: Man and Animal*, trans. Kevin Attell (Stanford, CA: Stanford University Press, 2004), 68.

12. Suzuki, *Zen Mind, Beginner's Mind*, 100.

13. John Daido Loori, *Riding the Ox Home: Stages on the Path of Enlightenment* (Boulder, CO: Shambhala Publications, 2002), 23.

14. Robert Duncan, *The Opening of the Field* (New York: New Directions, 1960), 7.

15. Trungpa, *Mudra*, 102.

16. Suzuki, *Zen Mind, Beginner's Mind*, 46.

17. T. S. Eliot, "Little Gidding," *Collected Poems: 1909–1962* (London: Faber, 1974).

18. James Ishmael Ford, *If You're Lucky, Your Heart Will Break* (Boston: Wisdom Publications, 2012), 52.

CHAPTER FIVE: TAMING THE OX

1. John M. Koller, "Ox-Herding: Stages of Zen Practice," ExEAS Teaching Unit, accessed May 30, 2023, www.columbia.edu/cu/weai/exeas/resources/oxherding.html.

2. John Daido Loori, *Riding the Ox Home: Stages on the Path of Enlightenment* (Boulder, CO: Shambhala Publications, 2002), 35.

3. Chögyam Trungpa, *Mudra: Early Poems and Songs* (Boulder, CO: Shambhala Publications, 2001), 82.

4. Shunryu Suzuki, *Zen Mind, Beginner's Mind: Informal Talks on Zen Meditation and Practice*, 50th Anniversary Edition (Boulder, CO: Shambhala Publications, 2020), 31.

5. Bill Morgan, *The Meditator's Dilemma: An Innovative Approach to Overcoming Obstacles and Revitalizing Your Practice* (Boulder, CO: Shambhala, 2016), 13.

6. Xenophon, *On Horsemanship*, trans. H. G. Dakyns, (Project Gutenberg, 2013), www.gutenberg.org/files/1176/1176-h/1176-h.htm.

7. Suzuki, *Zen Mind, Beginner's Mind*, 32.

8. Brené Brown, "Dare to Live Greatly," *Omega*, 2013, www.eomega.org/article/dare-to-live-greatly.

9. Sarah Maslin Nir, *Horse Crazy: The Story of a Woman and a World in Love with an Animal* (New York: Simon and Schuster, 2020), 129.

10. Suzuki, *Zen Mind, Beginner's Mind*, 37.

11. These words and song lyrics are from Milarepa's Hundred Thousand Songs, which has been translated in several versions. See, for instance, "Song of Paldarbom," lyric loosely adapted from the translation by Garma C. C. Chang and set to music by Winfield "Binny" Clark, YouTube, Jan. 2, 2015, www.youtube.com/watch?v=xLD2DoiDuoo.

12. Suzuki, *Zen Mind, Beginner's Mind*, 35.

13. Don DeLillo, *Point Omega* (New York: Scribner, 2010), 30.

14. Joan Sutherland, "Gaining Perspective on Habitual Patterns," *Buddhadharma* (Summer 2011), 33.

15. Chögyam Trungpa, *The Heart of the Buddha: Entering the Tibetan Buddhist Path* (Boulder, CO: Shambhala, 2010), 30.

16. Dilgo Khyentse, *Zurchungpa's Testament* (Boulder, CO: Shambhala Publications, 2020), 204.

17. Thupten Jinpa, *A Fearless Heart: How the Courage to Be Compassionate Can Transform Our Lives* (New York: Avery, 2016), 32.

18. Adam Phillips and Barbara Taylor, *On Kindness* (New York: Picador, 2010), 44.

19. Zakiyyah Iman Jackson, *Becoming Human: Matter and Meaning in an Antiblack World* (New York: NYU Press, 2020), 2.

20. Trungpa, *Heart of the Buddha*, 33.

21. Suzuki, *Zen Mind, Beginner's Mind*, 45.

22. Norman Fischer and Susan Moon, *What Is Zen? Plain Talk for a Beginner's Mind* (Boulder, CO: Shambhala Publications, 2016), 183.

23. Trungpa, *Heart of the Buddha*, 33.

24. Chögyam Trungpa, *Shambhala: The Sacred Path of the Warrior* (Boulder, CO: Shambhala Publications, 1988), 30.

CHAPTER SIX: RIDING THE OX

1. John Daido Loori, *Riding the Ox Home: Stages on the Path of Enlightenment* (Boulder, CO: Shambhala Publications, 2002), 44.

2. Charles Belyea and Steven Tainer, *Dragon's Play: A New Taoist Transmission of the Complete Experience of Human Life* (Berkeley: Great Circle Lifeworks, 1991), 49.

3. Martine Batchelor, "The Ten Oxherding Pictures," *Tricycle* (Spring 2000), https://tricycle.org/magazine/ten-oxherding-pictures.

4. Loori, *Riding the Ox Home*, 44.

5. Loori, *Riding the Ox Home*, 45.

6. Shunryu Suzuki, *Zen Mind, Beginner's Mind: Informal Talks on Zen Meditation and Practice*, 50th Anniversary Edition (Boulder, CO: Shambhala Publications, 2020), 54.

7. John M. Koller, "Ox-Herding: Stages of Zen Practice," ExEAS Teaching Unit, accessed May 30, 2023, www.columbia.edu/cu/weai/exeas/resources/oxherding.html.

8. Loori, *Riding the Ox Home*, 55.

9. Koller, "Ox-Herding."

10. Loori, *Riding the Ox Home*, 1.

11. Koller, "Ox-Herding."

12. Chögyam Trungpa, *Mudra: Early Poems and Songs* (Boulder, CO: Shambhala Publications, 2001), 84.

13. Josh Bartok and Chögyam Trungpa Rinpoche, "Searching for the Ox: The Path to Enlightenment in 10 Pictures," *Lion's Roar*, March 4, 2015, www.lionsroar.com/searching-for-the-ox-the-path-to-enlightenment-in-10-pictures.

14. Chögyam Trungpa, *1973 Seminary Transcripts: Hinayana/Mahayana* (Kalapa Media, 1973), 40 and 49, PDF.

15. Trungpa, 1973 *Seminar Transcripts*, 45.

16. Elihu Genmyo Smith, "No Need to Do Zazen, Therefore Must Do Zazen," *Tricycle* (Fall 2011), https://tricycle.org/magazine/no-need-do-zazen-therefore-must-do-zazen/.

17. Suzuki, *Zen Mind, Beginner's Mind*, 32.

18. Trungpa, *Mudra*, 84.

19. Chögyam Trungpa, *The Path Is the Goal: A Basic Handbook of Buddhist Meditation* (Boulder, CO: Shambhala Publications, 1995), 92.

20. Trungpa, *The Path Is the Goal*, 92.

21. Ian Baker, *Tibetan Yoga: Principles and Practices* (Rochester, VT: Inner Traditions, 2019), 272.

22. Suzuki, *Zen Mind, Beginner's Mind*, 134.

23. Toni Packer quoted in in Kazuaki Tanahashi and Tensho David Schneider, *Essential Zen* (San Francisco: Harper, 1995), 22.

24. Chögyam Trungpa, *The Collected Works of Chögyam Trungpa* (Boulder, CO: Shambhala Publications, 2004), 5:85.

25. Suzuki, *Zen Mind, Beginner's Mind*, 19.

26. Chögyam Trungpa, *The Collected Works of Chögyam Trungpa* (Boulder, CO: Shambhala Publications, 2004), 3:78.

27. "The Bodhisattva Vow from the Bodhicharyavatara by Shantideva," Nalanda Translation Committee, accessed April 28, 2023, https://static1.squarespace.com/static/57b4bb3a6b8f5b5b2c74b3d0/t/58fec92f579fb33b524dd201/1493092655271/Full+Bodhisattva+vow+copy.pdf.

CHAPTER SEVEN: FORGETTING THE OX

1. Josh Bartok and Chögyam Trungpa Rinpoche, "Searching for the Ox: The Path to Enlightenment in 10 Pictures," *Lion's Roar*, March 4, 2015, www.lionsroar.com/searching-for-the-ox-the-path-to-enlightenment-in-10-pictures.

2. Seng-ts'an, "Hsin Hsin Ming: On Trust in the Heart," trans. Arthur Waley, in *Buddhist Texts through the Ages*, ed. Edward Conze

(New York: Philosophical Library, 1954), 296–98. This and other translations of this poem are available at https://terebess.hu/english/hsin.html#1.

3. Shunryu Suzuki, *Zen Mind, Beginner's Mind: Informal Talks on Zen Meditation and Practice*, 50th Anniversary Edition (Boulder, CO: Shambhala Publications, 2020), 27.

4. Suzuki, *Zen Mind, Beginner's Mind*, 113, 115.

5. Norman Fischer and Susan Moon, *What Is Zen? Plain Talk for a Beginner's Mind* (Boulder, CO: Shambhala Publications, 2016), 5.

6. Chögyam Trungpa, *The Collected Works of Chögyam Trungpa* (Boulder, CO: Shambhala Publications, 2004), 3:140.

7. Trungpa, *Collected Works*, 3:140.

8. Jill Lepore, "Burnout: Modern Affliction or Human Condition?" *New Yorker*, May 17, 2021, www.newyorker.com/magazine/2021/05/24/burnout-modern-affliction-or-human-condition.

9. Jay Ogilvy, *Living without a Goal* (New York: Doubleday Business, 1995), 37.

10. Yulia Aleynikova, Ed Brown poem, Write Fresh Ink Retreats, Facebook post, December 11, 2019, www.facebook.com/groups/328258854639721/search/?q=A%20gentle%20rain%20settles%20the%20dust.

11. Chögyam Trungpa, *Cutting Through Spiritual Materialism* (Boulder, CO: Shambhala Publications, 1973), 25.

12. Jonathan Franzen, "Sherry Turkle's 'Reclaiming Conversation,'" *New York Times*, September 28, 2015, https://www.nytimes.com/2015/10/04/books/review/jonathan-franzen-reviews-sherry-turkle-reclaiming-conversation.html.

13. Chögyam Trungpa, *Mudra: Early Poems and Songs* (Boulder, CO: Shambhala Publications, 2001), 86.

14. Steven D. Goodman, *The Buddhist Psychology of Awakening* (Boulder; CO: Shambhala Publications, 2020), excerpted at www.shambhala.com/ego-personality.

15. Suzuki, *Zen Mind, Beginner's Mind*, 100.

16. David Chadwick, afterword to Suzuki, *Zen Mind, Beginner's Mind*, 144.

17. David Schneider, *Crowded by Beauty: The Life and Zen of Poet Philip Whalen* (Berkeley, CA: University of California Press, 2015), 23.

18. Taigen Dan Leighton, "Dropping Off Body-Mind, and the Pregnant Pillars" (Dharma Talks, Mt. Source Sangha, Bolinas, February 9, 2002), www.ancientdragon.org/dropping-off-body-mind-and-the-pregnant-pillars/.

19. John Daido Loori, "Dropping Off Body and Mind" (Dharma Discourse, *Koans of the Way of Reality*, Case 108, Zen Mountain Monastery, Fall 2002), www.abuddhistlibrary.com/Buddhism/C%20-%20Zen/Modern%20Teachers/John%20Daido%20Loori%20-%20Dharma%20Talks/Dharma%20Discourse%20Dropping%20Off%20Body%20and%20Mind.htm.

20. Chögyam Trungpa, *The Heart of the Buddha: Entering the Tibetan Buddhist Path* (Boulder, CO: Shambhala, 2010), 37.

21. Bartok and Trungpa, "Searching for the Ox."

22. Trungpa, *Collected Works*, 1:465.

23. Martine Batchelor, "The Ten Oxherding Pictures," *Tricycle*, Spring 2000, https://tricycle.org/magazine/ten-oxherding-pictures.

24. Sojun Mel Weitsman, "Suzuki Roshi's Practice of Shikantaza," in *The Art of Just Sitting: Essential Writings on the Zen Practice of Shikantaza*, ed. John Daido Loori (Boston: Wisdom Publications, 2002), 164–65.

CHAPTER EIGHT: FORGETTING OX AND OXHERDER

1. Lewis Hyde, trans., "Oxherding Poems," *Tricycle* (Spring 2011), https://tricycle.org/magazine/oxherding-poems/.

2. Paul Reps and Nyogen Senzaki, eds., *Zen Flesh Zen Bones: A Collection of Zen and Pre-Zen Writings* (Rutland, VT: Tuttle, 1985), 109.

3. Chögyam Trungpa, *Mudra: Early Poems and Songs* (Boulder, CO: Shambhala Publications, 2001), 88.

4. Trungpa, *Mudra*, 68.

5. T. S. Eliot, "Little Gidding," *Collected Poems: 1909–1962* (London: Faber, 1974).

6. Robert Rosenbaum and Barry Magid, *What's Wrong with Mindfulness* (Boston: Wisdom Publications, 2016), 30.

7. Robert Aitken and Kazuaki Tanahashi, trans., "Actualizing the Fundamental Point (Genjokoan)," thezensite website, accessed May 1, 2023, www.thezensite.com/ZenTeachings/Dogen_Teach ings/GenjoKoan_Aitken.htm.

8. Trungpa, *Mudra*, 88.

9. Trungpa, *Mudra*, 92.

10. William Blake, "To Nobodaddy," *All Poetry*, accessed May 1, 2023, https://allpoetry.com/To-Nobodaddy.

11. Shunryu Suzuki, *Zen Mind, Beginner's Mind: Informal Talks on Zen Meditation and Practice*, 50th Anniversary Edition (Boulder, CO: Shambhala Publications, 2020), 19.

12. Steven Heine, *Readings of Dogen's Treasury of the True Dharma Eye* (New York: Columbia University Press, 2020) 210.

13. Shunryu Suzuki, "Way-Seeking Mind, Part III" (Winter Sesshin, Tassajara Zen Mountain Center, California, December 1, 1969), 1, www.shunryusuzuki.com/suzuki/transcripts-pdf/69-pdf/69 -12-01V.pdf.

14. Kyabgon Traleg, *Mind at Ease: Self-Liberation through Mahamudra Meditation* (Boulder, CO: Shambhala Publications, 2004), 220.

15. Federico García Lorca, "Romance Sonámbulo," in *The Selected Poems of Federico García Lorca*, trans. William Bryant Logan (New York: New Directions, 1955), https://poets.org/poem/romance -sonambulo.

16. In Kazuaki Tanahashi and Tensho David Schneider, *Essential Zen* (San Francisco: Harper, 1995), 143.

17. Stefano Harvey and Fred Moten, *The Undercommons* (New York: Minor Compositions, 2013), 154.

18. John Daido Loori, *Riding the Ox Home: Stages on the Path of Enlightenment* (Boulder, CO: Shambhala Publications, 2002), 56.

19. Joan Sutherland, "Here at the End of the World," *Lions Roar*, April 7, 2020, https://www.lionsroar.com/here-at-the-end-of -the-world.

20. Chögyam Trungpa, *The Collected Works of Chögyam Trungpa* (Boulder, CO: Shambhala Publications, 2004), 5:306.

21. Tim Buckley, "Editor's Introduction," *Wind Bell* 8, nos. 3–4 (Spring 1969): 3, http://www.cuke.com/pdf-2013/wind-bell/69 -03-04.pdf.

22. Christopher Bident, *Maurice Blanchot: A Critical Biography*, trans. John McKeane (New York: Fordham University Press, 2020), quoted in Robert Pogue Harrison, "The Nothing Beyond Nothing," *New York Review of Books*, March 12, 2020, www.nybooks.com/ articles/2020/03/12/maurice-blanchot-nothing-beyond-nothing/.

CHAPTER NINE: ENJOYING THE SOURCE

1. John M. Koller, "Ox-Herding: Stages of Zen Practice," ExEAS Teaching Unit, accessed May 30, 2023, www.columbia.edu/cu/ weai/exeas/resources/oxherding.html.

2. Christian Dillo, *The Path of Aliveness: A Contemporary Zen Approach to Awakening Body and Mind* (Boulder, CO: Shambhala, 2022), ix.

3. Koller, "Ox-Herding"; Chögyam Trungpa, *Mudra: Early Poems and Songs* (Boulder, CO: Shambhala Publications, 2001), 90; Martine Batchelor, "The Ten Oxherding Pictures," *Tricycle* (Spring 2000), https://tricycle.org/magazine/ten-oxherding-pictures.

4. Trungpa, *Mudra*, 90.

5. Albert Low, ed., *Hakuin on Kensho: The Four Ways of Knowing* (Boulder, CO: Shambhala Publications, 2006), 42.

6. Trungpa, *Mudra*, 90.

7. Trungpa, *Mudra*, 90.

8. Trungpa, *Mudra*, 90.

9. Shunryu Suzuki, *Zen Mind, Beginner's Mind: Informal Talks on Zen Meditation and Practice*, 50th Anniversary Edition (Boulder, CO: Shambhala Publications, 2020), 21.

10. David Hinton, *China Root: Taoism, Ch'an, and Original Zen* (Boulder, CO: Shambhala Publications, 2020), 1.

11. Hinton, *China Root*, 1.

12. Christopher Lasch, *The Culture of Narcissism* (New York: W. W. Norton, 1979), 21.

13. Blanche Hartman, *Seeds for a Boundless Life: Zen Teachings from the Heart* (Boulder, CO: Shambhala Publications, 2015), 21.

14. Chögyam Trungpa, *Glimpses of the Profound: Four Short Works* (Boulder, CO: Shambhala, 2016), 270.

15. David Ross Komito, *Nagarjuna's "Seventy Stanzas": A Buddhist Psychology of Emptiness* (Boulder, CO: Snow Lion, 1999), 79.

16. Stephen Batchelor, "Nagarjuna's Verses from the Center," *Tricycle* (Spring 2000), https://tricycle.org/magazine/nagarjunas-verses -center/.

17. Tim Buckley, "Editor's Introduction," *Wind Bell* 8, nos. 3–4 (Spring 1969): 3, http://www.cuke.com/pdf-2013/wind-bell/69 -03-04.pdf.

18. For this and subsequent quotes on the *Lotus Sutra* and the trikaya, see Shunryu Suzuki, "The Trikāya," *Wind Bell* 8, nos. 3–4 (Spring 1969): 4–18, http://www.cuke.com/pdf-2013/wind-bell/69-03-04 .pdf.

19. Chögyam Trungpa, "The Five Buddha Families," Shambhala, accessed May 2, 2023, https://archive.ph/h9q9M.

20. Chögyam Trungpa, "Seasons Greetings," in *First Thought, Best Thought: 108 Poems* (Boulder, CO: Shambhala Publications, 1983), 193.

21. Joan Sutherland, *Vimalakirti and the Awakened Heart: A Commentary on the Sutra that Vimalakirti Speaks* (Santa Fe, NM: Following Winds Press, Cloud Dragon Dharma Works, 2016), 19.

22. Juliet B. Schor, *Plenitude: The New Economics of True Wealth* (New York: Penguin Press, 2010), 56.

23. Larry Yang, *Awakening Together: The Spiritual Practice of Inclusivity and Community* (Boston: Wisdom Publications, 2017), 39.

CHAPTER TEN: BEING IN THE WORLD

1. Martine Batchelor, "The Ten Oxherding Pictures," *Tricycle* (Spring 2000), https://tricycle.org/magazine/ten-oxherding-pictures.

2. John M. Koller, "Ox-Herding: Stages of Zen Practice," ExEAS Teaching Unit, accessed May 30, 2023, www.columbia.edu/cu/weai/exeas/resources/oxherding.html.

3. Kuoan Shiyuan, "The Ten Oxherding Pictures," trans. Lewis Hyde, Zen Literature, accessed May 2, 2023, https://terebess.hu/english/oxherd1.html.

4. Daisetz Teitaro Suzuki, *Manual of Zen Buddhism* (New York: Grove Press, 1994 [1934]).

5. Shinzen Young, "Zen Ox-Herding Pics – Part 1 of 3," YouTube, February 15, 2009, https://www.youtube.com/watch?v=x8aN9O73lgg.

6. Christian Dillo, *The Path of Aliveness: A Contemporary Zen Approach to Awakening Body and Mind* (Boulder, CO: Shambhala, 2022), 284.

7. Henri Bergson, *Creative Evolution*, trans. Arthur Mitchell (CreateSpace Independent Publishing Platform, 2012), 3. Kindle.

8. Chögyam Trungpa, *Mudra: Early Poems and Songs* (Boulder, CO: Shambhala Publications, 2001), 92.

9. Peter Schjeldahl, "The Walker: Rediscovering New York with David Hammons," *New Yorker*, December 15, 2002, https://www.newyorker.com/magazine/2002/12/23/the-walker.

10. Robert Aitken and Kazuaki Tanahashi, trans., "Actualizing the Fundamental Point (Genjokoan)," thezensite website, accessed May 1, 2023, www.thezensite.com/ZenTeachings/Dogen_Teach ings/GenjoKoan_Aitken.htm.

11. Trungpa, Mudra, 92.

12. Quoted in Peter M. J. Stravinskas, "'All the Way to Heaven Is Heaven': 7 Basic Steps to Holiness," The Catholic World Report, November 29, 2017, www.catholicworldreport.com/ 2017/11/29/all-the-way-to-heaven-is-heaven-7-basic-steps-to -holiness.

13. Seng-ts'an, "Hsin Hsin Ming: On Trust in the Heart," trans. Arthur Waley, in Buddhist Texts through the Ages, ed. Edward Conze (New York: Philosophical Library, 1954), 296–98. This and other translations of this poem are available at https://terebess.hu/ english/hsin.html#1.

14. Kazuaki Tanahashi, ed., Treasury of the True Dharma Eye: Zen Master Dogen's "Shobo Genzo" (Boulder, CO: Shambhala, 2012), 885.

15. Tanahashi, Treasury of the True Dharma Eye, 30.

16. Trungpa, Mudra, 92.

17. Shunryu Suzuki, Zen Mind, Beginner's Mind: Informal Talks on Zen Meditation and Practice, 50th Anniversary Edition (Boulder, CO: Shambhala Publications, 2020), 27.

18. Taigen Dan Leighton, preface to Daido Loori, The Art of Just Sitting (Boston: Wisdom Publications, 2002), reprinted online at Leighton, "Hongzhi, Dogen and the Background of Shikantaza," Ancient Dragon Zen Gate, February 21, 2019, www.ancientdragon .org/hongzhi-dogen-and-the-background-of-shikantaza.

19. Pema Chödrön, Comfortable with Uncertainty: 108 Teachings on Cultivating Fearlessness and Compassion (Boulder, CO: Shambhala Publications, 2004), 1.

20. Donald Allen, ed., The New American Poetry, 1945–1960 (Berkeley: University of California Press, 1994 [1960]), 424.

21. Kate Murphy, "Talk Less. Listen More. Here's How," *New York Times*, January 9, 2020, www.nytimes.com/2020/01/09/opinion/listening-tips.html.

22. Murphy, "Talk Less."

23. Sallie Tisdale, "Travel Guide to the End of Life," quoted in "Daily Dharma," *Tricycle*, accessed May 3, 2023, https://tricycle.org/dailydharma/travel-guide-to-the-end-of-life-2/.

24. Joan Sutherland, "Koans for Troubled Times," *Buddhadharma* (Spring 2008), www.lionsroar.com/koans-for-troubled-times/.

25. Alex Greenberger, "Bodies, Fabric Spirits, and Celebration: Senga Nengudi's Elusive Art Finds Joy in the Everyday," *Art in America*, April 28, 2021, www.artnews.com/feature/senga-nengudi-who-is-she-why-is-she-important-1234591161/.

26. Ashley Garrett, "A Conversation with Ann Craven," *Figure/Ground*, November 28, 2014, https://figureground.org/a-conversation-with-ann-craven/.

27. Batchelor, "The Ten Oxherding Pictures."

28. Nalanda Translation Committee, trans., "The Sūtra of the Recollection of the Noble Three Jewels," 1975/1980, www.nalandatranslation.org/wp-content/uploads/2016/09/sutra-of-the-recollection.pdf.

29. Suzuki, *Zen Mind, Beginner's Mind*, 62.

30. Chögyam Trungpa, *1973 Seminary Transcripts: Hinayana/Mahayana* (Kalapa Media, 1973), 122, PDF.

31. Josh Bartok and Chögyam Trungpa Rinpoche, "Searching for the Ox: The Path to Enlightenment in 10 Pictures," *Lion's Roar*, March 4, 2015, www.lionsroar.com/searching-for-the-ox-the-path-to-enlightenment-in-10-pictures.

32. Sojun Mel Weitsman, "A Bite of the Universe," in Rosenbaum and Magid, *What's Wrong with Mindfulness*, 137.

33. Suzuki, *Zen Mind, Beginner's Mind*, 19.

34. Shunryu Suzuki, "Lecture," (lecture, Tassajara Zen Mountain Center, Carmel Valley, CA, July 1968), http://www.cuke.com/pdf -2013/srl/68-03-04-July-Lecture.pdf.

35. PBS, "Bill Moyers Journal" (transcript, February 26, 2010), https:// www.pbs.org/moyers/journal/02262010/transcript2.html.

36. Leighton, "Hongzhi, Dogen and the Background of Shikan-taza."